THE WAY TO COACH

Leaders, Executives, and Managers

ANDREW
NEITLICH

Published by The Center for Executive Coaching,
Publishing Division, Sarasota FL

Every effort has been made to obtain permissions for material quoted throughout the book. If any required acknowledgments have been omitted, or any rights overlooked, it is unintentional. Please notify the publisher of any omission, and it will be rectified in future editions.

Library of Congress Control Number: 2016914086

Cover design by William Reynolds
Interior design and formatting by William Reynolds

Printed in the United States

THE WAY TO COACH
Leaders, Executives, and Managers

Part Three - More Coaching Conversations

Part Four - Coaching Situations
Individual Effectiveness

Part Five - Coaching Situations
Strong Relationships

CONTENTS

Part Six - Coaching Situations
Supporting Organizational Initiatives

Part Seven - Career Coaching

Part Eight - Business Coaching

Introduction

The Difference That Coaching Makes

Coaching has had a profound impact on my life. The best managers in my career were generous enough to be coaches as well as managers. They used coaching as a tool to help me reach new levels of success. By sitting down with me and asking probing questions, they helped me come up with my own observations, insights, and new ways of approaching problems. They gave me the capacity and confidence to advance my career and also to lead others, but these managers didn't just coach. They also mentored me, taught me, and, when required, directed me. I remember most the coaching conversations because they left me with lessons that are now part of who I am.

In contrast, my least effective managers came from the command-and-control school of management. They expected me to do what they said. Why? Just because. One of my worst managers once said, "Andrew, your job here is not to think but to execute." I'm not sure why he recruited MBAs from the top business schools if that was his philosophy. Regardless, I left that company - as did many of my talented colleagues - within only a year of joining.

Now that I run a coaching and leadership advisory practice, I enjoy the privilege of working with amazing clients. All of them recognize that even with the success they have achieved they can still get better. Some face challenges that hold back their careers and organizations. Others want a sounding board to test their ideas in a safe, confidential forum. Still others hire a coach to keep improving their game - the same way athletes have a coach to help them keep getting faster, stronger, and gain an edge. This work has proven to me that coaching can achieve extraordinary results.

At the same time, for the past fifteen years, I have run the Center for Executive Coaching, which trains and certifies professionals to become coaches. Approximately a thousand people have graduated from one of our training programs. When they arrive for training, they are already successful whether as leaders, business owners, or experts in a particular discipline. Almost all of them share that their most rewarding career experiences have involved both being coached and coaching and developing others to higher levels of performance. Some also note that they decided to become a coach after experiencing the benefits of coaching whether from a practicing coach or from a manager who took an interest in their development.

Some people reading this book are full-time coaches whether internal or external. Others are leaders and managers seeking to develop coaching as a skill. Some coach in a for-profit setting, while others coach in a nonprofit or government setting. To avoid confusion throughout this book, here is clarification of three terms.

First, when I use the word "coach," I am referring to anyone stepping into the role of coach. It doesn't matter whether you are a full-time coach or a manager who uses coaching as a skill to develop and engage your people.

Second, when talking about coaching, this book is focused on coaching people in organizations to be more effective in their roles. Sometimes this kind of coaching is called leadership coaching, executive coaching, management coaching, high-potential coaching, career coaching, development plan coaching, team coaching, or corporate coaching. Coaching may be defined by the sector, as in corporate coaching, nonprofit coaching, government coaching, and educational coaching. Coaches seem to love to make up new terms, and I am sure I have left out some possibilities. To keep things simple, I am going to call all of these things coaching. The key emphasis is on coaching professionals to higher levels of performance.

Third, to avoid having to write "the person being coached" every time we discuss the person you are coaching, I use the word "client" or the phrase "coaching client." Your so-called client might be an employee who has come to you for coaching, or it could be a colleague in an organization where you serve as an internal coach. Perhaps it is a paying client if you run a coaching practice. Even if the client is not paying you, I am still referring to the person being coached as a client.

Again, the emphasis should be on practicing coaching and getting results, not on splitting hairs about terminology. Coaching is fun and productive. Splitting hairs regarding terminology isn't.

Coaching is emerging from its infancy as a profession. Professional coaching associations can be found, and a common language for coaching and some clear core competencies define effective coaching. Research has documented the efficacy and returns of coaching, although common sense would indicate that receiving the support that effective coaching provides would have an impact.

Even as coaching evolves, a great many organizations, leaders, and managers haven't yet embraced it as a tool to develop and retain top talent. My intent with this book is to give you a practical guide without the jargon that unfortunately clouds many coach training programs today to get great results by adding coaching to your capabilities.

The rewards of coaching are fantastic. What leader wouldn't want the ability to help other people advance their careers, develop new skills, and move their organizations forward?

Enjoy!

Part One

FOUNDATIONS

What Coaching Is And Isn't

Coaching has many definitions, and many coaching associations have their own definitions of coaching along with sets of core competencies. This book defines coaching with a primary focus on coaching leaders, managers, and up-and-coming talent in organizations:

Coaching is an efficient, high-impact process of dialogue that helps highly performing people improve results in ways that are sustained over time.

Unlike traditional consulting assignments, coaching is efficient because it does not require invasive processes, large outside teams, or lengthy reports and analyses to get results.

It is a high-impact process because coaching typically gets results in short meetings, which can often last only a few minutes and are rarely longer than an hour. During this time, the coach and the individual being coached can generate important insights, gain clarity, focus, and make decisions to improve performance

Coaching is a dialogue. The coach and the person being coached are working together to make things happen. When you are coaching, you might speak 25 percent of the time, while the other person speaks 75 percent. Even if you are an expert in your field and know all the answers, you hold back to let the person being coached express concerns, challenges, and feelings. The dialogue allows the other person to determine their own answers and action steps, allowing the individual to not only solve immediate issues but also develop the capacity to keep improving.

Third, coaching works with high-performing people. It is not therapy meant to fix a person. As a coach in an organization, you work with people who are already highly functioning and successful. Like any of us, these professionals need support from time to time to perform better. Some might have serious blind spots, such as a leader who comes across as too abrasive, but coaching assumes that people have tremendous talent and potential.

Finally, your goal as a coach is to improve results in ways that are sustainable over time. The point of coaching is to achieve some sort of valuable outcome, usually related to improved performance, higher profits, career success, organizational effectiveness, or career and personal satisfaction. If you aren't helping people get results through coaching, you aren't coaching well. At the same time, coaching is about helping people improve their own capabilities and effectiveness so that the results and performance improvements last. To use the time-worn and famous quote, you are teaching people to fish, not feeding them for a day.

You can incorporate coaching into almost any role.

If you are a manager, coaching becomes a crucial skill to develop your people, improve performance, and gain leverage on your time.

Likewise, if you have a training role, coaching provides a way to sustain results. It makes common sense that following up after a training event reinforces learning and results. For instance, the coach can help the other person deal with specific challenges that might be preventing the training from having its full impact.

Similarly, if you are a management consultant, you probably already provide coaching as part of what you do. Coaching is the part of the engagement where you work one-on-one with clients to encourage them to make difficult decisions, step out of their comfort zone, stop destructive behavior, embrace change, and shift performance. For me, a long-time consultant, coaching is the fun part. Coaching lets you stop doing the analyses (and most of the time the client already knows the answer anyway), stop revising the PowerPoint presentation, and sit down face-to-face with the client to help them improve results. It's the part of the engagement where the client turns to you as their objective, trusted advisor—as a colleague and confidant.

It is also important to be clear about what coaching is NOT.

As noted before, coaching is not therapy. You are not fixing anybody. You are not delving into traumatic pasts. Good coaching certainly gets underneath the surface to look at perceptions, but the emphasis is on helping a healthy individual overcome challenges and be more effective. If you do work with someone who might need therapy, refer that person to a licensed professional.

Second, coaching is also not the same thing as management. Coaching is one tool that a manager can use, but it is not the only tool. Sometimes a manager needs to direct, tell, mentor, and/or teach. Coaching is a powerful skill but not the only thing that a good manager does.

Third, coaching is not consulting. Your primary focus is not to analyze and make recommendations. When appropriate and when you have permission, you can add a lot of value by sharing your own observations and insights, but coaching is more about having the other person develop their own insights and then take new actions to improve results.

Put another way, your job as a coach is not to be a "crystal ball" that magically provides an answer. As a coach, you will intervene and provide advice when appropriate. Successful coaches engage in dialogue with their clients and then customize a tool or solution that works for their unique solution. Sometimes there is no easy answer, and your value will be to support your clients in making decisions with incomplete information.

Fourth, coaching is not training or teaching, which focus on sharing knowledge and best practices and also helping people develop and hone skills. Learning usually occurs in a classroom setting, and the trainer or teacher leads the session. A coach might include teaching and training in the session, and good teachers and trainers coach, but the primary activities in each discipline are different.

Fifth, coaching isn't mentoring. Mentors are typically seasoned professionals within an organization who show less senior and experienced people the ropes. Mentors are great at pointing out how things work in an organization along with some of the hidden keys to getting things done and being successful. They also make introductions and sometimes pull strings. Again, there is overlap with coaching. The best mentors typically coach, and many coaches have years of experience to share with the people they are coaching.

Finally, coaching is not progressive discipline. Many organizations confuse the two, which sometimes causes coaching to be seen negatively. Progressive discipline, or probation, is a process of working with employees who are not performing, with the intent of documenting their poor performance and terminating their employment if they don't improve. In the past, this process was conflated with coaching. The word coaching was—and still is in some organizations—a euphemism for the last resort before firing someone. Today, coaching is seen as a standard leadership development tool. It is an investment in the talent the organization wants to develop and retain. Coaching should be separated from anything related to progressive discipline or probation.

Confused? Join the club. There is a lot of overlap among these different disciplines, and not everyone agrees on where the boundaries stop and start. My advice is that you not spend too much time obsessing about definitions. You can go online and see all sorts of self-appointed coaching police telling people what is and isn't coaching. Instead, do two things:

First, practice and keep getting better at coaching as you go through this book. You will learn firsthand about coaching and what it can do.

Second, and most importantly, if you focus more on having impact and helping the people you coach get results, everything will work out great.

Clearing Up Some Differences with Sports Coaching

Coach n 1: (sports) someone in charge of training an athlete or a team 2: a person who gives private instruction (as in singing or acting) 3: a railcar where passengers ride 4: a carriage pulled by four horses with one driver 5: a vehicle carrying many passengers; used for public transport.

-Source: WordNet ® 2.0 via www.dictionary.com

The above, dictionary definition of a coach is interesting because the first reference is to sports coaching. Many coaches who coach leaders, executives, managers, and up-and-coming talent don't like comparing what they do to what sports coaches do. When people think of the word coach, however, they usually think of sports coaches. Plus, it is hard to argue with the dictionary when it associates coaching with sports coaches.

Let's compare traditional sports coaches with the types of coaches described in this book - coaches who work with leaders, managers, and up-and-coming talent. Such coaches tend to meet with our clients in an office setting, where we sit down in a meeting room and coach. Coaching for us largely entails asking many questions so that clients can determine what to do on their own. We provide advice and observations but try to do so only when clients have exhausted their options.

During the heat of an athletic contest, when most people get to observe sports coaches, we don't see much of this kind of coaching. Sports coaches are much more active, drawing up diagrams, putting players in and taking them out of the game, calling time-outs, yelling at the referees, giving quick remarks to motivate the players, and shouting as they walk up and down the sidelines. They also have a role in recruiting players, cutting players, and setting salaries.

In other words, sports coaches are primarily managers. They manage games, and depending on their level of authority and relationship with the general manager, they also help manage their team.

Behind the scenes, though, top sports coaches sit down with the athletes on their teams and do indeed coach them. They watch tapes to learn what went well and what the athlete and team can do better. They ask questions and engage in a dialogue to understand the athletes' perspective about their performance. They make resources available for the player to train and improve, and then they try to connect with the players so that they take accountability for improving their own performance. Some coaches have more of a command-and-control approach, tending to tell players what they need to do. Others are better at engaging the players in a dialogue to understand what drives them, what makes them tick, and how they can take responsibility for improving their own performance.

Coaches who work with executives, managers, and up-and-coming talent can learn from sports coaches, especially the ones who know how to engage their players. Asking a never-ending circle of open-ended questions, as some coaching associations require, is not always the best way for a coach to get results. In real-world coaching, sometimes the coach needs to intervene a bit more proactively as a sports coach might. An effective coach sometimes makes observations, gives tough advice and feedback and, when needed, even gives a firm kick in the pants.

If you manage and coach a team of employees, the lines get even more fluid. Like a sports coach, you wear many hats, depending on your job description and span of control.

Moving away from the sports coach metaphor for a moment, notice the third, fourth, and fifth definitions of the word coach. These definitions focus on the coach as a vehicle. Personally, I like this more traditional definition best. Think of yourself as a railcar or carriage that gets people from where they are to where they want to be. You are a vehicle that moves individuals, teams, and sometimes the people in an entire organization from their current point A to a better point B.

Why People Who Work with Coaches Are Better

This week I started a coaching engagement with a young leader who hired me to become what he calls "a leader of leaders" within his Fortune 500 company. When we explored his aspirations during our first meeting, it occurred to me for the umpteenth time that leaders who hire coaches are just better: more open, more fun to work with, more willing to learn, more willing to stretch for outstanding achievements, more willing to take responsibility, more concerned about the development of their people, more willing to laugh at themselves, and more positive.

In this case, the up-and-coming executive shared some wonderful goals for himself, his employees, and his area of responsibility. He had the self-awareness and wisdom to know that employing a coach could help him have insights about the most effective and efficient ways to get where he wants.

To his credit, he is paying for the coaching with his own money because his company doesn't support external coaching. He had hired a coach a couple of years ago and got so much value out of the experience that he is doing it again, and I am privileged to be the coach that he chose.

Leaders like my new client come across differently from their colleagues who are not so coachable. They are like professional athletes who are committed to being the best and who hire a team to help them stay in shape and keep improving. They have that sense of drive, an internal fire, and the wisdom that an outside perspective is crucial for their ongoing improvement. These qualities are infectious and make them more attractive to others. One could argue that these attributes alone - even without a coach - will lead to success, and yet these individuals are still willing to hire a coach to get even further, faster.

Clearly, I'm not talking about people upon whom coaching is forced. That's the old way of coaching - in companies where coaching and progressive discipline are still synonyms or in companies that hire a coach as a last resort primarily as a way to document for legal purposes that they tried something before firing the employee. When coaching is forced on someone, he or she rarely wants to be coached.

Unfortunately, despite various studies proving that coaching provides important career and organizational benefits, many leaders still do not want a coach. They will sometimes point to members of their team and say to the coach, "Go fix them. They are the ones who need help." However, they don't see the benefits of coaching for themselves, at least until something really negative happens in their careers, and by then it is often too late.

There is a different feel to leaders who are closed to coaching, at least from my admittedly biased perspective. They come across as a bit more shutdown, unwilling to explore new possibilities, and perhaps even stagnant. They don't like asking for or listening to advice and feedback from others and tend to get defensive when constructive advice is offered. Sometimes they seem more concerned with other priorities than getting results, such as looking good, being the smartest person in the room, dominating others, or winning some sort of popularity contest. They often have some sort of behavioral blind spot, for instance, getting angry too quickly, avoiding appropriate conflict, or letting their egos get in the way of getting results and building positive business relationships. Like the villagers in the story about the emperor who had no clothes, no one in the organization dares to give them a hint that they have opportunities to improve, and they don't believe the messenger, usually from Human Resources, when he or she comes with bad news. Eventually, they get pushed out, never reach the next level, or burn out. This situation is a tragedy, because with a little bit of coaching and a mind-set of being coachable, they could find new ways to get results and thrive.

One other category of a leader is relevant to this discussion: the leader who has a coach but never does anything despite the coach's best efforts. These leaders like the status of having a coach but aren't really interested in making positive change. A coach is more like a status symbol to them, a way of saying, "Hey, I'm on the leading edge of the coaching trend. I have a coach with amazing credentials and a best-selling book. I'm getting enlightened as we speak. Now leave me alone." That's not the type of leader I am talking about in this chapter either.

Shown below are five attributes that I especially appreciate in leaders that hire a coach with the sincere intent of getting better, advancing their careers, and improving their organizations. You might have a different list or some tweaks to this one. If so, please let me know.

They are committed to continuous learning and improvement. By definition, coaching clients want to get better; otherwise, they wouldn't have hired a coach in the first place. It is refreshing to work with people who seek ongoing improvement compared with those who want to preserve the status quo, complete a list of tasks every day, and hope nothing changes.

Their high aspirations are exciting and often lead to great things. Leaders who seek out coaching usually have ambitious aspirations. They want to see great things happen, and people gravitate toward those with vision and a sense of purpose. At the same time, they hold themselves accountable for achieving their aspirations and goals, including ongoing gains in performance.

They see possibility in themselves and others. It is more enjoyable to be around people who see the potential for greatness all around them than to be around people who are cynical, apathetic, and perceive the people on their team to be subpar. This sense of possibility makes them more attractive to others and gets people aligned toward a common purpose.

They are willing to be vulnerable in ways that allow them to leapfrog over other leaders. The best leaders have some degree of vulnerability about them. It is not easy to learn the truth about how we actually come across to others compared with how we hope we come across to others. It is not easy to take responsibility for improving a strained professional relationship, to see one's own role in the situation, and proactively make amends. It is not easy to hear feedback from our colleagues and then resolve to improve. It is not easy to allow give and take when pushing an idea forward rather than win at all costs. This kind of vulnerability, however, ultimately leads to improved results, relationships, and success. Leaders who are vulnerable also tend to attract more followers—especially top talent—than those who are pushy, obnoxious, and unwilling to lighten up. By having just enough vulnerability, they are able to learn, grow, and get better.

They are more flexible in how they get results, which gives them more options. One benefit of coaching is that it often helps leaders develop new approaches to handle different situations. Many leaders are like the proverbial broken clock stuck on one time: They stick to a single style that is right once or twice each day and wrong the rest of the time. Leaders who are coachable understand the need to be flexible and have a range of styles and approaches for different people and situations. This allows them to lead more naturally and authentically instead of relying on long-standing patterns that make them rigid.

In essence, leaders who have coaches have a different quality about them and are better. I am so grateful to be in the coaching profession because it allows me to work with the best of the best.

Why Organizations with a Culture of Coaching Are Better

If an individual who works willingly with a coach is better, it makes sense that an entire organization filled with people who are receptive to coaching is better too.

Coaching is not a panacea that can solve all of a company's problems. It is also not the only tool available to develop talent in an organization, but it can make a company better, and it deserves a place as one of the most important tools to improve performance. Visit the International Coach Federation website (coachfederation.org) for the latest research about the benefits and results of coaching. According to most studies, coaching returns $4 to $8 for every dollar invested. The benefits of coaching to organizations include the following:

- improved loyalty by the people being coached
- improved relationships up, down, and across the organization
- improved teamwork
- improved productivity

Once you know how coaching works, it makes common sense that coaching brings the above benefits. Coaching enables people to discuss issues beyond analytic content. The people being coached start to focus on how well they relate to others, they learn about working with different styles, and they collaborate more willingly and effectively. They have open, honest conversations that are deeper than the usual progress reviews and often come up with innovative ideas that can have a major impact on their teams and organizations. People being coached are encouraged to seek out and listen to advice from others rather than getting defensive. As part of the coaching process, they also commit to making specific improvements in their behavior and attitude. They are better able to balance ego, results, and relationships in their work so that they make things happen while nurturing their relationships with colleagues. Would that type of process make a difference in your organization?

While a culture of coaching might seem touchy-feely, it isn't. Effective coaching includes metrics to track, measure, and achieve results. It also includes conversations to hold people accountable, get underneath the issues, and get things back on track.

Coaching works well in all sectors, including organizations with highly specialized, technical, scientific, or clinical professionals, because it helps people develop the softer skills that they might not have learned during their years of education. They can then take ideas and use influence to get buy-in and execute more quickly and effectively. From biotech firms to Wall Street financial companies, law firms, and emerging technology companies, coaching can broaden the skills and tools that employees need to get results.

It also makes sense that employees in organizations that support coaching are more motivated and loyal because they recognize that leadership is willing to invest in their development beyond the usual, generic, off-the-shelf training programs. High-potential talent quickly gets bored by the generic leadership training programs on the market, which is why it is estimated that billions of dollars are wasted every year on leadership training that doesn't even make a dent on performance. In contrast, organizations that encourage leaders and managers to coach and be coached are able to create personalized approaches to developing talent.

The substance of coaching is quite powerful, too, and helps people work better on teams, lead more effectively, and communicate with more impact. The content you will read in this book offers approaches to help people get better in these areas.

Where would you rather work: in an organization that bakes coaching into its very fabric or in an organization with a traditional command-and-control approach to getting things done? Where do you think the freshest talent coming out of the best schools wants to work? In this respect, organizations with a culture of coaching are also better because they are more likely to attract top talent.

Imagine a company in which every single leader and manager knows how to coach their team members to improved performance. Imagine that each leader and manager sits down with each team member and develops a personalized coaching plan to develop that team member and then follows through with that plan. Furthermore, imagine that as people receive coaching they are more receptive to listen to advice, to examine how well they relate to others, and to commit to making improvements. They have open conversations about their progress and keep working to get even better. What would be possible in an organization in which every employee is committed to this process?

It doesn't have to take much time to make this happen. Coaching can happen during normal one-on-one update meetings; it can happen in short bursts while doing rounds in the workplace; it can happen as part of implementing key strategic initiatives, and it can happen during both formal and informal performance reviews. If leadership is committed, they can create a culture of coaching.

Examples of Situations that Are Opportunities for Coaching

Coaching solves specific problems. The problem can be vague, as in "I just want a sounding board to bounce ideas around" or "I want to become a better leader." Usually, however, the client has a specific issue to address. Common challenges include the following:

- I am juggling too many priorities and feel overwhelmed.

- My career has reached a plateau, and I want it to advance.

- I have a conflict that is hurting my ability to get things done.

- Our team is not working well together.

- We need a strategy.

- We have a strategy, but it isn't being implemented.

- People are resisting change.

- I need a succession plan.

- I received feedback that I need to correct a certain behavior because it is hurting performance.

- My employees are not engaged.

- I need to change the culture.

- I need more leadership presence.

- I need to influence people with more impact.

- I need to manage my time better.

- I can't determine how to get the organization to embrace my idea.

- We need a stronger board of directors.

- I need to develop more leaders.

- Our organization has reached a point where we need to put into place systems and processes before we can improve.

- I need to prepare for my exit from this company.

- I want us to be better at collaborating.

- We don't execute well.

- I need a stronger personal brand.

- I am not getting along well with my manager.

- I need a strong network of business relationships.

- I love technology but not working with people.

- I want more accountability from my people.

- We need to change how we do things, and the organization is not moving quickly enough.

- I am spending too much time at the office and need to delegate more.

- I am too much of a perfectionist.

- We need to improve quality.

- We need to improve our revenues and profits.

Many more examples could be provided, but these are some areas where coaching is valuable. Coaching solves problems. When you hear someone complain about a pressing issue, you have an opportunity to coach them if they are willing.

This leads to the first rule of coaching . . .

The First Rule of Coaching

The first rule of coaching is that you can only coach people who want to be coached. It is a simple rule, and yet aspiring coaches break the rule all the time. Coaching only becomes possible when two conditions are met:

First, someone faces a challenge that is significant enough for that person to want to be coached. This condition is not easy to meet. For most people, deciding to get coaching is like deciding to go to the doctor. Nobody wants to go to a doctor because doing so makes us feel vulnerable and exposed. We only go when we feel enough pain. Being coached also makes us feel vulnerable and exposed at least until we build trust with the coach. For this reason, people rarely want coaching unless they have a big enough problem and enough pain to want support.

Second, permission must be granted. Either the coach asks permission to coach the other person, or the other person asks for coaching. Anyone with a spouse or significant other knows that coaching without permission is not coaching; it is nagging.

With this in mind, people don't naturally seek out coaching. Effective people in organizations typically believe they can figure things out on their own. They don't want help. They don't want others involved in their business, and they definitely don't want to be exposed. Often, they don't even think they have a problem!

Accordingly, the way to find people who want coaching is not by pitching coaching to people who probably don't want to be coached. Nobody wakes up in the morning and says, "I'm a horrible leader. I better go get some coaching today."

The way to find people who want coaching is by finding people who have problems that they recognize as problems and asking them if they would be open to coaching. Alternatively, someone with a problem might come to you and ask for coaching.

Complications arise when we make assumptions that people who should get coaching actually want coaching. For instance, I trained a coach who thought she had secured her first coaching prospect. She explained, "I know lots of middle managers at the company, and they tell me that the senior leadership team is doing all sorts of things that are demoralizing. They are abusive. They are arrogant. They don't listen. They don't seem to care, but I can't figure out how to get the senior leaders to hire me as a coach so they can change these behaviors."

In fact, senior leaders in this company don't necessarily want coaching. The middle managers would like to see them get coached, but there is no indication that the leaders themselves see a problem or want to change. The coach could work with the middle managers if they have the budget to learn to adapt to or cope with the senior team to be more effective, but as long as they are the only ones who acknowledge a problem the senior leaders are not going to ask for coaching.

Coaching someone who is not coachable is like trying to coach a vampire to stop biting. It's not going to happen. The vampire is made to bite! Maybe the villagers living near the vampire's castle want the vampire to change through coaching, but the vampire doesn't. The vampire might be open to coaching about how to recruit more vampires or how best to use his minions assuming he has a challenge in those areas. Likewise, the villagers might be open to coaching about how to protect each other from being bitten, but until the vampire realizes that he doesn't want to bite people anymore or someone can convince the vampire that biting is not in his interests, there will be no coaching on that topic.

Please heed this first and fundamental rule of coaching. Nobody wants unsolicited coaching.

How Coachable Are You?

A corollary to the first rule of coaching is that coaches should set the highest standard of being coachable. This sounds obvious, yet many people get into coaching more as an escape or as a way to show they are above other people. They hide behind their coaching certification, use jargon to show that they stand apart, or go to self-proclaimed transformational workshops with a bit of an air of superiority. Some want to be seen as gurus who are above it all. Some are rigid, defensive, and don't listen well. This is not good for the profession. If you are going to use coaching skills effectively, a good starting point is to develop your ability to be coachable.

Someone who is truly coachable is willing to learn from anyone and anything. Instead of getting defensive and taking things personally, the coachable professional uses both achievements and setbacks as opportunities to learn. That person is constantly trying to improve and committed to personal and professional growth.

When people offer advice or constructive feedback to someone who is coachable, that person listens to it, directs it to understand and learn more, thanks the other person, and makes amends for past behavior if they have not been as effective as they could have been. Then they consider the feedback and advice and decide how best to use it in the future. If the advice is valid and helpful, they use it to get even better.

The coachable individual also appreciates that different people have different ways of communicating, thinking, making decisions, relating to groups, getting things done, and leading. They even have different energy levels. Someone who is coachable works hard to develop a flexible style to work effectively with different people in different situations.

Perhaps the best way to develop coachability is by having a coach. At the same time, get into the habit of asking others for their advice about strengths you can build on and ways you can be even better. Listen to the advice. Feel any natural resistance you have to receiving it. Then take it in and process it with the intent of learning and improving based on how helpful the advice is for you. Here are some questions to answer to confirm that you are coachable:

- How open are you when people give you advice or feedback?

- How well do you respond to advice or feedback that points out a mistake you made or something you could have done better?

- How focused are you on constant learning and ongoing professional and personal development?

- How aware are you about styles that differ from you own? How well do you adapt to other people's styles so that you can build rapport with them and develop effective solutions?

What else can you do to be more coachable?

The Fundamental Coaching Conversation

The fundamental coaching conversation is called active inquiry, which combines powerful questions, active listening, and dialogue with the client so that the client receives insights to overcome challenges. Four steps are involved in active inquiry:

First, agree on the intent of the coaching session. Without a clear intent, the session will tend to meander or ramble along without achieving much of importance. Ask the client, "What would be a great outcome to achieve in our coaching session?" Take your time to be sure the client's intent is specific, measurable, and something both of you can achieve in the time you have.

Second, let the client know you are going to be doing active inquiry. For example, "To achieve this goal, I'm going to ask you some open-ended questions. The intent of these questions is to better understand the challenge you are facing and hopefully have you come up with some ideas to overcome it. Is that okay?" Setting up active inquiry in this way is helpful for a couple of reasons. Most importantly, if you don't, and then start asking the client open-ended questions, that person might get confused and think, "Why are you asking me all of these questions?" By setting up active inquiry as an exercise, however, you show that you have a process to help clients solve their problems. You aren't just asking a random set of questions but rather you know what you are doing. Finally, by asking permission to move into active inquiry, you confirm that the client is coachable.

Third, dive into active inquiry, which is the meat of the process. You ask open-ended questions to produce results. A good open-ended question begins with a "what," "who," "where," "when," or "how" and perhaps a smattering of "why" (if too many, you come across as judgmental or interrogative).

You focus on asking primarily open-ended questions and not yes/no questions because you want to know what the client is thinking. You want to understand the client's world view. Yes/no questions tend to close off the conversation, especially if the client's answer is "no." Watch out for questions that jump to such suggestions as "Have you tried Y?" or that clarify the past, such as "Did you do X?" Develop the skill of letting clients arrive at their own insights and conclusions. Open-ended questions do that more effectively.

At the same time, yes/no or closed-ended questions can occasionally be very effective. A closed-ended question can be provocative or stand out as an exclamation point. For instance, "Would you rather be popular or successful?" The number of effective open-ended questions is nearly infinite. You will read about many of them as the book progresses to some specific coaching situations. To get started, here are some examples:

- What are your ideas to solve the problem?

- If you had to make a decision now, what would you do?

- Where do you want to start to start making progress?

- What lessons can you apply from a time when you successfully dealt with a challenge like this before?

- Who can you go to for support?

- What strengths can you bring to bear on this problem?

- If you were giving advice to a colleague with this issue, what would you tell them?

- What resources do you control that can help?

- Who do you need to influence to make progress here?

- What do you see as the root cause of the issue?

- If you were in my shoes, what would you want me to ask you?

- What is the other person's perspective on this issue?

Good open-ended questions have a certain amount of voltage to them. You're not just sitting in a coffee shop and talking about how the client's day is going. You are doing your best to help that person improve. You don't have to spend the client's time getting up to speed on the situation or being trained by this individual. You don't have to delve into the past unless it is to discover other situations that can help resolve the current one. Focus on assisting the client to gain insights and direction and for discovering the best approach to solving their challenge.

Many leaders wonder why they can't just jump in and tell the client what they would do. You can, but that's something different from coaching. Also, if you want people you are coaching to develop professionally and personally, it is most effective to let them solve their own problems.

A metaphor that helps explain this is to imagine that your client is a steam boiler filled to the top with steam. Most successful managers and leaders are confident and sometimes a little arrogant. They already know the answer. Their tendency is to resist suggestions made by others. Active inquiry allows the steam to vent by giving clients the opportunity to share their thoughts. Once the steam vents, the steam boiler empties out. It has room for more steam, meaning that the client is more likely to be open to suggestions and ideas from others.

During this phase of active inquiry, your primary job as a coach is to listen. Ideally, you are talking 25 percent of the time or less, while the client talks 75 percent of the time. From time to time, reflect on what you have heard—both the content of what the client says and any emotions you hear—to be sure you are talking about the same thing. In this way, active listening becomes the key to effective active inquiry and coaching. As a colleague of mine keeps reminding me, "If you listen, the client tells you the next question to ask."

Sometimes clients say they have no idea and want you to jump in with what you would do. Resist the urge to be the hero. Tell them that you have some ideas but want to hear their thinking first. After being a coach for almost two decades, I can almost guarantee that when clients ask for your ideas too soon they are setting you up. Every time I have opened my big mouth with my brilliant ideas, the client has argued with me that my ideas are wrong. If you do step in with your ideas and the client rejects them, that gives you the opportunity to say, "Well, you asked for my ideas. I gave them to you, and you didn't like them. Your turn! What are your ideas?"

Fourth is to wrap up. Do this by asking what insights your client has had and, if appropriate and with permission, offering your own observations. This phase begins when the conversation loses energy, or when it feels it's appropriate to summarize. At this point, simply say, "Let's pause here. What insight or insights, if any, have you had so far?" Let clients tell you what, if any, insights they have had. Then make sure you heard them and ask what they will do after the coaching session to take action. If appropriate, create a specific action plan and commitment by the client to take action. Challenge the client to agree to specific deadlines where it makes sense.

If you don't agree with the client's conclusions, ask permission to provide your perspective. Remember, however, that the client ultimately has to decide the right course for him or her. You are not a guru.

If you are aligned with the client's insights and you still have some observations of your own, ask permission to share them. Coaching is not a passive process, and clients usually want to hear your suggestions. You might say, "Do you mind if I share an observation?" Then, if the client is open to it, share it and find out what the client thinks about it. Don't just let it hang out there and end the session abruptly, as I have observed some coaches do.

At the end of the session, ask clients what was most valuable for them. Doing this is a great way to end the session and confirm whether or not you achieved the session's intent.

This process can take five minutes, thirty minutes, or an hour. Generally, the coach and client weave in and out of these steps during the course of a coaching session. Start with a goal, move into active inquiry, summarize and confirm any insights, and then keep moving ahead through active inquiry.

The best way to learn how to do active inquiry is by doing it. Coaching is a practice. Find some friends and colleagues, ask them about an issue they are facing, and ask permission to practice active inquiry with them. Work hard at listening, asking open-ended questions, and not jumping in to solve their problems. At some point, if you join a coach training program, such as the Center for Executive Coaching, you can even have your coaching conversations reviewed confidentially so that you keep getting better. Regardless, ask your client for advice about what you did well and what you could have done better.

Later on, you will read about an in-depth coaching process. For now, if you can lead active inquiry, you can coach. The flow of a session is quite simple, and consists of eight steps. Part of this was covered in the previous section.

The eight steps to conduct a single coaching session are:

1. Get clear with the client about the intent of the session.

2. Explain the active inquiry process and ask permission to dive in.

3. Use active inquiry to help the client improve.

4. Ask the client what insights they are having, confirm that the client is moving toward the intent of the session, and then get back to active inquiry.

5. Confirm next steps and what the client is accountable for doing. If and when appropriate, ask permission to share your own observations and insights, and get the client's feedback.

6. Schedule the next meeting or time to check in to follow up.

7. Ask the client what was most valuable from the coaching.

8. Confirm that you achieved the desired intent of the session.

There is no correct answer about how long a coaching session should be. For external coaches, sessions run between thirty and sixty minutes. If you are a manager, you might be able to coach a colleague or employee through an issue in a matter of minutes. On the other hand, sometimes an issue is so complex that it requires several sessions to tease out and resolve.

If you can run a single coaching session and make progress, you can set up multisession coaching engagements. Simply take small steps toward helping the client achieve their goals and keep getting better.

The Six Most Important Questions to Ask in a Coaching Session

One: "What would be the most valuable outcome you can achieve in our session?" This question focuses the session on a specific outcome. If the client doesn't have a clear, measurable, specific outcome, the session is unlikely to go anywhere. Even if clients simply wants a sounding board to check the wisdom of their idea about an issue, that at least tells you both what the client wants out of the session. Alternative wording is: "What outcome would make this session the most valuable hour of your week?"

Two: "What are your ideas to find a solution?" By asking this question, you jump right to the client's perceptions rather than interrupting with your own. Alternatives include "Where do you want to start?" and "What do you see as the key areas to discuss?" Frame the question to come from the highest and broadest level of logic to learn the most you can about the client's own thoughts about the issue.

Three: "What are your insights so far?" Ask this question after conducting some active inquiry. It will stimulate the discussion and help clients crystallize their thinking. Listen for how closely the client is to making progress on their stated outcome.

Four: "What would you like to discuss now?" Use this question to let the client guide the process. You learn more about clients when you let them guide the process instead of when you direct it with your questions.

Similarly, if the client is at a fork in the road and has brought up a few issues or points, you can summarize them and ask, "Which of these - or perhaps another avenue - do you want to discuss now?"

Five: "What are next steps?" By asking this question at the end of the session, the client has accountability to take action and keep making progress.

Six: "What was most valuable for you in our discussion?" Finally, this question adds value to your coaching. Listen for how closely you came to achieving the client's intent during the session, but sometimes the client gets value that is different from what was expected. Check to be sure that clients received what they wanted. If not, get back to active inquiry either now or by scheduling a future meeting.

Bad Coaching

Sometimes the best way to learn how to do something is by learning how not to do it. With that idea in mind, this article shares 14 examples of bad coaching. As you probably already know, coaching is partly the process of asking powerful questions to help the client deal with a challenge and improve. The coach works in partnership with the client to concentrate on certain issues, being focused, attentive, and reflecting back what has been heard. The coach offers suggestions only as a last resort and only with permission. In normal coaching conversations, the coach talks no more than 25 percent of the time. In contrast, here are examples of what not to do:

Fixing. If you are in a position to coach someone, you likely have experience and knowledge. You are also probably accustomed to stepping in and solving problems for people. When coaching, it can be extremely tempting to just give the client the answer, but when you jump right into solving the client's problem for them, you aren't coaching them. You could be advising, directing, teaching, or telling, but you aren't coaching.

The problem with fixing the client's problem is that just because you know the answer and would be able to implement it doesn't mean your client can. Coaching allows you to explore the best answer given where the client is right now along with their own unique talents, experiences, and style. The right solution for you might not be the right solution for the client. At the same time, even if your solution is correct, that doesn't mean your client is ready to implement it. Coaching allows you and the client to explore what challenges they face ahead.

What if you can't focus on the coaching because you are so sure you know the answer? If you are really certain that you are smart enough to know the right answer for the client, I suggest saying, "Do you mind if I jump in? I have a lot of experience with this issue, and I think I have a possible solution . . ." Share your idea, but let the client decide if they are ready to accept it. Then decide if you should continue being a consultant and advisor or if you should get back to being a coach. The latter means that you once again ask open-ended questions based on what the client wants to do. The former means that you use facts and logic to keep making your case. Be explicit with the client whether you are wearing the hat of a consultant, teacher, manager, or coach. Otherwise, your client might get confused.

I used to see myself as a smart guy who could solve any problems. I left coaching sessions feeling great about myself, but clients didn't implement my suggestions. When I allowed clients to solve their own problems, however, they felt smart and also felt that I was providing great value. *Don't fix. Coach.*

Knowing the answer and manipulating. If you know the answer, don't torture the client into figuring it out on their own with a series of Socratic questions. That's not coaching. At best, it is teaching the way they do in law school. At worst, it's manipulation—your attempt to get the client to come to the same conclusion as you have about a decision. From the client's point of view, it can feel condescending, tedious, and obnoxious to have to endure a series of questions knowing that the coach already has the answer.

Coaching is for situations when you and the client jump into the unknown. Don't play the game called "What's in my pocket?" If you already know the answer you want the person to also know, and you are not flexible about it, don't torture them. Simply tell them.

I worked with one manager who had a tendency to play this game. After interviewing his employees, I discovered that they called this manager's process "torturous self-realization." They loved his coaching style when it made sense for him to coach them, but when he already knew the answer, his employees found his approach to be inauthentic, tedious, and an inefficient use of time.

Interrupting. Don't interrupt when you coach. This deceptively simple rule can be hard for coaches who process information quickly. If you interrupt, you might cut off the client just when they are about to say something crucial. Get comfortable with silence. Wait a beat or two to be sure your client has finished speaking. Sometimes silence is the best coaching question of all because it encourages the client to think more deeply about the issue and go beyond the usual.

Distracted coaching. If you are in a noisy place, have crises to handle, are on the phone, or checking your email on your laptop, you are not in a position to coach. Coaching requires focus. Also, your clients deserve your attention. Don't coach when you are distracted.

Stacking questions. Stacking questions means that you ask your client more than one question at a time. For instance: "Tell me about the people involved in this issue. Also, what do you see as the main ways to resolve the issue? And, when you do resolve it, what are your action steps?" Even though the coach might be thinking of many different questions, a client can usually focus on, let alone remember, only one question at a time. Be patient. Let the process unfold. Ask one question at a time. If you do, you might also find that the next logical question is different from you had expected.

Checklist coaching. Checklist coaching means that you already have a list of questions to ask. There is no need to listen and no room for creativity or flexibility. Sometimes coaches falling into this habit don't even seem to be listening to the client. They ask one question, maybe grunt acknowledgment, and then move to the next. The client doesn't feel heard. The coach is more like a journalist conducting an interview than a coach. Instead, let the coaching process unfold naturally. Ask questions based on what you hear the client tell you. If the client doesn't seem to know what to say, you might introduce a different line of inquiry to ignite new ideas, but avoid rote, checklist-based coaching.

The Diagnostic. The diagnostic sounds like this: "Have you tried A? Have you tried B? Have you tried C? Have you tried D?" It's similar to having an algorithm or flow chart and similar to a doctor trying to diagnose a disease. This kind of approach is good for solving problems and for consulting, but it is not good coaching—good coaching asks open-ended questions and allows the client to come up with their own ideas. If you think a particular situation warrants a diagnostic approach, let clients know this is what you are doing so that they don't expect coaching.

Hiding suggestions. Some coaches hide their ideas in the form of a question, thinking that asking any type of question is good coaching. For instance:

"Have you tried X?"
"What about trying Y?"
"When will you set up a meeting with him to discuss this?"

It is better to be less directive and to ask questions that let clients lead the process. For instance:

"What are your ideas to solve this challenge?"
"What can you try?"
"Who can help?"

Bringing up some sort of fad book or trend. Some coaches are suckers for the latest trend or fad. Whether it is taking emotional intelligence far beyond where the initial author intended, claiming pseudoscientific applications of neuroscience, becoming a fan of the latest approach to personal transformation, or glomming on to the latest positive psychology guru, you can bet there are coaches waiting in line to share it with clients. These coaches come across more as evangelists pushing a particular philosophy. They make the coaching profession seem flaky. Worse, prospects view these coaches the same way we think about religious evangelists who knock on our doors on Sundays. We want them to go away.

Don't look for fads. Let the client's problem dictate your approach instead of pushing an approach and hoping it solves a problem for the client. Ask great questions, listen, and focus on the client's specific situation rather than forcing the client into a specific box. Applying frameworks or concepts from various disciplines can be valuable, but wait until the client's situation calls for it.

Never-ending, open-ended questions. Some coaches believe you can never offer advice or observations to a client. They insist on only asking open-ended questions. As a result, their coaching feels more like therapy. It also becomes frustrating. One executive who came to me for coaching after firing a coach who did this called this form of coaching "an expensive waste of time."

A balance exists between jumping too quickly to suggesting solutions and not offering observations or insights at all. It is perfectly acceptable to offer your ideas and insights. In fact, clients expect it. If you wait until you have thoroughly explored the client's issue and possible solutions from their point of view and then ask permission to share your insights, the client usually appreciates it.

Caring more than they do and getting frustrated. Sometimes it feels that you care more about the client's goals and aspirations than the client does. They simply won't do what they need to do to achieve the goals they claim they want to achieve. It's frustrating to feel this way.

Many parents also face this issue, for instance, when their child declares they want to go to Harvard, yet won't do their homework. When this happens, avoid the temptation of getting too attached to your client's goals and becoming disappointed.

You can certainly talk openly about the client's lack of effort and coach them about what might be going on to prevent the required actions, but if you start judging the client, become exasperated, or even chide them during coaching sessions, you have jumped into the realm of bad coaching.

Getting trained on the client's time. You can coach a client without being an expert in their field or even about the situation they are facing. If you find you are asking clients to bring you up to speed on key terminology, how to do their job, or in-depth play-by-play about what happened recently, you might be doing things that are valuable to you but meaningless to the client. These types of questions are called situational questions. A few can be helpful in the way a bit of salt can enhance a meal, but you are not helping anyone if you get carried away.

One of the powerful aspects of coaching is that you don't have to have content knowledge to ask the kinds of questions that help the client improve. This statement might not make sense right now, but you will discover it is accurate the more you coach. Once you realize this, coaching becomes easier, more fun, and more effective.

Doing the client's dirty work What do you do if the client asks you to coach employees who are not performing as they should? One option is to go and coach them, but be careful. Sometimes clients ask the coach to step in and coach members of their team when what they really want is for you to do their dirty work for them. It is often better to coach your clients on how they can be more effective in leading and influencing the other person.

For instance, I worked with a client who was leading a major performance improvement program. He asked me to talk to one of his executives who wasn't participating in the program and coach him to get on board and find opportunities to improve productivity in his area. What would you do in that situation? In my judgment, my client wasn't asking me to coach this executive. He was asking me to influence the executive to get on board with the program. That's my client's job! On further exploration, I learned that my client was a bit afraid of this executive and didn't like confronting him. So we worked on strategies for my client to get over this fear and how best to influence this executive

Remember: Coaching isn't about stepping in and doing a client's work. It is about helping clients be more effective so that they can do the work without you.

Failing to put in place ways to track progress and measure results. Like any other profession, coaching is about getting results. If you don't agree on a clear intent and outcome with your client, you won't know if you deliver value. If you don't put a way to measure progress in place, you won't know how your client is doing. If you don't track progress, you won't know when you have achieved the desired outcome(s). Any subject for coaching – from improved confidence to new attitudes and behaviors, stronger relationships, and better individual or team performance – and be measured if the coach and client are thoughtful enough.

Find Your Coaching Style

If you are a manager, you know that different leadership and communication styles work better with different people and in different situations. The same is true for coaching. Most seasoned coaches adapt to the situation and needs of the client. At the same time, almost all coaches have a natural style that fits them best. A few adjectives that define different coaching styles include edgy, nurturing, contemplative, patient, intuitive, positive, intense, high-energy, relaxed, logical, visionary, provocative, and peaceful. One way to define your style is by looking at how you balance ego, results, and relationships.

First, coaches need some degree of ego to be on equal footing with highly successful managers, executives, and up-and-coming talent. The coach who emphasizes ego a bit too much, however, comes across as arrogant and might have trouble stepping back and letting the client do the work.

Second, coaching is meaningless if the coach and client don't achieve results. Meanwhile, the coach who overemphasizes results tends to come across as too forceful and directive, even to the point of hurting relationships.

Third, the coach and client should have trust, rapport, and a strong working relationship. Otherwise, the client won't open up and be willing to be vulnerable. On the other hand, the coach who emphasizes relationships too much might not say what needs to be said to get results. That coach might be more interested in being popular than in helping the client with open, honest conversation.

Different situations, organizational cultures, and clients call for a different balance of these three attributes. For instance, a coach working with a Wall Street CEO might need a different style than a coach who works with an up-and-coming manager in a small nonprofit organization. Even with a natural style, the savvy coach adjusts to the client and situation. For instance, I had the opportunity to interview one of the most successful college basketball coaches in NCAA history. When I asked him how he coached individuals on the team, he replied that in general there are three types of players. The first wants the coach who puts his arm around the player's shoulder. The second responds best to tough love, or what this coach called "kick in the pants coaching." The third type does best when the coach calls the player's mom. His job as a coach is to get to know his players and adapt his style accordingly.

What about you? What is your natural style as a coach? Do you prefer to tell it like it is and be a bit forceful? Do you set a completely positive tone and emphasize what's working well? Do you step back and try for a neutral tone? There is no right or wrong answer, but the more you can adapt your style to what's right for the situation, the more effective your coaching will be.

Suppose your client has just gotten some negative feedback about a project they are leading. Because of this feedback, they are feeling down. Depending on the client, this is probably not be the best time to get on the client's case and reinforce the negative feedback. It's probably better just to listen, let the client vent, and perhaps help the client talk about what's working well and how they can use their talents to get back on track.

Similarly, what style would you use if your client has failed to follow through with an action plan for a few weeks in a row? Let's assume you have already explored some of the underlying reasons why the client won't act, and the client told you they had resolved those. Perhaps it is time to add a bit more edge to your coaching style, maybe even questioning whether or not the client is really committed to achieving their stated goals.

Another way to adapt your style is by completing an off-the-shelf assessment of your client. A validated, reliable assessment tool will give you insights about your client's natural thinking style, communication style, behavioral traits, and even values. For example, if you know that someone is more direct and bottom line in their thinking and communication, you would coach them differently from somebody who needs to go into minute, step-by-step detail about issues. Similarly, you might move at a different pace with a client who processes information very quickly compared with a client who needs time to process information.

External coaches have a bit of an advantage compared with internal managers who use coaching as a tool to develop their people because they can build a brand based on their natural and unique style. They become known for solving specific issues in specific ways. They can attract clients that are comfortable with their style and approach. In contrast, managers inherit a diverse group of employees and colleagues. They can't choose their coaching clients the way that external coaches can and have to be more flexible.

Take a moment to define your natural style as a coach. What types of people seem most comfortable for you? Which types of people would be more challenging? In which situations or with which people do you see yourself needing to adapt? Finally, how willing are you to adapt and be more flexible depending on the situation and the individual?

The Sublime Art of Asking One Question that Changes Everything

The best coaches do less, not more. The more you talk, the less you learn about a client and how that person is thinking about challenges they face. The more you step in and solve the client's problem, the less you allow the client to develop. Coaching is about building capacity and developing people, not about showing how much you know. Consider the ideal of finding just one question to ask during a coaching session - a question that somehow changes everything for the client.

Perhaps you have had the good fortune of being in a meeting with an executive who had a similar gift. That person patiently listens to all the points of view in the room and then asks a simple question that changes the way everyone thinks about the issue. Something like this happened in the carbonated beverage industry and changed the entire vision, strategy, and conversation among its biggest competitors. Imagine a strategic planning meeting at one of the biggest companies in the industry. As usual, everyone is talking about how the company can increase share of market among carbonated soft drinks. Suddenly, someone asks, "What would be a different way to think about market share than share of beverages sold?"

This simple question led to a massive insight: "What if we stop thinking about share of the carbonated beverage market and think about share of stomach?" Now the people around the table see the opportunity to sell other beverages, such as sports drinks, fruit juice, and bottled water. They also see the possibility of marketing snack foods, restaurants, and anything else related to food and beverage consumption. The entire focus of the company - and soon the industry - expands dramatically, as does its growth potential. One question changes everything.

As a coach, unlike with this example, you don't have to come up with earth-shattering questions every coaching session or even every engagement. The idea of asking one question that changes everything is ideal, but it's not possible to do this all the time. Not every coaching session has major breakthroughs or cathartic moments, but the concept of one-question-coaching is a good one to keep in mind to make sure you are focused on listening and asking questions that bring high impact and value to the person you are coaching. The best coaching questions are often the simplest, such as the six key questions described in an earlier chapter. Even asking clients for their ideas to solve a problem can open up possibilities.

As you practice coaching, think before you ask a question. Consider if it will be beneficial for your client. Does your question have a little bit of voltage to it so that it gets the client thinking? Does it allow the client to see new possibilities, see things in a new way, and at least move on to insights and action? By thinking about these questions, you are on the path to the idea of asking one question that changes everything.

Getting Beyond
the What and the How

Some coaches worry that they can't coach people without significant content knowledge. For instance, what if you don't have an MBA? What if you don't have clinical experience and are asked to coach physicians or nurse managers. Most organizations have many people who are thoroughly familiar with highly technical content. They also have more than enough people who can develop action plans and process maps. Even still, they don't execute or get things done. How can this be when organizations invest so much in people with the right education and training?

It's because a third aspect is involved in getting results beyond the "what" and the "how." It is often invisible to leaders and managers, especially in highly technical organizations. The third aspect involves looking below the surface:

- how leaders or managers appear to others
- the impact they have when communicating
- how they build and nurture relationships up, down, and across the organization
- how well they navigate the politics of the organization
- how effectively they engage and mobilize people
- how they resolve conflict
- how aware they are of other people's styles, motivations, and values - and adapts to them or not

- their perceptions and thinking style and how these either move them ahead or hold them back

- their natural filters and orientations when making decisions

- how they lead and work on teams

- how they react to change

- the conversations they have and don't have

- how they carry themselves in high-pressure situations

- how and with whom they spend their time

- what they reward and what they punish

- how they influence others

The above attributes are only a few of the areas where a coach goes beyond the what and the how. Coaching is powerful and valuable because the coach sees things in the spaces between analyzing and planning. Coaching is able to uncover the issues that keep organizations with top talent from getting things done and being as effective as they can be. As a coach, you have the opportunity to focus your discussions on areas where most leaders, managers, and up-and-coming talent don't spend enough time.

This focus on the third, unseen domain has two sides to it. On the one side, some leaders question the value of coaching. They see it as soft. The areas that coaching explores weren't part of their years of training, and by extension, aren't relevant. On the other side, once you can demonstrate the ability to use coaching to get better results, you will earn the respect and admiration of your clients.

Ethics and Confidentiality

As with any profession, coaching has developed a set of ethical guidelines. The International Coach Federation has one of the most detailed, and you can visit their website to read them. Generally, the guidelines state what you would expect and are straightforward:

- Don't misrepresent your credentials as a coach.

- Disclose conflicts of interest and avoid coaching engagements that have significant conflicts of interest.

- Set up a clear contract with the client.

- Don't get romantically involved with your clients.

- If the client wants to end the coaching relationship, let him.

- Maintain confidentiality.

The last one deserves discussion. The first coach I ever had burned me badly by breaking confidentiality. At the time, I reported to the CEO of the company and was having a conflict with him. I assumed that everything we said in our coaching sessions was confidential, but the coach blabbed some of my more candid thoughts about the CEO to him directly, which caused serious damage to our relationship.

Coaching works best when it is confidential. Otherwise, the client won't be as willing to open up to you. Unless clients share that they are thinking of hurting themselves or others or that they are doing something illegal, you should not tell anyone else. Not his manager. Not Human Resources.

If coaching works, the results should speak for themselves. No one other than you and the client need to see the sausage being made. Even if clients share they are looking for another job or thinking about starting a company, that should remain confidential. The vast majority of employees are looking for another job and/or thinking about starting a company! You don't have to snitch on them. Ditto if the client talks negatively about colleagues. Who doesn't feel negatively about their colleagues from time to time?

When you set up a coaching relationship, if you don't want to hear certain things from the client, such as the fact that they are actively searching for a new job, let them know up front. Don't set them up to regret the coaching relationship later on. Confidentiality gets tricky when the person you are coaching is also reporting to you. In that case, you have to make it clear about when the conversation is truly off the record and when it is on the record and can be used in performance reviews or promotion decisions. If you don't feel comfortable or able to put up a wall between these two domains, then be sure the employee knows you will treat the coaching conversation as any other discussion between you.

I will never forget the sting of that coach when she violated confidentiality with me. Please don't give your coaching clients a similar experience.

The Attitudes of the Coach

A significant part of being a coach is how you show up to clients. How you show up has a lot to do with your attitudes or orientations. If you have the right orientations and are competent with coaching skills, your clients will be delighted. Shown below are a few attitudes that define how the effective coach appears.

Be curious. Come into coaching conversations without knowing everything. Instead, put your judgments aside and be curious. Learn as much as you can about how clients think about their situation. Before you jump in and fix things, discover how the client would solve a challenge. Ask questions and listen. Let the client be the smartest person in the room. Being curious while not needing to know the answers is a powerful attitude to have in coaching, career, and life.

Have a dialogue. Coaching is a dialogue between two people. Together, you are working to help the client have insights and move to a new, more effective place. Don't tell. Don't teach. Don't fix. Yes, you can offer your insights and observations, but be patient and wait until you have explored the client's view in depth. As noted earlier, try to speak less than 25 percent of the coaching session.

Balance ego, results, and relationships. When a previous chapter invited you to better understand your natural coaching style, we discussed the importance of balancing ego, results, and relationships. It is worth repeating this principle. With each client, in each situation, find that balance. If you push too hard, the client might get results (or at least agree to do what you want during the session), but you will damage the relationship. If you don't push hard enough, you might preserve the relationship, but the client won't get results, and, of course, the relationship will suffer, too, because it is inauthentic. If the coaching session is too much about you and how smart and successful you are, both results and relationships suffer. Find that balance during every coaching conversation.

Be open and honest. The effective coach is on equal footing with clients and is comfortable having open and honest conversations. If clients don't do what they said they would do between sessions, the coach mentions that and asks permission to explore why the client is being accountable. If the coach observes a behavior that might be hurting the client's effectiveness and ability to achieve stated goals, that is mentioned, and the coach asks permission to discuss it. The coach feels comfortable saying what needs to be said—all while still balancing ego, results, and relationships.

Empathize. Coaches not only listen to what the client is saying but also empathize with how the client is feeling.

See possibility. When clients are stuck, mired in complaints and negativity, the effective coach creates a sense of possibility. The coach is not unrealistic about what is possible, but that person's way of speaking and acting encourages clients to keep pushing forward in the face of uncertainty and difficult challenges.

Stand for the client's aspirations and potential. The coach is a stake in the ground for what clients can be and do. That's who the coach is. If the client wavers, thinks too small, or has doubt, the coach does not because the coach represents his or her aspirations and potential. The coach represents the client's most ambitious, noble, and inspiring goals. If needed, the coach challenges clients, reminding them of their goals and providing a little push to keep them moving in the right direction.

Sometimes doing this can be challenging because coaches might feel they care more about the client's aspirations and sees more potential for the client than the client does. In this case, the coach is open and honest and expresses concerns while also staying positive and emphasizing what's possible.

Build capacity. The coach is not working with the client just to get it done. Rather, the coach wants to help clients improve their capabilities and performance over the long term. Coaches don't step in and just do it. Instead, they detach themselves just enough to let the client determine the best course of action while developing professionally.

All of the above attitudes are connected like pearls on a necklace. You can't practice one without practicing all of them. Which of these strengths do you have? Which are more challenging? Your answer might change from client to client.

Here is a piece of advice to strengthen client relationships: Before a coaching session, take a moment to get grounded in each of these attitudes. Ask yourself which attitudes are strong, and which might be missing or weak in your relationship with the client. Commit to maintaining or building on what is working and improving what is missing or weak. After the coaching session, take a moment to reflect on how the session went. Go through the same process so that you remain grounded in these attitudes and keep strengthening your ability to show up as representing them.

Finally, if you had to build your own list of attitudes, what would you add, delete, or edit? The above list works for me and many other coaches but may not be perfect for you. Give some thought to the list you would create, and continue trying to keep getting stronger in those attitudes.

When Managers Coach

It is hard for managers to coach employees because managers wear so many different hats. Sometimes the manager has to be directive. Sometimes they have to provide information. Sometimes they have to probe and confirm that the employee is on the right track.

Coaching is only one part of a manager's toolkit. There is a time and place to do it.

Managers should use coaching when:

- Discussing the employee's long- and short-term development so that the employee develops their own professional development and career plan.

- The employee has a high-stakes conversation looming, and the manager can serve as a coach and role-play partner.

- The manager wants to re-engage an otherwise good employee whose performance has slipped.

- The manager is flexible on the outcome or at least how to achieve the outcome.

Managers should not use coaching when:

- The manager just wants something done. In this case, the best way is to communicate clearly what they expect.

- The manager needs to be directive. For instance, they know the answer. That's not a time to ask open-ended questions hoping that the employee will guess. Similarly, if the manager has specific feedback to give the employee or expectations to set, that is not the time to coach, but coaching can come after the employee accepts the feedback and wants support deciding what to do next.

- The manager is not flexible on the "what" or the "how." They know the outcome they want, and they know how they want it done. In this case, there is no reason to coach.

Much of this book is about creating a long-term coaching process. For managers, coaching happens both during just-in-time situations and over the long term. The manager coaches the employee through immediate challenges, helps develop a plan for professional development, and serves as a sounding board when appropriate.

I believe that the best managers are those who budget time each week with each employee to meet, discuss progress, and provide coaching as needed. The format is fluid depending on what the employee needs at the time. Managers who coach in this way develop their employees, engage them, and tend to earn their loyalty.

Part Two

THE COACHING PROCESS

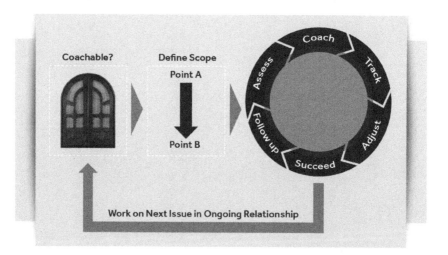

Overview of the Coaching Process

If you plan on coaching somebody for more than a single session, you should follow a more detailed coaching process. Seven steps are involved in the process diagrammed above. Here is a brief description of each step followed by more details.

Be sure that coachability is in place. Without coachability, the entire coaching process shuts down. Coachability means that your client has given permission for coaching to take place.

Define goals, scope, and contract. Set a clear goal or goals with the client. Then agree on the scope and boundaries of the coaching relationship.

Assess. Take time to understand the root causes of the client's challenge. Get the data you and the client need to develop the most effective and efficient coaching plan.

Coach, track, and adjust. Most of the coaching process is about coaching, tracking progress, and adjusting as needed on the way to helping clients achieve their goals.

Succeed and celebrate. In today's organizations, few leaders or managers take the time to celebrate and acknowledge results. In the coaching process, take time to step back and acknowledge achievements as they happen.

Work on the next issue. Coaching is about having a long-term relationship with the client. As the client achieves one goal, identify the next challenge. Every single leader and manager has room to keep growing.

Follow up. Sometimes clients slip, even after achieving initial success. Build in time to follow up with the client and make sure that everything remains on course and results are sustained.

Let's now look at each step in more depth.

Confirm and Establish Coachability

You can't coach somebody who isn't coachable. Being coachable means being receptive to advice, trying out new ideas, and listening to tough feedback. For this reason, establishing coachability is not only the start of the coaching process but also the gateway to effective coaching. Anytime that coachability does not exist, the coaching process shuts down. Many executives are not particularly coachable. They think they already know or can figure it out. Some need to be in LOTS of pain before they ask for, or take, anybody else's counsel. As a coach, it is your job to create a coachable environment between you and your clients.

As I write this, a show called *Trading Spouses* is on television. In this show, two wives switch families for a while. During tonight's episode, one of the wives is a professional motivational speaker. When she goes to her new family, she naturally begins "motivating" them just as she does with her real family. How do you think her new family reacts? They want to kick her out. The family isn't receptive to her ideas. They are not coachable, at least not by her. They are not coachable because they don't think they have a problem and because they haven't agreed to be coached by her. They don't know her, are still getting used to having a stranger in their home, and certainly haven't asked for her ongoing opinions. This woman started coaching her new family without creating an environment conducive to the reception of her advice.

Nobody wants unsolicited advice. Lots of people don't even want advice when they ask for it (i.e., "Does this dress make me look fat?"). Yet, many of us love giving unsolicited advice. We intervene without permission. In personal situations, this behavior is called "nagging."

Don't assume your client is coachable simply because they have asked you for coaching. Coachability is a mind-set that comes and goes, much like the tides. Every time you sit down with a client, you have to be sure that he or she is coachable. You can do this in three ways:

First, the client can ask for coaching by requesting your opinion or counsel. In this case, if you have tough advice to deliver, you should let the client know and confirm they are receptive.

Second, you can ask permission. For example, "Joe, I've listened to what you have to say about the situation and have some ideas, but first I want to be sure you are open to hearing some tough advice."

Third, if the client seems to be resisting your input, you can be assertive. "Joe, you said you were open to my coaching. I don't mind if you have logical issues with what we are discussing, but it seems like you are not even giving the coaching a chance. I need you to be more coachable. At least take a moment to consider some of the questions I am asking."

You should constantly be assessing your clients and your relationship with them to be sure they are coachable. If they are not, stop the session and re-create a coachable environment. When a client isn't coachable, there are two possible reasons why:

First, it could be the client, who might be distracted, or who might have a more urgent issue to discuss. The client could also be feeling too vulnerable.

Second, it could be you. Maybe you are pushing too hard or not hard enough. Perhaps you are not listening well. You might be directing the conversation where the client doesn't want to go.

Start by pointing the finger at yourself before you blame the client.

Consider different approaches. Talk openly with the client. Executives and managers are by nature a challenging group. They aren't going to simply sit back and allow you to pronounce your findings. They will want to go back and forth with you and eventually arrive at their own conclusions. Some might want you to serve as a "sparring partner" (as one of my clients calls me), so they will push back. You constantly have to earn the right to be their coach. None of this means that your clients are uncoachable. It simply means that they are smart, thoughtful individuals. Therefore, you should not claim that your client is uncoachable too quickly.

On the other hand, if you do get a client who is truly uncoachable, after an appropriate amount of discussion and chances to get back on track, you might have no choice but to terminate the coaching agreement.

In other words, you constantly have to balance two tensions with clients. On the one hand, you have to stay on your toes, provide value through coaching, and earn their respect. On the other hand, you also have to make sure your clients are open to coaching, open to hearing uncomfortable advice, and open to new ideas that may take them out of their comfort zone.

Set the Foundation for a Successful Engagement

Define Goals, Scope, and Boundaries

This step has two parts. First, define what would constitute a successful engagement for your client. In fact, the first question any coach should ask a client is: "What would a successful coaching relationship achieve for you?" Even better, ask: "What would make this engagement the best and most valuable career development experience of your life?" Your job is to get specific, measurable results for your client. Start every engagement by defining those results. A well-defined outcome is:

Measurable. You can prove that you got the results through metrics. Different situations call for different approaches. For instance, if clients want to change a behavior, you should be prepared to interview their colleagues over time to find out how often they observed the old and new behavior(s) in question. Likewise, if the client wants to improve the way he or she spends time, then you should measure how s/he spends time as your coaching engagement progresses.

Specific. "Specific" means that you are getting finite, concrete results. "I want to feel better" is not specific; "I want to increase sales in my department by 25%, from $10 million to $12.5 million" is specific

Time bound. A good outcome definition includes a deadline. Without a deadline, there is no accountability. "Someday" is not a deadline. "By January 31 of this year" is a deadline. Work with your client to define aggressive but specific and measurable results, with a deadline. Once you do, you will notice a gap between where the client is and where the client wants to be. In the above example related to sales, the gap is $2.5 million (let's say the deadline is within twelve months). It will be helpful to your coaching work to define that gap. When you begin the assessment phase, you can then develop a structured, logical process for understanding the root cause of the gap and how to move quickly to the client's desired future state.

The second piece of the coaching foundation is setting scope and boundaries, or contracting. On any engagement, it is essential for you to be clear about the scope and boundaries of your work. What will and won't the engagement cover? What types of subjects are within bounds and out of bounds? When is the engagement done? What are the ground rules for this engagement? These and other critical questions are important to answer up front and often throughout the engagement.

The following are some of the key scope-related questions to discuss with a client before an engagement begins. Don't simply ask the questions that follow and expect your client to answer them. Have your own suggestions ready to propose.

Scope

How often do we meet, and for how long? A coaching engagement can range from a couple of sessions to a year or more. Meeting frequency can vary from once per week to every other week, monthly, or even quarterly once the client gets traction and just needs to check in occasionally. Work with your client to determine the best duration and frequency. If in doubt, start with weekly meetings and adjust from there. Also, I have found that it is hard to see sustainable results with anything less than a three-month commitment, and I usually won't coach a client for less than six months.

When does the engagement begin and end?

What kind of follow-up is included after the engagement ends? I build in at least one follow-up session after the formal coaching period ends, which allows me to check in with the client, address any remaining challenges, and be sure that the results from our coaching are sticking.

What kind of assessment will be done?

How many people will be interviewed (if there are interviews)?

Who will be interviewed and for how long?

How do we track results?

Who is involved in this engagement and who is not?

Who handles logistics of setting up any interviews?

Boundaries

What questions can be asked when conducting interviews and what questions or topics are out of bounds?

Is it okay to share findings with anyone else?

What kinds of topics are within bounds in discussions with the client and which are out of bounds (e.g., personal issues)?

What political land mines should I avoid when speaking to any colleagues or working with you?

Should interviews with your colleagues remain confidential? My preference is to allow what people say to be made public but to keep the identity of the person who says it confidential. At the same time, I agree to remove any comments that might reveal a specific individual.

What do I do if you don't keep your word or do any assignments that you agree to do?

What do I do if you don't seem to be coachable?

What happens if you have to cancel or reschedule a session? My policy is that the client agrees to give seventy-two hours' notice. Coaching is meant to be a privilege and a top priority.

In addition, I like to create a set of ground rules up front with my clients, starting with the following list:

The client agrees to be coachable. This includes listening to advice from colleagues and from the coach.

We will be open and honest with one another. This includes giving each other honest feedback and advice.

We will do our respective assignments on time.

We will eliminate distractions during our sessions in order to focus on our work. No cell phones, other calls, interruptions, or checking email while we work.

Everything the client says during sessions is to be kept in the strictest confidence.

As the engagement progresses, you and the client may find that you need to renegotiate the goals, scope, and boundaries, which is normal. Sometimes goals clients thought they had change. Sometimes the client has new priorities. Sometimes the coach or client notices a behavior that is getting in the way of the coaching and has to request a change. For instance, I once worked with a client who traveled all over the world. He started calling me on my cell phone during his business hours, which was sometimes the middle of the night for me. I requested that he either pay me more to answer my cell at all hours of the night, or that he call me during my business hours. He chose the latter.

Assess the Client/Situation, Diagnose, and Design

The assessment phase is critical for a successful engagement. This phase sheds light on how your clients can move from where they are to where they want to be. With a sound assessment, you can determine the best intervention(s) to help your clients improve. Some of your clients may not have the patience for a lengthy assessment phase. Some clients think they already know the answer, but you have every right to structure an assessment that gives you the information you need to help your client succeed.

At the same time, you have an obligation to be efficient during your assessment process. Many coaches (and consultants) are sloppy during their assessment. They do what the consulting firm McKinsey & Company calls "boiling the ocean." Like a doctor who orders every test imaginable, these coaches do all sorts of surveys, interviews, and analyses—almost by rote—and still don't necessarily gain many insights. The way to be efficient during your assessment is to structure your thinking about what might be causing your client's problem ahead of time. When you have a solid structure in place, it is easy to map out an efficient and effective assessment process. You can assess the client in the following ways:

Off-the-shelf assessments give insights about the client's thinking and communication styles, behavioral traits, values, career preferences, and other specific traits (e.g., response to conflict, energy level, relationship to change, and relationship to risk). You can choose from among many assessments on the market. Some are highly validated, while others are more like fortune cookies. Most coaches use at least one reliable assessment that helps clients have insights about their style and adapt to a specific situation. Examples range from the Myers-Briggs Type Inventory, DiSC, Birkman, Profiles International, and dozens more. If you use an assessment, be sure to get trained in how to use it properly, how to avoid misuse (e.g., not all assessments are legally allowed to be used to screen for employment), and the reliability and validity of the tool.

A 360-degree verbal assessment is a confidential assessment in which the coach interviews people up, down, across, and sometimes outside the organization. This is different from a 360-degree review, which goes through Human Resources and is used for performance reviews. During the 360 process, the coach asks people about the clients' strengths, what they can do better, and other advice appropriate for the client's situation. Done properly, the 360 is a confidential process that lets clients know how they come across to others—without giving away who said what. This is my favorite approach to assessing leaders and managers because I can get to know the client's colleagues and discover the real impact the client has with other people.

Active inquiry is a powerful conversation to work with the client to get to the root causes of a challenge.

Your own impressions can be useful to assess the client and the situation. Don't invalidate your own instincts. As long as you ask permission to share your impressions and the client is open to hearing them, the way the client comes across to you can be revealing.

The client's job description can help you be clear on their role and what they are expected to achieve, but be sure to probe more deeply about what people expect from your client and that might appear in the formal job description.

The organization's strategic plan can give you insights about the clients' key initiatives and how aligned they seem to be with the organization's mission, values, and priorities.

Performance reviews and the organization's competency models can provide important data about how clients are doing and the skills they have to develop.

The client's professional development plan, if they have one, will give you a clear picture of where the client wants to head in the organization and how they plan to get there. A good professional development plan includes short- and long-term career goals followed by the work experiences, relationships, new skills, education, and other activities that will achieve the goals. If clients don't have a development plan, you can create one with them. Doing this gives you the opportunity to hold the client accountable for achieving the plan, including talking with others in the organization to support them.

Observing the client in action, for instance, in a team meeting, can give valuable insights too. Does the client show up on time? What does the client's body language say to others? How much do clients say, and how much do they listen? How well do they include everyone? What is their style?

The assessment process can help a client be more engaged in the coaching process. For instance, assume you are working with a professional that has a reputation for being abrasive. Abrasive behavior is tolerated in many industries and companies, especially when the leader or manager is a superstar in other areas. A good example is in healthcare, where numerous physicians have been labeled abrasive or even disruptive once they switch from medical practice to more administrative duties. That's because many of them never had training about working in organizations or haven't learned that the behaviors that might work in a surgical suite or emergency room do not work well in a more administrative setting. Initially, physicians might not be open to the idea that their behavior in meetings with nonclinicians is ineffective. Their behavior might actually be a blind spot for them. When you complete a 360 verbal assessment, the client might say, "Yes, that is what they have told you, but they don't understand the pressures of being a physician. Most of the people you interviewed are nonclinicians, and they just don't get it."

Next, you might diplomatically tell the physician that based on a couple of sessions together you also notice that this person has some behaviors that could be perceived as abrasive. The client might reply, "So what? You are not a physician either."

Third, you might do a validated assessment. For instance, the ProfileXT puts clients on a bell curve that compares them to other people in similar positions so that clients can benchmark themselves on certain thinking styles and behavioral traits. The physician now has validated data that might show that this person is an extremely fast processor, has a high energy level, and is also not as accommodating or manageable as the individual's peers. This data, which is reliable and validated, and which adds a dimension to the previous feedback, might get the physician to start to notice a pattern.

Fourth, you might observe clients in a meeting and take notes when they roll their eyes, interrupt, or even leave the meeting early because they are bored.

Suddenly, you have enough data from different sources for the physician to recognize that there is a problem, and that it is in this person's best interests to work on some new behaviors. At the Center for Executive Coaching, we call this approach to assessments "nowhere-to-hide coaching."

Different situations call for different assessments. For instance, when two people have a conflict and want coaching to resolve it, I might assess by interviewing each person separately and doing an off-the-shelf assessment to get a sense of their different styles. I don't need to do a 360 verbal assessment of both of them or observe each in meetings. I can get the information I need with a simpler approach.

Once you have assessed a situation, your next step is to diagnose it and create a coaching plan to help your client get the desired results. Sometimes all you need to do is set up an action plan with your client and a way to check in to be sure that the client is taking action. Or you may need to develop a more in-depth and creative plan. As a coach, you are working with a relatively blank slate and have the freedom to develop a coaching agenda that you think will do the best job.

Coach, Track, Adjust

Your coaching work either moves toward results or it doesn't. If you find that you and the client are off track, make a midcourse correction. Client progress rarely follows a direct, linear path. If it did, your services would not be as valuable as they are because anybody could coach.

A fundamental requirement when coaching is that you find a way to track results, which you can do in many different ways. If the issue is a behavior that the client wants to change, you can have the client ask people to rate how often they see the new behavior in action. If the issue is about time management, clients can track their use of time and report back on productivity. If the client wants to be more influential, you and the client can identify situations for the client to influence people more effectively and track how successful they are at achieving their goals. If the issue is more feelings based, for instance, when the client lacks confidence or feels stress, you can have the client rate their confidence or stress levels at different times and track improvements. Even if the client simply wants a sounding board, you can still set goals each session for whether or not clarity has been achieved.

There is always a way to set goals and track. Without putting this kind of process into place, coaching has a tendency to meander and not provide clear value. Take 100% responsibility for the impact your coaching is having. If you and the client are not on track, determine how to get on track—without blaming the client or being a victim.

Succeed and Celebrate

When the client get results, whether by achieving a short-term milestone or by realizing the overall goal of the coaching process, acknowledge the results and celebrate with your client. Acknowledging and celebrating doesn't mean you have to throw a party. Many executives and managers are bottom-line, self-motivated people. For them, getting a result is rewarding in and of itself. Also, new behaviors usually lead to improved response from colleagues and better results, which is the best reward. Usually, it is enough for the coach to remind the client about the starting point, acknowledge what has been achieved so far, and confirm what these results mean to the client and that person's organization.

The easy part is for the coach to acknowledge results. The hard part is getting the client to do it. In many organizations, especially with driven and highly educated people, leaders and managers are pretty hard on themselves. They assume that when results happen they would have happened regardless of their contributions. This is where the coach can help them recognize their contribution. Aside from creating a positive environment, this part of the coaching process also helps clients get better at talking about their contributions and promoting themselves (appropriately) in their organizations.

Choose the Next Situation/Goal

A good coach keeps clients for life or at least for a very long time. After you achieve one goal with a client, the client should see the value that you bring. Clients who are coachable want to keep growing and getting better. Find something else to work on, and repeat the process. Sometimes clients want to move right into the next goal, and sometimes they want to take a break. Let the client guide you, but at the same time listen for new initiatives, challenges, and professional development opportunities where you can bring value.

Follow-up

The final part of the coaching process is the follow-up. Build follow-up sessions into your engagements with the client. By doing this, you make sure the client does not backtrack or let gains slip away. Also, for external coaches, follow-up sessions allow you to stay in touch with your clients and can lead to additional work and referrals. Finally, by following up, you show the client that unlike many professionals you don't just disappear when the real work begins.

For instance, I worked with a coaching firm that provided clients with a free "10,000 mile checkup." About three months after an engagement ended, we came back to assess ongoing performance and results. We could identify any obstacles to ongoing success and develop additional interventions to regain momentum and results. Of course, you can't follow up if you don't put a sound tracking and measurement system into place as part of your initial work. Be sure that you have metrics in place, and that your client continues to measure results after you are gone.

What Coaching Really Looks Like

Of all the professional services, coaching is one of the easiest to scope out and plan. It's not like we are creating the critical path for building a rocket ship or even developing a project plan for a team of software consultants. If you plan on coaching a client for more than a single session, the process is simple. All you have to do is choose how often to meet, agree on the questions we discussed about scope and boundaries, conduct any relevant assessments up front, and jump into coaching conversations that move the client toward their goal(s). If the goals change, adjust the coaching accordingly.

I typically meet with a client weekly at first and then every other week or even monthly as the client makes progress. Some coaches meet monthly from start to finish. I suggest setting a six-month engagement with clients. I'll go for three months to start if absolutely required but have found that it takes at least six months to make significant progress. Some coaches insist on a one-year contract for an executive and 18–24 months for a team or for the owner of a growing business to see measurable change.

Let's assume you are coaching a leader who wants to get better. I call this the leadership tune-up. A coaching plan might include the following:

- An introductory session to agree on goals and the rules of the road as well as to set up assessments.
- A week or so to complete the assessment(s).
- A meeting to review the assessments and agree on the coaching plan.

- Regular coaching sessions for achieving the goals of the engagement. During these sessions, we work toward the overall goal; discuss current issues, especially as the relate to the overall goal of the coaching; put into place a behavioral coaching process if appropriate; and introduce other topics related to leadership if time permits.

Built into the above process are regular check-ins to evaluate progress, measure results, and determine whether or not to meet more or less frequently.

Keep it simple!

Sample Coaching Plan

Coaching plans vary based on the client's needs. Here is a sample coaching plan for a client that wants to improve as a leader.

This plan has three columns. The left column shows the session number. The middle column shows the primary work being done during that session or sessions. The column on the right shows a sampling of possible issues to discuss and methodologies to cover, depending on the client's professional development needs.

You can see that the beginning of the process sets goals and expectations, completes the assessments, and then reviews the assessments to set goals. The rest of the process combines behavioral coaching, coaching on current issues, and discussion of specific issues about leadership as time and client interest permit

After six months, it is important to conduct a second assessment phase to measure and track progress. Also, the behavioral coaching process builds in monthly feedback and advice.

This plan is one of many possible plans, but it provides an easy template to model.

Illustrative Coaching Plan

Session	Topic/Activity	Potential Curriculum
1 (Orientation/Setup)	Confirm fit. Set initial goals. Review ground rules. Set up assessments. Introduce Leader's Dashboard. Identify participants to be interviewed for confidential verbal 360.	Leader's Dashboard follow-up Behavioral change coaching with peer support Perceptual shifts for leadership
Between Initial Session and Session 2	Clients complete assessments and Leader's Dashboard. Coach interviews participants for verbal 360.	Engage and mobilize Influence others with impact
2 (Initial Session – 2.5 hours)	Review assessments and Leader's Dashboard with client. Review verbal 360. Homework: Choose one behavior that will have significant impact on performance; clarify goals so that coach and client can create an individual development and coaching plan.	Communicate powerfully Manage up Have a strong powerbase Resolve conflict
3	Determine behavior and set up behavioral coaching process. Review and agree on development plan and coaching plan.	Lead change Lead teams/team dynamics Execute effectively
4 +	Coaching begins. Emphasis is on behavioral coaching first and then Leader's Dashboard, current issues, and curriculum in the right column based on their goals and needs. At the end of every month, the client receives feedback/data about behavior change and discusses with coach. Do second set of assessments as required to measure progress.	Time management Success in a new role Manage personal domains/balance Specific issues as they emerge

The Coach's Week

Over time, your coaching practice and how you spend your time will evolve. Initially, if you have no clients, your week is all about getting clients.

Once you have clients, set some boundaries. Allocate two days per week to marketing and developing new coaching solutions/products. Don't coach clients for more than three days every week. If you do, you might never be able to extricate yourself from the "trading time for dollars" trap. The two days don't have to be actual calendar days. You could break up your marketing and product development time into a few half days.

There are two extreme models for coaches. The first is the "coaching factory." In this model, you sit on a phone and coach clients one after another. Some coaches can coach up to ten clients a day with this model, but I've never had the energy to be able to handle more than six. Still, six clients per day, three days every week, adds up to eighteen clients paying a monthly fee. You can make some good money with this model, and that's before add-on solutions, such as facilitation, training, and strategic planning retreats. The downside of this model is that you can burn out relatively quickly.

In my own case, my practice has evolved from the factory model to having just a few great, loyal clients who pay me a lot of money for my advisory services. I coach, train, consult, and sometimes even jump in and serve as an interim manager. Coaching is often the way in the door and leads to additional work as I learn more and develop trust and credibility.

In between these extremes are many options. For instance, suppose that instead of a weekly coaching program you offered only monthly sessions and say that you require a one-year commitment from the client, and that you throw in free off-the-shelf and 360-degree verbal assessments in exchange for the one-year commitment. This approach opens up your time, reduces your burnout factor, and allows you to see more clients.

Similarly, many companies are starting to prefer group coaching. This is a win-win for coach and client. You charge less per person but make more money for your time. The client organization gets more people involved in coaching, and the collaboration and sharing among group members is valuable. The public version of group coaching is offering monthly peer support groups for clients, with occasional one-on-one coaching or support built in.

Sample Contracts

Shown below are three sample proposals/contracts that you might use with clients. Two are for external clients, and one is for internal use. Note that my contracts are short and sweet. I close the engagement first and send a summary of our discussion. I have never had a problem with this approach. At the same time, I can't give you legal advice and strongly suggest that if you don't feel comfortable with a loose letter of understanding like this one you should consult an attorney in your area.

Example One: Leader of Leaders

Jim,

Thank you for your time last week to discuss your interest in coaching.

You indicated that you would like a coach to work with you as you become a leader of leaders and advance your career to oversee several offices.

To that end and given that you are paying out of pocket, I propose the following approach:

- A six-month coaching engagement as a start. We begin in November or December depending on your schedule.

- The ProfileXT assessment up front, which will provide us with quick and important insights about your thinking and behavioral traits. It will show how you might adapt to communicate more effectively with your team.

- As appropriate, a confidential 360-degree verbal assessment to learn more about your impact on key employees and your manager.

- One-hour coaching sessions every other week that will:

  - Set specific goals and track them throughout our engagement to ensure progress and value to you.

  - Based on what the assessment discovers, identify one major new habit to put into place to improve performance.

  - Discuss current challenges, and use those as examples to improve your leadership flexibility and capabilities.

  - Cover a coaching curriculum based on any of the following topics, as warranted by our assessment and desired by you: engage and mobilize employees, resolve conflict, develop leaders/succession planning, communicate with impact, influence effectively, set strategic direction, develop strong relationships throughout the organization, become more aligned with and improve your relationship with your manager, create a high-performance culture, juggle many priorities/ manage time more effectively, and shift limiting perceptions that might be holding you back. We can cover other topics depending on the challenges you face.

  - Leave you with specific ideas and accountability to improve performance and achieve your goals.

Ongoing email support is also included for the term of our agreement.

For our coaching relationship to work, I ask that you agree to the following:

- The coaching relationship is important to you, and you are committed to achieving the goals outlined above.

- You will attend all coaching sessions on time.

- You commit to the full six months of coaching unless we achieve your goals sooner.

- If you need to reschedule a coaching session, you will do so with at least seventy-two hours' notice. Otherwise, I am under no obligation to make up that session.

- During coaching sessions, you will be present, with no external distractions (e.g., cell phones, other people, and email).

- You will complete any assignments on time that you agree to do.

- You will be open and honest during the sessions, which includes giving advice to me about how you can get more value from sessions.

- The agreement we have includes weekly sessions and email. It does not include unscheduled calls or calls after business hours.

- You understand that I rely on referrals to build my business. Therefore, if you are pleased with our coaching relationship, you agree to serve as a reference and/or have at least one meeting with me outside of our coaching meetings where we discuss possible introductions to people you know who might also find value in my services.

Your investment for the engagement is $18,000. Payment will be made 50%, or $9,000 before we begin the engagement, and 50%, or $9,000 after three months. This engagement is about achieving your goal. If we achieve your goal sooner than six months and you do not wish to continue, you agree to make payment in full.

My goal is that you achieve a five to ten times return on this investment. If you don't believe that this is possible based on your aspirations, we should not continue.

I am excited about working with you and helping you take your career to its next phase. Please sign below to indicate that you accept the above terms.

Sincerely,
Andrew Neitlich
Director
Center for Executive Coaching

These terms are agreed to on this date _____ by:

_____
James Smith

_____
Andrew Neitlich

Example Two: New President

Bill,

Thank you for your time to discuss your interest in executive coaching. You indicated that you would like a coach with the following scope:

- Leadership development and onboarding in your new role as president.
- Assessment of leadership skills with direct reports and colleagues at the corporate office.
- Navigating culture dynamics at your business unit and the corporate office.
- Succession planning advice and team assessment for future growth.

To that end, I propose the following approach:

- A six-month coaching engagement with weekly meetings. We will meet once per month in person as schedules allow and then the remainder by phone. Our coaching sessions will discuss the above issues, beginning with a clear intent and outcome and then working to achieve insights and accountability on the way to the desired intent.

- The ProfileXT assessment up front. This highly validated, reliable assessment will provide us with quick and important insights about your thinking and behavioral traits. It will show how you might adapt to communicate more effectively with your team.

- A confidential 360-degree verbal assessment up front to learn more about your impact on key colleagues and personnel.

Ongoing email support is also included for the term of our agreement, and we can arrange an immediate telephone coaching call during business hours in rare time-sensitive situations.

For our coaching relationship to be productive, I ask that you agree to the following:

- The coaching relationship is important to you, and you are committed to achieving the goals that we set during the coaching

- You will attend all coaching sessions on time.
- You commit to the full six months of coaching unless we achieve your goals sooner.

- If you need to reschedule a coaching session, you will do so with at least seventy-two hours' notice. Otherwise, I am under no obligation to make up that session.

- During coaching sessions, you will be present, with no external distractions (e.g., cell phones, other people, and email).

- You will complete any assignments on time that you agree to do.

- You will be open and honest during the sessions, which includes giving advice to me about how you can get more value from sessions.

- You understand that I rely on referrals to build my business. Therefore, if you are pleased with our coaching relationship, you agree to serve as a reference and/or have at least one meeting with me outside of our coaching meetings where we discuss possible introductions to people you know who might also find value in my services.

The fee for this engagement is $18,000. You agree to pay $9,000 up front and $9,000 at the end of the third month. This engagement is about achieving your goal. If we achieve your goal sooner than six months and you do not wish to continue, you agree to make payment in full.

My goal is that you achieve a five to ten times return on this investment. If you don't believe that this is possible based on your aspirations, we should not continue.

I am excited about working with you on these important issues! Please sign below to indicate that you accept the above terms.

Sincerely,
Andrew Neitlich
Director
Center for Executive Coaching

These terms are agreed to on this date _____ by:

_____

Bill Jones

_____

Andrew Neitlich

Example Three: For Internal Coaches

Coaching Agreement
Coach:
Client:
Client's Manager:
Date:

Coaching defined:
Coaching is a dialogue between a coach and a leader with the intention of finding creative ways to solve challenging problems, improve team and unit performance, accelerate progress on key initiatives, and advance the leader's career.

Up to three goals during the engagement (subject to change as the engagement progresses):

1.
2.
3.

Scope:

We will meet every week starting on _____

After the first three months, we can meet every other week or even less frequently depending on need.

Initial term is twelve months. At the end of six months, we will evaluate results and decide if you see value in extending the engagement for the additional six months.

The engagement will include a ProfileXT assessment as well as a 360-degree verbal assessment of up to twelve people that know you well in a professional setting.

Confidentiality:

Everything discussed is confidential. Nothing said in the coaching session will be shared outside of the coaching relationship, including with your manager or Human Resources or in your performance review. The only exceptions are if you indicate that you are, will, or wish to harm yourself or others, or that you are doing anything illegal within [COMPANY NAME]. The only status update we will provide if asked is whether or not you are showing up for your coaching sessions; results are expected to show up through improved performance in your role.

My responsibilities to you as your coach:

- My commitment is to your professional and organizational success.
- I will fully prepare each meeting to ensure that your time is well spent.
- I will be available and supportive as your coach, including between meetings as needed.
- I will be open, honest, constructive, respectful, and professional.
- I am open to your advice about how to bring more value to your experience in this program.

Your responsibilities:

- The coaching relationship is important to you, and you are committed to achieving the goals outlined above.

- You are open to receiving coaching, including willing to hear advice.
- You will attend all coaching sessions on time.
- If you need to reschedule a coaching session, you will do so with at least seventy-two hours' notice.
- During coaching sessions, you will be present, with no external distractions (e.g., cell phones, other people, and email).
- You will complete any assignments on time that you agree to do.
- You will be open and honest during the sessions, which includes giving advice to me about how you can get more value from sessions.
- You agree to provide an honest review of the coaching program in the middle and at the end of the engagement so that we can assess the program and make improvements.

Signed by:

Coach:

Client:

Client's Manager:

Date:

Conceptualize and Improvise Programs that Meet Client Needs

Don't limit your thinking about how to serve your clients. Develop a broad portfolio of coaching solutions to offer the market.

In my own case, I use a consultative selling process to listen to a prospect's needs and develop a solution. I can respond to any issue that comes up, and I don't need to guess at what every single prospective client will need. Together, we develop the approach that works best.

For instance, suppose that a prospect tells me they are having trouble getting members of their team to work effectively together.

I'll ask them a number of questions to learn more about the issue and what it is costing them. Then, assuming it makes sense, I'll say something like, "I think I can help. I have a coaching program specifically about creating a high-performing teams. It starts with an assessment of your team and, depending on what the assessment uncovers, takes about sixteen weeks to complete. At the end of it, your people will have a clear goal, be committed to achieving that goal, and know how to communicate with each other to succeed. Would you like to talk more about this?"

Similarly, suppose that a prospect says they are about to begin a strategic planning process and wish they had a simple approach to follow because no one on the team even agrees on the strategy. After probing a bit, I'll say, "I have a simple, powerful three-part strategic planning process that takes about three or four months to complete, which has helped organizations in your industry get clarity about strategic direction, set priorities, and actually make sure the strategy gets done. Would you like to talk more about this?"

Notice that the above examples result in single coaching engagements. That's okay with me. I know that if I do well, I'll continue to work with the client on general leadership issues or find a new issue to explore through an extended engagement.

The above approach requires improvisation and knowledge of the different coaching methodologies presented so far.

In addition to this approach, I advise you to create the following off-the-shelf coaching solutions that you can market:

- **Choose specific issues and market solutions to them.** Create coaching packages that focus on specific needs in your target market. Any of the solutions described in this book could be coaching packages that you market, and you can also combine different solutions in new ways. You can choose a single issue or a broad theme that combines specific issues into one larger area (e.g., leadership communication coaching, power and influence coaching, organizational development coaching). If you market a coaching package, you need to specify the problem you solve, the benefits your solution provides, how long the program takes, a high-level peek at the framework you use, why it is unique, and proof that it works. If you need testimonials about your program(s), give a speech in which you lay out the solution and ask audience members for testimonials about what they liked best about your content. The goal of each package, in addition to getting results for the client, is to find new issues to work on, become a trusted advisor, and convert the client to a regular coaching client.

- **Offer a leadership academy.** A leadership academy teaches key leadership competencies to up-and-coming managers in your market. It can combine one-on-one and group coaching, assessments, team projects, and monthly facilitated meetings

- **Start with an assessment to gain a foothold.** Assessments are a low-cost way to get in the door. Many coaches start with an assessment, use it to understand the client's situation and build the relationship, and then convert the client to a coaching engagement from there.

- **Create a hybrid coaching model.** Coaches are not part of a union. You can be a coach, consultant, facilitator, trainer, and even interim executive. Feel free to create a client solution that uses all these things. For instance, when I work with clients on improving employee engagement, the solution usually includes surveys, interviews, facilitated sessions with the leadership team, one-on-one coaching with executives and managers, trainings, and ongoing follow-up.

- **Leadership circles.** A leadership circle is a meeting of noncompeting, like-minded leaders. For instance, one healthcare consulting firm offers a leadership circle made up of top executives from hospitals around the country. One executive per major market is allowed to preserve confidentiality. You can create a leadership circle for executives in your niche market. Then, if your first is successful, expand by offering a circle to other types of executives in your market (e.g., if you offer one for CEOs, offer a new one for their second in command, for the CIO, for the CFO). You can also transition your one-on-one clients into a leadership circle when appropriate. This is better than losing a client who no longer wants such an intensive coaching experience.

- **Group coaching.** Almost any coaching program that you offer for one you can also offer for many. You might do a weekly or monthly group coaching program and in between these sessions provide an additional one-on-one coaching session monthly or quarterly for every member of the group.

- **Weekly, monthly, and quarterly options.** Don't let yourself get fixed in the mind-set that you have to have one-hour weekly coaching meetings. You don't. Perhaps you start weekly for a few months and move to monthly and then quarterly maintenance. Or, as many top executive coaches do, you might meet monthly for at least a year with the client because at the executive level in major corporations less time is better than more.

You may still be thinking:

- With which of the above should I start?
- How long should each of these sessions be?
- I still don't know whether to meet weekly or monthly.
- How much do I charge?

Fortunately, there is no standard process in the market. If there were, every coach would be a commodity. You have to learn about your market, introduce and test out different programs, and determine what works best for your style and the clients who come to you.

If in doubt, come up with ONE one-on-one and/or group coaching program that solves a pressing issue in your market. Include an assessment process up front and twelve weeks of coaching. Test that out, learn, and keep making progress.

Part Three

MORE COACHING CONVERSATIONS

Overview

We already introduced active inquiry, the most fundamental coaching conversation. While all coaching conversations could fit under the umbrella of active inquiry, additional conversations are worth knowing.

Setting goals and defining the problem. Coaching is ultimately about achieving results. It is much easier to achieve results if the coach has clear conversations with the client to set goals and define the problem.

Listening. If an effective coach speaks only 25 percent of the time, then what do coaches do during the remaining 75 percent? They listen. Listening as a coach is more than being present and reflecting on what the client is saying. Listening is an active process that helps the coach discover the best question to ask next.

Appreciative inquiry. This is a form of active inquiry in which the coach focuses on the positive, on what's working, and on building momentum. It works best when the situation is emotional or the client needs support.

Accountability. Accountability conversations include agreeing on what the client will do between sessions and helping clients move forward when they don't do what they agreed to do.

Shifting the conversation when a client is stuck. A coach can ask questions to help a client get unstuck. The situation dictates which questions to ask.

Role play. Role play is an effective way for the client to hone a crucial conversation, practice a public presentation, or plan to resolve a conflict

Presenting observations with impact. Certain conversations help the coach present observations without coming across as too coercive or pushy.

Letting the client guide the process. When the client and coach have a number of potential directions they can go, the coach uses this type of conversation to let the client guide the process.

The following chapters cover these conversations in more depth. Also, at the end, a chapter gives you guidance about conversations that can help you when you feel stuck during the coaching session.

Agreeing on the Problem and Setting Goals

While we discussed problem definition as part of the coaching process, conversations to agree on the problem and define goals deserve additional clarification. Coaching begins with a problem the client wants to solve or an opportunity the client wants to achieve. Both lead to a goal.

Without a clear problem statement and goal, the coaching will meander. A problem defines a point A and a better point B, with a deadline. For instance:

- I need to increase profits in my unit from $1 million to $1.5 million by the end of the year.

- We need to reduce voluntary turnover by our top talent from 15% to 5% per year by December 31.

- I want to be promoted from branch manager to district manager within the next two years.

Sometimes the coach has to ask questions to help the client set a specific goal. For example, suppose the client states a goal as, "I want Joe to be more engaged in my project." The term "engaged" is pretty vague. If I were coaching this client, I would want to know more about what it would look like if Joe were engaged in the project. If the client went to Joe and said, "Joe, I need you to be more engaged," Joe might reply, "What do you mean? I am engaged." With more questioning from the coach, the client might clarify that Joe should attend three team meetings per week, participate at each meeting, and also speak positively about the project. Now we have something to work with.

A good coaching question to clarify the goal is, "Tell me more about what it would look like if you did achieve this goal?" The reason for defining the problem and setting goals is to be specific enough that there is no doubt about whether or not the goal is achieved. The client will receive value, and the coach knows the session or engagement delivered results.

Sometimes it is hard to define a problem as precisely as the coach might want. Some clients resist getting specific. Some situations are murky. Sometimes the client simply wants to talk things out with an objective listener. All you can do when it comes to goal setting is try your best. At some point, you might feel that you are beating the proverbial dead horse, and the client will want you to move on.

If you let the conversation move forward with an unclear goal, don't be surprised when the session doesn't seem to go anywhere. To paraphrase the Cheshire Cat, if you don't know where you are going, then any direction will get you there. Once the goal is as clear as possible, the coach can keep the conversation on track, for example, asking the client for guidance whenever it seems the conversation is rambling or when the client seems to be discussing a different topic. For instance:

- "I want to check back with you about the initial intent of the session. You mentioned you wanted to achieve X during our meeting. It seems like we are now talking about Y. Let me know if this is okay with you or whether Y connects back to your initial intent."

- "How are we doing in terms of achieving the goal you said you wanted to achieve at the start of the session?"

- "I know you said you wanted to achieve X at the start of the session, but you seem to be talking much more about Y. What would you like to do at this point in the conversation?"

Listening

In almost any form of communication, listening gives you the keys to the kingdom. This fact is even truer in coaching. The coach should be listening 75 percent of the time in a coaching session. Otherwise, you are teaching, mentoring, preaching, directing, or training. Given how much time the coach spends listening, it makes sense to listen with purpose.

First, if you listen well, the client tells you the next question to ask. Once you are present and really hear what the client is saying—both the logical and emotional content as well as what the client isn't saying—coaching becomes easy. The client tells you where to go next! You do much less but get much more. For instance, suppose a client indicates frustration with a conflict. What question is the client telling you to ask?

Many questions can be asked at this point: How would the client like the conflict to be resolved? What is the best approach to resolve the conflict? What does the client know about the other person's style? Where is the common ground? Where is the client willing to be flexible? Where is the client not willing to give ground? What motivates the other person in the situation?

All these questions can be beneficial but they jump ahead a bit and make some assumptions about what the client knows and doesn't know and where the client wants to go. All the client has shared so far is that they have a conflict and are frustrated. What if you added nothing to the conversation beyond what the client has told you? Why not ask, "What would you like to discuss here to get the most out of our time?" It's a simple, high-level question. It assumes nothing and provides the coach with the maximum opportunity to learn from the client and go from there. It also gives the client the opportunity to share what they want to do next. By the way, suppose you can't figure out what to ask the client next. Something you can do—maybe once or twice per coaching session at most—is ask, "If you were the coach, what question would you want me to ask right now?" It works!

Listening comes in many forms, both productive and unproductive. If you have ever taken a $99 hotel seminar about active listening, you know that distracted listening is not helpful. When coaching a client, especially by phone or computer where you can't be seen easily, be sure you are focused. Be present. No matter how much you are tempted, don't multitask, for instance, by typing an email or checking your smart phone for messages while you and the client are talking.

The $99 seminar also teaches you to listen just to listen without fixing, judging, or interrupting to offer your opinion. A slightly more expensive listening seminar might show you how to listen for nonverbal cues and emotions. From there, listening as a coach gets interesting. You can listen by:

- paraphrasing what the client is telling you to be sure that you heard correctly

- reflecting back the emotions you notice to be sure you are empathizing with how the client feels

- understanding the client's interests, commitments, aspirations, and point of view

- drawing a mental map about how the client structures their thinking about an issue

- identifying where the client might be stuck

- observing for how well the client's aspirations and work effort match up

- noticing how coachable the client is

- discover the client's top priorities and values

- identifying the client's communication style

- finding out how aware the client is or isn't about how others are affected

- hearing what the client is not saying

- uncovering the perspectives the client is considering and those the client isn't

- seeing blind spots the client might have in their perceptions or thinking

- identifying limiting perceptions about the issue

- acknowledging the talents and strengths the client has

- finding ways to appreciate the client for their work so far

- noting what gets the client excited and passionate

- determining where the client seems to want to go with the coaching conversation

There are many other ways to listen with purpose. The art of coaching is largely about developing the capacity to listen, which is one of the reasons why developing a culture of coaching in an organization helps leaders, managers, and up-and-coming talent be more effective. By learning to really listen intently, employees learn how to be more collaborative, have more impact, and work more effectively together.

Appreciative Inquiry

Appreciative inquiry is as much a style for a coach as it is a subset of active inquiry. Appreciative inquiry is the same as active inquiry except that the coach emphasizes the positive. Some coaches have a purely appreciative style. Others use appreciative inquiry in situations when the client feels especially vulnerable, is not especially open to criticism, responds best to praise and the positive, or seems to have thin skin.

Appreciative questions are questions that help the client identify how to do better, build on what's working, find support, use their strengths, and consider positive possibilities:

- What's working that you can build on?

- What strengths can you bring to bear on this issue?

- What's a small step you can take to get some traction?

- Who supports you?

- Who can you go to for resources or support?

- What has worked in other areas of your life that you can apply here?

- You mentioned a successful project you did last year. How can you take the lessons from that and apply them to this challenge?

- What becomes possible when you succeed?

- How can you make this initiative the most remarkable of your career?

- How can you make this coming quarter the best financial quarter in the company's history?

Accountability

There are two types of coaching conversations for accountability: the easy one and the hard one. This kind of coaching is a lot like comedian Jerry Seinfeld's observations about rental car companies. According to him, it is easy to take a reservation and hard to keep a reservation. This first accountability coaching conversation is akin to taking a reservation for a rental car. The second is more like keeping the reservation.

The easy conversation—the equivalent of taking a reservation for a car rental—happens when the client gets clarity, and it is time to take action. Your job as a coach is to ask the client what they will do next. Get as specific as possible so that there is no doubt about whether or not the client did what they said they would do. Even here sometimes you have to add a little bit of edge to your coaching and challenge a client who might be thinking too small or holding back. For instance, I recently worked with a client who wanted his branch to be the first one in the nation to implement a new organizational initiative. When I asked him what specifically he would do to make this happen, his plan was vague. He needed some tough coaching to commit to an ambitious, specific goal and a plan to achieve it.

The harder conversation—the equivalent of keeping the car rental reservation—happens when clients don't do what they said they would do. When this happens, it can be challenging to decide how forceful to be. Consider what happens when someone declares a New Year's Resolution to eat less and work out more and then seems to give up. Why does this happen? It isn't rocket science to control portion size, eat fewer snacks, count calories, and navigate to the gym. Something else must be going on beneath the surface. The same is usually true when a client doesn't do what the two of you agreed on. Possibilities might include the following:

- The client isn't really serious about achieving the goal.

- The client isn't accurately calibrating how much work it will take to achieve the goal.

- The client doesn't want to do the work required to be successful.

- The client doesn't have the skills or knowledge to take the action they said they would take.

- The client has time management issues.

- Something else came up that was a bigger priority and might even shift the focus of the coaching.

- The client has limiting beliefs or fear that prevents action.

Given all the unknowns, it makes logical sense to start off by being gentle. Use active inquiry to find out what happened and what the client's considerations were for not taking action. Then discuss those considerations and ask the client to recommit. The coaching could include anything from talking about and working through the client's challenges to role playing, identifying small steps to take instead of large steps, choosing a less ambitious goal, coaching to manage time better, or coaching to shift limiting beliefs. The most effective way to coach a client who isn't taking action is by asking the client for their suggestions. For instance, "How can I best support you so that you do what you committed to do, assuming this is still your intent?"

If the client continues to avoid accountability, perhaps for weeks, then it might be effective to add more edge to your approach. For instance:

- "It's a been a few weeks now, and you've not followed through on your agreement three times in a row. How important is this goal to you?"

- "The current action plan doesn't seem to be working for you. What's plan B?"

- "What's really going on here?"

- "It feels like I care more about getting this done than you. How can I best support you at this point?"

Holding a client accountable is not about judging, blaming, yelling, telling the client what to do, doing the work for the client, or getting impatient. It is about working with the client to find out why the client won't take action and either resolving those challenges or changing the original goal.

Shifting the Conversation
when the Client is Stuck

All coaching is supposed to help the client get unstuck or move ahead more quickly than they are now. Later in this book you will see examples of methodologies that help get people unstuck in specific situations they face. They range from helping clients change their perceptions to addressing specific issues, such as a conflict, engaging employees, or juggling multiple priorities. At the same time, certain conversations can be helpful in general when your client seems stuck.

First, you can ask the client to look at the issue not as a client but as someone giving advice:

- "If you were in my shoes, what would you want me to ask you right now?"
- "Let's say a friend or colleague were in your situation. What advice would you give him or her right now?"

Second, sometimes clients get stuck somewhere on the way to results, which don't just happen. To get a result, someone first has to have a vision about what's possible, develop ideas to make the vision a reality, evaluate and choose from among many ideas, take action, follow up in the face of challenges, and move on to the next goal after getting results. Along the way, there are many places where a client can get stuck, or turn from optimistic to negative or even cynical. Following are some coaching tactics to help clients along the way.

When the client falls into negativity, complaint, the status quo, frustration, or cynicism, take them back to their vision. With an inspiring and large enough vision, immediate challenges tend to seem small. It is easy to do: "I hear that you are upset. That's actually a good thing because when people are upset it shows that they care. Let's go back to your initial vision. Tell me about what got you so excited about this initiative in the first place."

Sometimes your client gets stuck in the past. Perhaps that person believes that because something failed before it will fail again. Perhaps they resent somebody involved in the new initiative due to some past conflict or offense. If vision doesn't get them back on track, you might have to challenge them to be willing to stop holding onto the past. Either they have to make amends, forgive, or choose to go in a different way from before.

When clients are having conversations about vision, sometimes they get stuck in the excitement of describing an inspiring future. They can't get past vision. These types of clients are often visionaries by nature. They are the dreamers. They are great at talking about an exciting future and can even get others aligned and engaged, but by never leaving the conversation about vision, their colleagues eventually get frustrated. They wonder, "What are next steps? How do we take action?"

To get a client unstuck when they can't seem to get out of the vision conversation, ask, "What are specific ideas to realize your vision?" This will shift most people to brainstorming ideas. Some people love to do this and will never stop unless someone helps them along. They are natural idea generators. The coach can ask, "How do you go about prioritizing these ideas?"

Now the client has to evaluate various ideas. This requires data and analysis. Just as some people are natural visionaries or idea generators, some are natural analysts. These individuals can fall into the trap of analysis paralysis. The coach can help them by saying, "Given that there is never perfect information, if you had to make a choice now, what would it be?" Or, "If you need to do one more round of analysis, how can you make sure that it is the final round before you make a decision?" Once a decision is made, some managers and executives agree on what has to be done, but nobody raises their hand to take action or develop a formal plan. The coach can ask, "What happens next?"

Next, some leaders, managers, and entire teams take some action but quickly get frustrated when things don't move as quickly as they would like. They fall back into negativity and frustration. The coach can take them back to the vision to get them motivated again and also ask them to come up with a contingency plan. At the other end of the spectrum, clients can get so stuck in tasks that they forget about the larger vision and goals. The coach can help them align their work with the actual results they want to achieve.

Finally, once results happen, some clients get stuck here. Rather than acknowledge their success and move on, they bask in the glory of the last successful initiative. They resist moving on to the next idea that will help realize their vision or to a new vision for what's possible beyond what has been achieved. They are like Dorothy and her friends when they fall asleep in the poppy fields near the Emerald City. Now the coach can ask, "What can you do now to keep the vision moving forward? What's the next opportunity or idea to pursue?"

These types of shifting questions are quite powerful. Many leaders and executives are skilled at having a certain type of conversation, such as visioning, brainstorming, or developing action plans. The coach looks for opportunities to keep making progress.

Role Play

Role playing with clients can make a significant difference in their effectiveness. When a client has a high-stakes conversation, role playing and rehearsing almost always helps the client have insights about how to be even better during the real event because you and the client have a chance to observe what is already working and areas that need improvement. You also have the opportunity to test out different strategies and learn which approaches work best. When you role play a high-stakes conversation with the client, here are a few suggestions:

- Be very clear about the goal of the client's conversation or presentation. Make sure it is specific. Otherwise, you won't know whether or not the client is achieving their goal.

- Videotape or record the client. Recording gives clients the opportunity to watch themselves in action and draw conclusions about whether or not they really have the impact they intend to have.

- Ask the client for advice about how you should play the role of the other person. What is your style? What objections should you raise? Play with scenarios in which you are more or less difficult in the role of the other person.

- Before jumping into formal role play, let the client vent for a couple of minutes. This is a way for the client to get out everything they can't say in polite company but really would like to say. Let the client swear, insult the other party, and say things as harshly as they want. Sometimes what the client says during this venting time turns out to be the best approach; some clients hold back and don't say what needs to be said.

- How the client opens the conversation is what usually needs the most work. Clients tend to ramble, give too many reasons, or go in a different direction from their stated goal. Give the client about two minutes to open. Then stop and review. Spend enough time on the opening so that the client starts off efficiently and effectively.

- Let the client go first when it is time to discuss how they did during the role play. Don't behave like the stereotypical acting coach who barks out instructions. As with all coaching, after a bit of role play, ask the client what they think worked and what could have been better. Then get back into the role play. From time to time, if it seems the client is missing something major, ask permission to make a suggestion and then share your idea. Less is more.

- Experiment with different approaches. Most people have a natural communication style, which isn't always the right one to use in a specific situation. Role play allows you and the client to try a variety of styles and approaches. The phrase "role play" has the word "play" in it. Treat the experience like a playground. Have fun. Keep it loose. That will help the client relax and keep improving.

Presenting Observations with Impact

The coach enables the client to have insights and move forward. His primary tools are powerful questions and insightful listening. Some coaching purists take these facts a bit too far. They believe coaches should never provide advice or their own observations. This philosophy makes no sense, especially if you have expertise and knowledge and the client values your input. Why wouldn't you share observations and insights that can help the client improve?

Unfortunately, as noted throughout this book, leaders, managers, and high-potential talent are not always open to hearing advice. They have to be coachable, and clients can go in and out of being coachable more frequently than we wish. Therefore, if you have observations to offer your client, you have to present them in a way the client is willing to hear. Following is a suggested approach to do this:

- First, let the client explore issues on their own through the powerful questions that active inquiry requires. Remember the metaphor of the steam vent. Your clients need to vent and let out some figurative steam—to create space before they are open to your advice.

- When the client seems to have exhausted an issue and you still believe you have something valuable to offer, ask permission. For instance, "Do you mind if I offer an observation?'

- If the client says yes, then offer your observation, insight, or advice.

- Let the client respond. I have observed coaches who will give their advice, leave it hanging, and then say, "Okay, time is up. See you next time." Don't do this. Give your advice the respect it deserves. Ask the client for their thoughts about it.

- Don't take it personally if the client doesn't accept your suggestion. Avoid getting into an argument or a debate. Your clients don't have the same experience, style, or attitudes as you do. Ultimately, the client has to be accountable for getting results and will do so their way and at their pace. If you want the client to do it your way, you are no longer a coach. You are either a manager, a consultant, an advisor, or a teacher.

- Help the client get clarity about how they will integrate their own insights with your advice. What happens next? What will the client do and by when?

Letting the Client Guide the Process

It takes a specific type of conversation to let the client guide the coaching process. Avoid stepping in right away and directing the coaching conversation with your own lines of logic or checklists.

At the very beginning of a session, ask clients what they want to achieve. Then before asking for a data dump about the situation ask what the client's ideas are to get there. If you reach a fork in the road, let the client choose which direction to go. For instance, suppose the client tells you three reasons they have for being unproductive. Avoid saying, "I really like that first reason. Let's start there." Instead, let the client guide the process by asking, "Which of the three would you like to discuss first?"

Similarly, it is common for a client to start a coaching session with one goal in mind and then identify new challenges and goals. The client might gain more value by discussing the new issue rather than the original one. The only way to know for sure is by asking the client. For instance, "We started the session with the goal of resolving a conflict you are having, but now you are talking about the overall culture of your team. Which would you like to discuss in the time we have left?" At the end of the session, ask the client what value they got from the session and what they will do next. Ask what they want to discuss next time.

The client will tell you about the coaching they want. The most effective coaches realize this and do less rather than more. They let clients tell them which way the conversation should go. They don't need to be the smartest person or the hero saving the day. Coaching is about working with already effective people. Give your clients the respect they deserve, and let them guide the process.

When You Are Stuck

At some point as a coach, you will get stuck. Coaching is hard, and not all clients are as aware and coachable as we might like. It is the coach's job to determine what to do when they feel stuck. Here are some common situations:

The client asks you for ideas right away.

When the client asks for your ideas to solve their problem, this is a trap to avoid. If you give the client your answers before taking time to understand the client's situation, you are likely to give advice that might work for you but won't work for the client's experience, skill, style, and perceptions. You set yourself up for the client to resist your ideas and get into a debate.

Instead, tell the client that you have some ideas (assuming that you do) but want to understand their thinking first. After all, you both have different styles, and what's right for you might not be right for the client. If you can't help yourself or the client insists on hearing your ideas, let the client know they probably won't like them, because—again—you are not the same person. If the client doesn't like what you have to say, this gives you the opportunity to reply, "I told you that you wouldn't like my ideas. Now it's your turn. What would you do in this situation?"

The client still has no idea what to do.

If the client seems stuck, some questions that can help include the following listed on the next page:

- "What advice would you give to a colleague with the same problem?"
- "What skills do you have that apply here?"
- "Who can you go to for advice?"
- "Who has handled this situation really well in the past? What did they do?"
- "What are situations outside of work that you handled that are similar to this? What worked that you might apply here?"
- "If you could do anything at all with no fear or repercussions and money and time were no object, what would you do?"

One question that will seem completely ridiculous but works much of the time is: "If you did know the answer, what would it be?" This question somehow gets beyond logical thinking and encourages the client to be creative. I can't explain why, but it works a good percentage of the time.

You run out of questions to ask the client.

What if you draw a blank and run out of things to ask the client? Here are three options:

First, ask the client what they would ask if they were the coach. This is a great way to learn about the client's thought process in the moment.

Second, take a moment to summarize what you have heard and confirm you and the client are on the same page. Then ask the client where they want to go from here.

Third, ask the client what, if any, insights they have had up to this point. This might open up new areas to discuss.

The client rambles, and this frustrates you.

Some clients seem to ramble on and on. If you have a client who does this and it frustrates you, it will be hard for you to focus on what they are saying. You might feel that you are three steps ahead of the client and already know the answer.

The best approach in this situation is patience. Some clients will have different ways of communicating from how you communicate. They could be more process oriented and need to go into the details. Also, they might appreciate taking time to think things through out loud with you. Recognize that you are providing value to the client by letting them process their issues. Don't worry about whether or not you are getting to talk enough. Don't fret if you can't always be the superhero who saves the day with your fast, brilliant insights. Be patient and wait for your opportunity to share your observations or challenge the client to think bigger if appropriate.

Another approach is to ask the client about how the coaching is going. For instance, "I want to be sure you are getting value from our sessions. I notice that you are doing most of the talking, and I'm not sure if that is working for you or not. Please let me know." If the client is all over the place, ask them where they want to focus. For example: "I hear you talking about three things: X, Y, and Z. Which of these is most important to discuss now?" Or, "When we first started, you said you wanted to talk about X. Now you are talking about Y. Help me understand how they are connected or which one you want to focus on now?" Of course, if the client is working specifically with you to be more concise, then you do have an opportunity to challenge the client to express their thoughts more efficiently.

The client doesn't keep their agreements.

Coaching clients are typically busy people with many priorities. Sometimes they have to cancel sessions. Sometimes they come late. Sometimes they don't do what they said they would do. Keeping the busy schedules of most coaching clients in mind, I suggest that you start out gently. Ask what happened and what you and the client can do to prevent that from happening in the future.

If the client continues to break their agreements, this can be a sign that they also break agreements outside the coaching session. A 360-degree verbal assessment can confirm if this is true. If it is, then focusing on these behaviors can lead to insights about the client's habits and perceptions and help them be more effective. At some point, you can change your style to have a bit more edge. For instance, "You are late for the fourth time in four sessions. Is our coaching relationship important to you?"

The client is emotional.

Sometimes clients get emotional. That's a sign of powerful coaching, although it is not required, and you shouldn't feel that you need your client to experience a major catharsis when you coach them. If the client gets emotional, roll with it. Give the client the time they need to process their emotion. Ask what they would like to do.

Sometimes the client will want to keep moving ahead. Sometimes the client needs a few minutes to calm down. And sometimes the client will be so distracted that rescheduling the session is best.

You already are 100 percent sure that know the answer, and you don't need to ask more questions.

We have covered this issue before, but it is so important that it is worth repeating. Again, wherever possible, coaches are most effective when they let the client work things out. However, let's assume that the client has an issue that is right smack in the middle of your sweet spot of expertise. For instance, they might be wrestling with an operational issue, and you happen to be an expert on operations in the client's industry and even company. If you know the answer so certainly that you can't focus on coaching the client anymore, simply call a time out and say, "I hope you don't mind, but I feel like I need to break out of my coaching role for a moment. I happen to be an expert in this area. Do you mind if I put on a consulting or advisory hat for a bit?"

***The client has other distractions
that are more urgent than the current coaching.***

Ask what the client wants to do. Some clients will want to talk through the urgent issues and need to do so before they can focus on the stated intent of the coaching. At other times, clients might need to reschedule the session to a better time. Again, let the client guide the process.

If a pattern of having constant fires continues, you might ask the client if they want to discuss it in more depth. Constantly fighting fires and having urgent issues come up prevents effective strategic focus and often leads to burnout. It also can serve as a way for the client to avoid having conversations about the main goal of the coaching.

Coaching Clients on Giving and Receiving Feedback

One surprise and disappointment for me as a coach has been how unwilling many leaders, managers, and employees are to give and receive feedback. Feedback is one of the most valuable gifts we can give and be given. How will anyone get better if they don't welcome feedback and advice from others?

It makes some sense that people in corporations don't like or want to give and receive feedback. Why stick one's neck out for a manager, colleague, or employee if the other person isn't receptive, might take it personally, and negative consequences could result?

As a coach, you can help your clients be more open to feedback. If you were to ask any leader or manager how to give and receive feedback, they would know what is required. Here is a list of guidelines, and you can edit or add to it according to your own experience.

To receive feedback from someone:

- See it as a gift, not a threat. Be open to it.
- Don't take it personally.
- Thank the other person for the feedback.
- Direct the feedback so that it gives you the most value.
- Don't argue or debate unless there are rumors or inaccuracies circulating about you. In that case, stick to facts and logic without getting emotional.

- Consider whether or not the feedback is true, if it is helpful, and whether or not you will do anything about it.

- If you get feedback from more than one source about an issue, it is probably accurate or at least perceived to be accurate.

- Take action based on a desire to be successful, not wanting to be right, smart, look good, or liked.

To give feedback:

- Ask permission. Don't give feedback unless permission is granted and the other person is open to it.

- Make sure that the purpose of your feedback is to help someone get better, not to hurt their feelings or stir the pot.

- Bring specific examples that you have personally witnessed.

- Tell the person what you appreciate about them, what you don't like, and what you want them to do differently. Give them reasons that matter to them about why they should consider the feedback. For instance, how will changing their behavior help their reputation, results, or career?

- Balance your the need to achieve results and the desire to maintain or even improve the relationship. Don't push too hard. Don't be so vague that the other person has to guess.

- Focus on one thing. Don't overwhelm the other person with a long list of areas to improve.

- Let the other person guide the conversation so that it brings them the most value.

- If you sense that the other person is getting emotional, back off and reconvene another time.

In practice, when two people are meeting, these guidelines go out the window. The person receiving the feedback gets defensive. The person giving the feedback isn't clear enough or gets too aggressive. Things spiral downward. People build up resentment.

As a coach, you can work with your clients so that they are more open to receiving feedback and more comfortable and effective giving it. If you implement behavioral coaching or a 360-degree verbal assessment process, they will have no choice but to receive feedback. Role-play with them. In some cases, you can even attend the meeting to observe, mediate if needed, and make sure conversations stay within bounds.

Part Four

COACHING SITUATIONS: INDIVIDUAL EFFECTIVENESS

Overview

Each chapter in this section covers a different issue that leaders, managers, and up-and-coming talent face and that improve individual effectiveness. The next sections raise issues related to building strong relationships and using coaching to move organizational initiatives forward. The topics covered in this section include:

- Get grounded: Who does the client need to be as a leader?
- Coach to change or develop a new behavior.
- Coach to shift a limiting perception.
- Communicate simply and powerfully.
- Influence others.
- Manage time and overcome overwhelm.
- Think comprehensively about an issue.
- Develop leadership presence.
- Coach on the personal realms.

Get Grounded: Who Does The Client Need To Be As a Leader?

If you are coaching a leader, executive, manager, and up-and-coming talent to be a better leader, a great place to start is by helping the client get grounded about who they need to be as a leader. The client answers a series of simple but profound, important question to clarify who they are and what they stand for. Before you coach somebody else on this topic, please answer these questions about your own role as a leader. The questions are:

- "What is your vision for your area of responsibility?" Help clients define where they are taking their organization in the future.

- "What is your vision for your career?" Coach clients on their vision for what they can make happen in their career.

- "What are your core values as a leader?" Values are fundamental attributes about how the leader shows up.

- "What do you stand for as a leader?" Leaders stand for more than making money or surviving the next layoff.

- "What is your purpose?" In other words, what contribution do you want to make, and why?

- "What is your unique edge as a leader?" Coach the leader to clarify what sets them apart from others. The answer could include talents, strengths, skills, knowledge, relationships, and past experiences upon which to build.

- "What are your top priorities as a leader?" Answering this question helps the leader to focus their time.

- "What are the metrics that measure your success?" While vision, mission, and values are crucial, they mean nothing if the leader fails to achieve results.

- "What are the key behaviors and attitudes that you will model?" Leaders send messages with every decision they make and action they take. By determining key habits to model, leader can send consistent messages and show others what they really stand for.

- "Who are your key relationships?" Leaders engage, mobilize, and work effectively with other people to get results. They nurture professional relationships while also   continuing to improve.

- "What is your plan to continue to develop professionally and personally?" Leaders never stop growing.

The above questions are not easy to answer. One approach is to give these questions to your clients to contemplate on their own time before meeting with you. Ask clients to write down their answers to each question in a concise document. Then have a coaching session to follow up. Ask the client about which questions they would like to discuss and help them develop clarity. After the coaching session, the client can refine the answers to these questions in more depth. The outcome of this work is that clients have a living, breathing document about their most important priorities and what they stand for as a leader. The two of you can bring it out from time to time to discuss it, update it, and handle any current challenges. Meanwhile, clients have a short document that helps them stay grounded and focused as a leader.

The Center for Executive Coaching Leader's Dashboard

Instructions: Please complete the Leadership Dashboard before our next coaching session to the best of your knowledge. Don't worry about being perfect. We will review it during our next coaching session and then use it throughout the coaching process as a way to track progress and opportunities.

The focus of this Dashboard is on your area of responsibility, whether the entire organization or a piece of it. You can also do a second Dashboard with each space filled out specifically for your career (e.g., your vision for your career, key initiatives for you to take to advance your career).

Here is a glossary of terms in the Dashboard:

- Vision: This is how your want your area of responsibility to look over the next two to five years. Discuss briefly where you want your area of responsibility to be in the future.

- Mission: Describe the "why." What difference or contribution do you want your area of responsibility to make here? What gets you excited about the impact your area of responsibility can have?

- Values: What are the top three to five values that are non-negotiable for you and the people who report to you in your area of responsibility?

- Edge: What are the unique talents and capabilities that set your area of responsibility apart? Think about the unique qualities, attributes, gifts, strengths, and value. What do others say your area of responsibility does best? What should it do best? One way to phrase this question is, "Unlike others in our field, we . . ."

- Initiatives: What are the most important initiatives that currently define your success and are where you should focus your time for your area of responsibility? List the three that should account for most of your focus

- Performance metrics: What are the most important performance metrics that define the success of your initiatives and overall success for you and your area of responsibility?

- Relationships: Who are the most important people who are critical to your success and the success of your area of responsibility? Be sure to consider relationships up, down, across, and outside the organization.

- Development opportunities: What are the experiences, assignments, skills, educational opportunities, and other professional development opportunities that will advance your ability to lead your area of responsibility? What behaviors and attitudes do you know you can build on, start doing, do less, or eliminate?

Dashboard Area	For Your Organization or Area of Responsibility
Vision	
Mission	
Values	
Your Edge	
Initiatives (Top 3)	
Performance Metrics (Top 3)	
Key Relationships	
Top Development Opportunities	

Coach to Change or Develop a New Behavior

One of the simplest and most powerful forms of coaching is behavioral coaching. In a behavioral coaching process, the coach works with the client to discover and change one behavior that will have the biggest impact on their performance. Behavioral coaching can be valuable in a number of situations:

- As part of general leadership coaching, the client wants to find the one behavior that will make the biggest difference in their performance. Baseball offers a useful metaphor for this situation. A baseball player who gets eight hits out of thirty at bats has a batting average of .267, which is considered to be mediocre. If that player can get just one more hit in every thirty at bats—only one more hit—his average goes up to .300, which can make him millions in additional salary. And yet, one more hit out of thirty is an increase of only 3.3%. If he can make even one more hit out of thirty, he has a .333 batting average, which can make him an All-Star. What we are looking for today is that one behavior for you that will be the equivalent of getting one or two more hits at work. We are looking for you to choose one behavioral change that might seem minor but can lead to major improvements in results.

- The client has a behavioral blind spot that is holding back or even derailing their career. For instance, they exhibit a pattern of behaviors that show up as arrogance. Alternatively, perhaps they avoid conflict in ways that hurt productivity.

- The client has a limiting belief, perception, or attitude that is holding them back. Behaviors are expressions of our beliefs, perceptions, and attitudes. By combining perceptual coaching with behavioral coaching, the client can provide tangible evidence that the new ways of thinking are taking root.

- The client is trying to change the habits of the entire organization and first needs to model those same behaviors. Leaders go first.

Behavioral coaching has the advantage of being measurable. The client either makes the new behavior a habit or doesn't. We can observe and monitor results. There is nowhere to hide. The approach has two parts.

First, choose a behavior. The client chooses a simple, specific, and measurable behavior to start doing, stop doing, do more, or do less. The key is that this behavior is simple, specific, measurable, and stated in a positive way. Examples include letting people finish speaking, smiling more, praising the team more often, criticizing privately instead of in team meetings, making eye contact, giving employees informal feedback once each week, and confirming understanding after giving instructions

Avoid subjective patterns, judgments, and conclusions. For instance, arrogance is a subjective conclusion that we make about someone after observing a variety of behaviors that come together. Specific behaviors under the umbrella of arrogance might include interrupting, making dismissive comments, rolling eyes, folding arms, sighing loudly when others speak, raising one's voice, and making personal attacks. Different people express arrogance in different ways.

Subjective themes, such as arrogance, should be avoided because coaching works better when choosing one simple behavior rather than a whole pattern. People don't respond well to subjective labels. If you were told that you were arrogant, sloppy, passive-aggressive, abrasive, difficult, stubborn, or that you lacked integrity, how would you respond? In contrast, if you were challenged to let people finish speaking without interrupting, you would probably be more accepting.   Also, behaviors that fit a pattern, such as arrogance, usually go together. If you choose one behavior to work on with a client, they will also need to discuss the others. In other words, by choosing a specific behavior, the coach and client handle the overall pattern regardless.

A final reason to choose a simple and specific behavior is that the behavioral coaching process includes getting feedback and advice from colleagues. During this process, colleagues comment on both the specific behavior in question as well as other things they notice. The client should ultimately choose the behavior. If you did a proper assessment, you and the client will have plenty of data from colleagues, performance reviews, an off-the-shelf assessment, the client's own observations, and what the sponsor of the coaching has to say.

Once you choose the behavior, the second step is to make the new behavior a habit. It takes time and support to create a new habit, especially for already successful professionals. The process requires the coach and client to work together for anywhere between six months and a year before the new behavior fully takes root. Of course, during this process, there is plenty of time for coaching on other issues to help the client keep getting better. Shown below is a step-by-step process based on cognitive psychology to coach a client to make a new behavior a habit.

First, take notes. To start the process, ask the client to take notes about incidences that happen while they try to make the new behavior a habit—both positive and negative. What happened? When? What was the trigger? What worked? What did they learn? What will they try next time? By taking notes, you and the client have data about what's really happening. You can look for patterns and also coach the client to tackle each challenge one at a time. As the coaching progresses, the client should see the notes emphasize more and more positive results.

Second, build in a monthly 360-degreee feedback process. This process takes courage, but it works beautifully. It is very loosely based on a process that pioneering coach Marshall Goldsmith showed me when I had the chance to shadow him almost two decades ago. (For more information about the way Marshall Goldsmith currently teaches this process, read his book *What Got You Here Won't Get You There*).

To begin the feedback process, coach and client choose around five allies who will offer monthly feedback. Their time commitment is not more than twenty minutes per month. Every month the client asks each person, in person or by phone (not email!), how often they observed the new behavior, overall advice about what the client has been doing well and, if applicable, one thing that the client could be doing better. Each person rates how often they observed the new behavior used productively, using a scale of one to five.

The client's job is to receive the feedback professionally, avoid getting defensive, ask questions to direct the feedback in a useful way, and thank each person for the advice. You might have to role play with the client and coach them to get better at receiving feedback with grace. The client's goal is to go three consecutive months getting an average score of at least a four or a five in terms of how often their colleagues see the new behavior. This is a great way to create an open, transparent culture where people trust each other enough to give and receive advice. After all, how many teams and organizations do you know where leaders give and receive feedback and advice as naturally as they cash their paychecks? It also ensures that the coaching process includes a way to measure and track results and know when the client has achieved the goal.

Third, work with the client to stay on track while they still take notes and get feedback. A number of proven ways can be used to support and reinforce a new habit. If your client experiences challenges staying on track and you believe that additional support is needed beyond the coaching, use any of the following techniques. Add no more than one per coaching session or you risk overwhelming the client.

Preplanning

Before an event that is likely to challenge the client, you can help them preplan what they will and won't do in the meeting. Athletes do the same thing before going into a big game. They visualize different scenarios and how they will react when those happen during the game.

Self-talk

When the client feels the temptation to go back to old ways, it helps to talk to themselves about what they will and won't do and also the consequences that are likely to follow. Self-talk can be both positive and negative. Positive self-talk convinces the client about what they will do and the good things that will result. For instance, "Joe is driving me nuts in this meeting, but I am going to relax and let him finish. If I do, then he will feel more engaged and is more likely to do what he needs to do. Also, my career will move ahead."

Negative self-talk emphasizes the consequences. For instance, "If I don't smile when I am happy, people will get mixed messages about how I really feel and also think I am angry. I'll be known as the office sad sack, and my career will never go anywhere." Talking out loud to oneself works best, although for obvious reasons this is not a good tactic to use in public setting.

Rewards

We don't like to think of ourselves like Pavlov's dogs, but rewards do reinforce desired behaviors. Rewards are often built into the process. When client use more effective behaviors, they get better response, have more impact, and get better results. Sometimes, however, the client can also choose additional rewards.

Role play

Role play helps the client get comfortable with new behaviors that involve interacting with others.

Practice, drills, and repetitive training

These activities can ingrain new behaviors. They work well with individuals and teams. For instance, many health systems run drills in anticipation of a major disaster or health crisis. Similarly, you can test individuals with different scenarios that might challenge them in everyday situations.

Stress reduction

When we are stressed, we are more likely to fall back into automatic ways of doing things. Stress reduction can take many forms that can work for clients. Please be careful about evangelizing about your own favorite form of stress reduction. Just because you love hot yoga or meditation doesn't mean that the client will respond the same way. Stress can be relieved in many simple ways: scheduling time to work out, walking around the office campus, changing one's diet, getting a good night's sleep, leaving for work a bit earlier to avoid traffic jams and being late for the first meeting, improving time management skills, and taking a few deep breaths when upset or angry.

Support network

Ask clients who else can support them in making the desired change. For instance, a trusted colleague might be able to send signals during a meeting to remind the client to avoid old behaviors and focus on new ones. He or she can also talk to the client after the meeting about what worked and could have been better.

Self-coaching

At the beginning and end of every day, clients can have a coaching session with themselves about the new behavior. Have them ask themselves questions they would want a coach to ask, share insights that they would want a coach to share with them, and acknowledge what has worked and what they will work on to keep improving.

Conversations that set boundaries

If clients discover that their old patterns of behavior are triggered by others' actions—especially actions that step over the line and infringe on their boundaries—they might need to assert appropriately. For instance, if someone consistently misses deadlines and this causes great stress for your client, it might be time for your client to have a conversation that influences this person to change his or her ways.

Anchoring to negative and positive emotions

By anchoring old behaviors to negative emotions and new behaviors to positive emotions, old habits are more easily broken, and new habits are more easily formed. This technique comes from Neuro Linguistic Programming.

For instance, remembering the poor performance review about the behavior that led to coaching is an example of anchoring to negative emotions. Similarly, some people use elastic bands on their wrist as reminders; they tweak themselves with the band when they are tempted to go back to the old behavior.

On the positive side, clients can imagine how their career will progress after achieving the goal and how they will feel. These positive feelings can help them stay on track. Another way to use the elastic band, or a bracelet, is to put it on the left wrist after doing the desired behavior and on the right wrist after making a mistake.

Vision

Having your clients create a vision statement—and even draw it and post it in their work area—is a great way to keep a goal in mind and stay on track. The client can map out what becomes possible once they make the current behavior a habit. They can refer to their vision as constant encouragement to stay on track. This approach is closely related to anchoring to positive emotions.

Lessons from past successes

Ask clients about when they made a change in the past and what they did to stay on track. Perhaps they lost weight, got in shape, stopped smoking, or applied a new skill at work. Use that success to identify strategies that work best for your client.

As you can see, behavioral coaching is a straightforward, simple process that can have a major impact.

Coach to Shift a Limiting Perception

In one sense, all coaching is perceptual. You and the client discover new ways of thinking about a problem and have new insights about how to make progress and come away with new approaches and action steps. Our attitudes and perceptions shape how we see the world. A bunny rabbit could be a cute and cuddly animal, a tasty meal, a pest that eats crops, a disease-carrying vermin, or an important part of the ecosystem— depending on who is looking at it. The same variation in perception is true for us at work, with all sorts of situations, people, and decisions. What is interesting is that each unique viewpoint is correct; none of them are right or wrong. Too many times we let our perceptions get in the way of our progress because of the level of "fact" we place on them.

As a result, sometimes clients have attitudes and beliefs that are so pervasive and have a significant cost on their productivity and relationships that they will benefit from a focus on shifting perceptions. These ways of perceiving might have served the client in the past but now hold them back. In fact, many of these perceptions probably came about as defense mechanisms or ways to cope and started early in the client's childhood. They occur automatically in the blink of an eye, and the client is often not aware they are reacting on autopilot. Such reactions tend to come up especially during times of stress when the client doesn't have the space to make a conscious choice.

In fact, these perceptions are so pervasive that clients often don't even know they have them. Usually, you can't ask a client, "What are your limiting beliefs?" and expect a good answer. Rather, you will uncover these beliefs after working with a client for some time. You will find

them in recurring things that the client says and does—explanations
for why things happen the way they do, all or nothing judgments about
people or situations, and subjective statements about how the world
seems to them.

Coaches can help. Note that we are not talking about therapy. If you
are working with someone who seems to have a very deep issue, shows
signs of mental illness, or talks about hurting themselves or others,
refer them to a licensed mental health professional immediately. We are
talking about perceptions that show up for the client at work, and that
we can help the client deal with in a work situation. We can do this
without asking about the client's childhood, parents, or getting into any
deep traumas.

The results are phenomenal. Clients have new ways of seeing things,
can grow into new roles, and move on with less effort and stress. They
have more choices and enjoy a greater sense of freedom. Meanwhile, by
dealing with these issues at work, clients often apply their insights to
areas outside of work too.

To start, let's define two common types of limiting perceptions: false
priorities and limiting beliefs about oneself.

False priorities

Sometimes we set priorities for ourselves ahead of getting results or
being successful. A great question to ask your clients when things are not
going well and where they seem to have lost track of outcomes is:
"Would you rather be _____ or successful?" Common false
priorities include the following:

- Look good. Some people would rather look good than get results.
  Of course, getting results is the best way to look good, but some
  people shift blame, take credit, and do all they can to look good,
  even at the expense of results.

- Enjoy prestige. If you would rather have the fancy title, think about who has the best office, compare the things you have to what others have, and are not thinking primarily about results for customers and for your organization, this one might be a false priority.

- Be right. Some managers are all about being right. This is the "I told you so" mentality, which also shows up when a manager wants to win at all costs, including cost to relationships and to the team.

- Get credit. Would you rather get credit or be successful? Some managers don't get results because they care too much about making sure everyone knows they are the ones who came up with the idea or made things happen. As a result, others don't want to play along. Share the credit.

- Be smart. In professional services firms, such as law firms and consulting firms, sometimes people would rather be seen as the smartest person in the room than come up with practical ideas that actually get implemented.

- Be funny. There is a great payoff for being funny, but using humor can also be a strategy to avoid getting results.

- Be interesting or eccentric. Ditto.

- Be liked. Newer managers often struggle with this, especially if they come through the ranks. They don't want to lose their friends, who now report to them, and so they go for popularity over making tough decisions and being respected.

- Have peace and harmony on your team. Many of us avoid conflict at almost any cost. In fact, appropriate conflict is important to having good, open discussions and exploring different angles of a decision. Conflict taken too far is unproductive, however, and managers need to find that right balance between avoiding appropriate conflict and pushing too hard.

- Be perfect. Some of us have the perfection syndrome. We want perfect data. We fall into analysis paralysis. We keep trying to perfect products and ideas instead of testing them and improving as we go. In today's world of Internet marketing, the need for perfection can be a liability.

- Be the hero. Some would rather let the team fail and then jump in and be Superman.

- Get attention.

- Be above it all. This is the aloof manager who won't deal with the masses.

- Dominate, thwart, or sabotage someone else.

- Escape or hide out. Sometimes we avoid issues when the going gets tough instead of facing up to them.

- Avoid being involved. If you tend to throw your hands up when things go wrong, this is a potential issue to discuss.

- Say, "I told you so!" This is the blamer and also a different way of being right instead of getting results.

Limiting beliefs about oneself

The second category of limiting perceptions is beliefs that we hold about our own self and that hold us back. For instance:

- I am not good enough.

- I am not smart enough.

- I can't trust other people.

- I need to be in control.

- I can't make a decision without perfect information.

- I can't let anything leave my office until it is perfect.

- Anytime I fail, it means that I am a failure.

- I am not likeable.

- I think that conflict is bad.

- No one can do it as well as I can.

- I can't find good people.

- I need to be liked.

- This project (or company) is my baby.

- Only I can get this done.

- I need to stay in control.

- Amazing things never happen to me.

- I can't show people my human side.

The approach to handling these perceptions is similar to behavioral coaching because the bulk of the work is about making new habits. In the case of perceptual coaching, you work with the client on new ways of perceiving as well as on new behaviors that reflect the changed view. The tactics that create new habits—note taking, getting support, preplanning, and so on—are the same as what we covered in the last chapter. The only new wrinkle is helping the client come up with new beliefs, perceptions, attitudes, and ways of thinking.

One challenge in doing this is that it is extremely difficult to help someone eliminate a perception or habitual way of thinking that they have held for years. Think of the mind as a vinyl record. Our thoughts are like the grooves in the record. The longer we have held the thought or belief, the deeper the groove. Our core perceptions and beliefs are so deep that they are hard to erase. In fact, if the client were to challenge the belief by saying it isn't true, all they would do is wake up the old belief. For instance, suppose you are working with someone who doesn't trust people. You can debate logically with that person all day long about the fact that some people are trustworthy and some aren't, and it won't make any difference to them. You can challenge the client to repeat, "I can trust people," but that will only cause them to remember all the reasons why they can't trust people.

The only way out of this challenge is to help the client choose an alternative perception and make it a habit. It takes commitment, discipline, and practice, but it is proven to work.

For instance, you can use the "if/then" format as a template to reframe a limiting belief about oneself. Many of our limiting perceptions are blanket statements. What we can do is come up with a narrower, more specific statement of what we can do to get a result. For instance, if we don't trust people in general, we can say, "If I give my employees the training, support, and resources they need, they will get the job done." Notice that the word "trust" doesn't appear here. You don't have to compete with the long-standing belief about not trusting others. What's compelling about this approach is that the client takes a blanket statement and turns it into a statement where they control their situation with simple things that they can do.

For clients with false priorities, you can use the same if/then template. In this case, you build on the client's need for a particular outcome— such as looking good or being liked—with a new path to get there. Suppose a client values being popular, sometimes at the cost of saying what needs to be said and getting results. A reframing might be: "If I assert appropriately about what I expect, people will get better results, their careers will advance, and then they will gravitate toward me."

A second approach is to come up with a mantra, which is a short statement that the client repeats again and again. In the case of not trusting employees, the mantra might be: "Support them. Support them. Support them." If the client needs everything to be perfect before taking action, a mantra might be: "Take small steps. Take small steps."

A third approach to reframe a belief is to choose a creative alternative. For instance, an alternative to the belief "conflict is bad" might be that appropriate assertion is an important tool for any manager. Patrick Lencioni is a master of creative alternatives, for instance, in his book The Five Temptations of the CEO. For each of the five temptations he reveals—status, being popular, harmony, invulnerability, and the need for perfect information—he offers a creative alternative: results, being respected, appropriate conflict, trust, and making quick decisions. It is not easy to come up with a creative alternative, and sometimes you and the client can look to business authors and experts for ideas.

A fourth approach is to help the client come up with a metaphor that will help them see things differently. I worked with a client who felt he didn't have anything valuable to offer. When we explored the issue, he shared that his parents owned a farm and eventually sold it to become financially independent. My client, who was a consultant, believed he had nothing valuable to offer because "value" to him meant having something tangible, such as a farm and the products that a farm produces. Eventually, he realized that "My knowledge and expertise are my farm!" The metaphor of a farm allowed him to break through to new ways of thinking.

Examples of reframing:

LIMITING PERCEPTION	REFRAMED
I can't trust other people to get the job done.	If I provide ongoing training, resources, and support and if I follow up, people will do what needs to be done.
Everything must be perfect.	By testing and improving and by taking small steps along the way, we eventually achieve perfection.
I am not smart enough to move up.	If I focus on outcomes and the needs of our customers, rewards will follow.
Conflict is bad.	Appropriate assertion, negotiation, and feedback are powerful tools to achieve my goals.
I need to be loved by everyone.	My family loves me. I want my employees to respect me.

It is not your job as a coach to give the client a bright and shiny reframed belief. You can offer suggestions and ideas, but the client has to embrace and own the new belief. Steps in this process include the following:

- Clients first have to agree that a current perception or belief is no longer serving them. Otherwise, they won't be coachable. You can ask the client permission to share your observation that the client might have a way or perceiving things that isn't working, but only the client can agree and choose to get coaching to reframe their thinking.

- Let the client know that you can't eliminate the current belief or perception. Remember the metaphor of the vinyl record.

- Offer to reframe the perception and then coach the client to make the new way of thinking a habit.

- Show the client different ways to reframe, and give examples like the ones above.

- Ask clients to choose a new way of perceiving that works for them. This can take some time. Give clients the space they need to come up with ideas. You know they have found something when their facial expressions, body language, and tone of voice shift to become more positive and relaxed.

- Ask the client about new behaviors and outcomes that become possible with the new perception. This step is crucial because it allows the new beliefs and attitudes to show up and get results.

- Work with the client to make the new perception and associated behaviors a habit. Use the behavioral coaching process from the previous chapter.

An alternative: creating a new, positive perception from scratch

For some clients, the perceptual issue is not so much about limiting ways of perceiving but rather that they have the opportunity to generate new attitudes and ways of thinking from scratch. It is a great practice to identify positive perceptions, key leadership attitudes, and more productive ways of perceiving the world and work to make those habitual. You don't need any kind of leadership guru to help you with this work. I am sure you and your clients could come up with a lengthy list of key leadership attitudes and perceptions.

If you would like some idea joggers, here are six attitudes that have worked with some of my clients:

One: "Yes, and . . ." This attitude comes from the world of improvisational acting and comedy. "Yes, and . . ." is about accepting what the other person says and building on it. At most organizations, the default attitude is "No, but . . ." Leaders build on ideas, on vision, and on possibility. They welcome new ideas and the contributions of other people. They explore ideas before shooting them down. Even if you are skeptical or don't like the idea at first, the "Yes, and . . ." attitude at least means you work with the other person to understand his or her thinking and see what it could make possible. Imagine meetings where people share their ideas and aren't shot down immediately—where people thank them for the idea, build on the idea, and try the idea on. That is the spirit of "Yes, and . . ."

Two: Vision. Leaders have vision. Vision alone is not enough to get results, and executing on vision can be extraordinarily difficult, but vision is the starting point. Leaders see the big picture. They shift perspective to the future, then back to the present, and then set a course back to the future. They have an inclusive vision beyond their own small and petty wants. When setbacks happen, the leader brings people back to the vision of what's possible so that the setback seems small in comparison. The leader becomes a source of confidence, possibility, and resolve, even when others feel down, are doubtful, or don't want to do the hard work required to succeed.

Three: I care. This is a tough one because we live in cynical times, and we have seen many leaders in the past that care only about themselves and not about their organization, customers, or employees. Authentic leadership is fundamentally about caring, caring about the success of each employee, caring about key strategic initiatives, caring about the organization's success, and caring about the customers and the value they get from the organization's products and services. In other words, the leader is engaged. It is certainly easier to get results, including those that serve one's own aspirations, when your client cares.

Four: I can. I am accountable and responsible. Leaders get things done and have a positive attitude that challenges can be met. If a leader says he or she will do something, it happens, even if the leader doesn't feel like it, even if others are in the way. Most importantly, leaders take responsibility for their impact and results. If I have a meeting with someone and it doesn't go the way I wanted it to, it is not the other person's responsibility. It means I didn't communicate effectively, and I need to regroup and come up with a better approach. If my relationship with my boss is not as strong as it could be, I don't blame my boss. I take responsibility for understanding my boss and improving it. The leader identifies what is working and what isn't and takes steps to build on what's working and address what isn't without drama. It also doesn't mean stepping in and micromanaging or doing all the work but rather taking responsibility for influencing others to do their part too.

Five: Focus on outcomes while finding a proper balance of managing relationships and ego. It is relatively easy to get results, one time, if the leader doesn't care about relationships, but we are in our careers over the long haul. We need to balance relationships, results, and our ego. Starting with ego, the fact is that leaders have healthy egos. At the same time, they also keep their egos in check. They give credit. They accept responsibility. They would rather be successful than right, smart, or the one with the fanciest car. Without keeping our egos in check, we get our priorities wrong. Next, the leader has to get results, but if the leader pushes too hard, that person hurts relationships. They come across as obnoxious, arrogant, or too forceful. This works once, but it kills relationships. Third, the leader has to balance ego and results with relationships. If the leader focuses too much on preserving relationships, that individual avoids tough decisions and doesn't get results. A leader balances all three: ego, results, and relationships.

Six: The success laboratory. Finally, leaders keep learning and getting better. If leaders don't get results, they don't keep doing the same thing over and over, hoping that something changes. They don't have a tantrum or give up. They learn. A poor result is nothing more than data. It doesn't mean anything. We say, "Hmmmm . . ." and develop another approach. We keep learning. Similarly, a good result becomes something we learn from and try again until we know exactly when that approach works and doesn't. Success becomes a science. We build on what works and eliminate what doesn't. We take small risks to keep learning. In marketing, we don't roll out a multimillion dollar campaign without first testing it on a small scale. If it works, we roll it out gradually. If it doesn't, we tweak it and try a small test, or we get rid of the idea and try something else. We don't put our careers on the line with huge bets, but rather we take a measured approach to learn what works. The same is true in almost any discipline at work, and it also applies to leadership. Most people take results much too personally. The attitude of seeing work as a success laboratory deals with this problem.

Again, I'm not suggesting that the above six attitudes are the only ones or the right ones. You as a coach can help clients develop positive attitudes in many ways. I have worked with clients to develop many other attitudes, including resilience, ability to handle ambiguity, persistence, courage, and creativity.

Perhaps your own organization has a set of values or desired attitudes. Still, if you take all six of these attitudes together, you have a leader who makes things happen, sees possibility, has a positive attitude, and keeps learning and getting better—all while building positive relationships. The ultimate goal of perceptual coaching is that the client discovers that they can create their own emotional state based on what will be most effective in a given situation, and that they don't have to be reactive. Perceptual coaching can be incredibly powerful, whether you are reframing current beliefs or helping make new beliefs and attitudes habitual.

Communicate Simply and Powerfully

You can help an executive, manager, business owner, or up-and-coming talent to improve their communication in many ways. This chapter focuses on three areas that come up frequently.

Giving a public presentation

First, you can coach your clients when they have a major public presentation coming up. Public speaking can be a nerve-racking experience. I know a CEO of a Fortune 500 company that was waiting to go onstage to make a presentation to a group of 1,500 people at a conference. Backstage he shared, "What they say is true. Public speaking scares me almost as much as dying a painful death."

You don't need to be a Broadway star or radio personality to help your clients become more comfortable before a major presentation and also help them improve their speaking skills. All you have to do is watch them give the presentation. You can videotape it and perhaps even invite a few trusted colleagues to review it. Ask your client what they think worked and what they want to keep improving. Review the videotape to make sure your client sees how they really come across. Ask any audience members for their advice about what worked and what could be better. Then repeat until the client is more comfortable and has the impact they want to have.

There are dozens of things that clients don't even know they are doing when presenting that are hurting their impact. Examples range from death by PowerPoint to a poor opening; a rambling middle;

a mushy end; issues with voice volume and tone; hand and facial gestures that don't work; using empty words, such as "um"; and pacing back and forth across the stage like a tiger. You can even buy any of the thousands of public speaking books on the market before you coach your client, or Google a list of top public speaking tips to become an instant expert. As always when coaching, please let your client guide the process. Ask what they liked and didn't like, where they might want advice, and what they want to do next to keep refining the presentation.

Communication style flexibility

Second, many leaders and managers suffer because they have only one or two communication styles. An approach you can use to help your client develop greater flexibility is to use parts of the body as a metaphor for different styles of communication. Different situations call for different styles. You and your client can brainstorm together and then role play to discover and practice the best style for a given situation.

Left Brain. The left brain represents facts, logic, data, and reasons. We communicate from the left brain when we want to convince someone that, logically, an idea makes sense. The best way to do that is by finding reasons and facts that matter to the other person. A good format for this is, "I suggest X. Here's why . . ." and then give two but no more than three of the best reasons you can to support your suggestion. If you give more than three reasons, you dilute your argument. For instance, "Joe, I suggest you start coming to the project meetings on time. First, you are losing credibility by coming late, and if you start coming on time the team will regain respect for you. Second, your manager is noticing this behavior, and so not coming on time is not good for your career." In this case, I used negative reasons. I could have also been more positive: "By coming on time, you'll show your manager that you are committed to this project, and you are more likely to advance your career. Also, your team will respect you even more than they already do."

A second approach that uses the left brain is called the rule of three. For some reason, we can't remember many more than three points at a time. We communicate most powerfully when we use this rule. To practice the rule of three with your clients, challenge them to answer the following questions:

- What are up to three talents you have?

- What are up to three things that your organization does better than any other?

- What are three traits you require from prospective hires?

- What are three performance goals you must achieve to be successful?

Finally, you can play a game called "That's exactly why . . ." with your client. This is a great game for using your left brain. Proposing ideas is a start but not enough. Your client is likely to receive objections, and it is important to be able to respond. This game is great practice for doing that. Here is how it works: Your client proposes an idea to you. Then you say, "No," and give a reason. The reason doesn't have to make sense. It just has to be a reason. The client's job is to then say, "That's exactly why my idea makes sense" and tell you why. For instance, suppose you say, "I suggest we go to Chinese food for lunch. You have said you wanted to try something new, and a great new Chinese restaurant has opened right next door. You also said you want to eat healthier, and this restaurant has a low-calorie menu." As the coach, you might reply, "No. I've never liked Chinese food." You could give any reason, from "Chinese food makes me queasy" to "I don't like the color of your shirt today and don't want to be seen in public with you."

Challenge your client to come up with a good response to whatever you say. For instance, suppose you have told the client, "I just don't like

Chinese food." Decide what would be a good response that begins with "That's exactly why you should come with me today." One example might be "That's exactly why you should come with me today. Flexibility is the sign of a great leader, and coming with me for Chinese food will be a great way to develop more flexibility." Another might be "That's exactly why you should come with me today. I don't like hamburgers, but you dragged me to that hamburger joint last week. Today, it is only fair that I get to take you to a place you think you won't like." Another might be "No worries. This place has a great salad buffet and other non-Chinese dishes, and the kitchen staff is very responsive to your custom requests."

The reasons don't have to be great. The key is that your client is willing to try. You are helping your client build the muscle of responding to objections using facts and logic. Make sure the facts matter as much as possible to the other person.

Right brain. The right brain is where we paint pictures with words, use metaphors, and tell stories that help people see your point of view and that can even move them emotionally. Human beings used to sit around fires telling stories because stories connect powerfully with people. As leaders, each of us should have an arsenal of stories that we tell: stories about how we overcame challenges to achieve a success; stories about what our mentors taught us; stories about our favorite characters from the movies, literature, and history and how their lives apply to current challenges. We don't want to overdo it and be seen as a blowhard, but we do want to mix it up by using stories from time to time. Your clients should be able to do the same.

If you have clients that could benefit from a bit more of the right brain in their communications, challenge them to tell you one story about some event or someone who has had an impact on their career and life. It could be the best boss they ever had, the best team they were ever on, an incredible challenge they overcame, or a huge lesson they learned the hard way. At the same time, images and metaphors are also powerful ways to make points, ways that connect to our right brain. Challenge your clients to think of a metaphor, movie, historical situation, or book that relates to a leadership challenge they are facing. For instance, we can use any number of movies to help motivate someone or a team facing challenges and in need of a turnaround: Rocky is the most overused. You can coach your clients to think of a current movie that applies to their team and how they might use it to communicate their message more powerfully.

Gut. The gut is where we go when we want to hold our ground. It works well when we want to come to terms with the other person, for instance, when negotiating a contract, asserting our needs and wants, and evaluating performance and setting expectations.

Let's suppose we want something and are willing to give something in return. That is a basic negotiation. The format is "If you give me X, I'll give you Y." Notice how this is different from using the head, from using facts and logic. Here we are exchanging things we control. We all control certain things: time, credit, our knowledge, access to us, access to our information, access to resources we control, kind words, and more. For instance, "Joe, if you work for me this weekend, I'll take you and your wife out to dinner next weekend." You can also use negative incentives, if the situation calls for it: "Joe, if you keep coming late to meetings, I'll stop covering for you to your boss." This approach works well when someone is stepping over your legitimate needs and boundaries, such as coming late to meetings.

It works even better if you add a few other statements, for example, what you appreciate or like that the other person is doing, what you don't appreciate or like, and what you expect: "Joe, I really appreciate the knowledge you bring to these meetings, but I don't like that you come late. I want you to start coming on time. If you do, I'll give you more control over the agenda. If you don't, I won't let you lead the product development piece of the project."

This is how we assert appropriately. It works when we match the incentives we offer to the situation. For instance, if Joe has only recently started coming late to meetings, you probably don't want to threaten that you will report him to the CEO of the company. Or, if he reports to you, you probably want to use informal influence first before threatening to put him on probation or firing him. If you have a client who is uncomfortable asserting, you can role play some situations where he has to speak from the gut.

Communicating from the gut also comes into play when we evaluate someone's performance. This is a great way to give informal feedback to each employee or team member instead of waiting for formal reviews: "Mary, I really appreciate the work you are doing on this project, especially the quality of your analyses. If there is one thing I'd like you to change it is that you share your ideas more often in meetings. Going forward, I challenge you to offer up at least one idea every week in our team meetings. If you do, I'll open up opportunities for you to lead a team and work with you on taking more responsibility on the way to the title of Director." Encourage your clients to keep this positive, and only bring up negative incentives if they have been giving this feedback for a long time and an extra push is needed.

Heart. Whereas the head and gut feel directive, the heart is more open. We ask for advice and help. We apologize for past mistakes and offer to make amends. We ask questions and listen. We acknowledge, recognize, celebrate, and thank the other person for his or her talents and contributions. The name says it all: we really are speaking from the heart. This doesn't mean we are wishy-washy. We can still be quite firm, and yet we ask questions and direct the answers we get by listening, reframing, and asking new questions. For instance, "Joe, I'm worried. You keep coming to these meetings late. I feel like I'm doing something that might be causing this, or maybe there is something about these meetings that turns you off. I really want you to come on time because you bring a lot to the team, and I really value your expertise. Please give me your ideas. What will it take to make that happen?"

Now we can listen to Joe. We can be firm and ask questions to involve him while still directing his response. Suppose Joe says, "These meetings are a waste of time and go on too long." Instead of getting defensive, arguing, or pushing back that Joe should come on time anyway, we can involve him again, "I had no idea you felt that way. What ideas do you have to shorten the meetings? How can I make them more valuable for you?" We listen to Joe again. It is up to us to accept his ideas or ask questions to clarify them. Joe might say, "Well, if you could get that agenda out before the meeting and cut Steve off so he doesn't babble, that would be a start." Now we can reply, "I can absolutely get the agenda out. I had no idea Steve was part of the reason you were coming late. Give me some help here. I don't want to embarrass Steve. What are ways I can keep him from dominating meetings without embarrassing him?"

Do you see how this works? We might not be flexible on the outcome we want, but by asking questions, we show we are flexible about how we get there. This only works when we need someone's commitment. If you want them to comply, communicate from the gut. If you want him or her to agree intellectually, communicate from the left brain. As with each of these communication styles, preplanning and role play are effective ways to practice with clients.

Communicating from the heart only works when your clients are willing to be open and honest. If they already know the answer, they are being manipulative if they try to force people to their point of view with questions. In that case, coach the client to just be authentic. Suggest they come out and say what they want and involve people in how best to make that happen.

Spirit and vision. Two communication approaches, spirit and vision, often go well together. We communicate from the spirit and with vision when we want a colleague or our entire team to feel more excited, enthusiastic, engaged, aligned, and energized. This is the realm of the preacher, the politician, and the inspirational speaker. Here, we tap into our shared, deeply held values and our past experiences. We build on the strength of our past relationship. We can also bring up our shared or complementary talents. From there, we paint a picture of a compelling future, a shared vision that others feel part of. We can also insert some of the right-brain methods of communication by using colorful metaphors, telling stories, and referring to heroes from history, literature, and the movies. In other words, communicating with the spirit and with vision incorporates and goes even further than what we covered when we were talking about communicating using the right brain.

Communicating with spirit and with vision is a great way to kick off teams or reengage teams and people that might be down or tired and need that extra push. It is a great way to recruit new hires by getting them excited about what's possible. For instance, "Sue, we both believe in high quality and in going the extra mile. I know we are tired after working nonstop for two months for this very challenging client. Now imagine that together we make a final push to the finish line. We are like the Boston Red Sox coming back from 3 games to 0 to beat the Yankees in the playoffs. A month from now, we are on vacation with our families, glad to be off this project, but also thankful for the huge bonus we received for completing it. At the same time, the firm acknowledges us for our breakthrough work and what it makes possible for others on new projects like this. We are seen as pioneers and thought leaders. What do you see as possible if we make this final push?"

Did you notice how the language changed to use "we"? Did you notice the shared values and history? And did you hear the vision? Here, you include the other person in shaping the vision. You share your vision and then ask him or her to share his or her vision. You are creating a shared, inclusive vision of what's possible. Similarly, one can use spirit and vision to explain to an employee and team about where your organization has been, the values everyone shares, and where the organization is heading. Then your client can ask the employee or members of the team to share their vision about how they fit in and what they see everyone achieving together. Everyone comes together as a team with a shared sense of alignment.

Legs. Finally, we use the Legs when things go wrong while we are communicating. Have you ever been in a meeting where the other person got upset or new facts emerged that threw you off? When this happens, we find a way to excuse ourselves—not to run away but to come back and reconvene when we have had a chance to review our strategy. For instance, "Jill, I see that I said something that got you angry. That was not my intent. Could I suggest we break for lunch and come back to discuss this at 2:00 after we've both had a chance to cool down?"

We might also use this strategy if new information has emerged that causes us to have to rethink our approach and come up with a new plan. If you are coaching a client who is about to go into a high-stakes conversation, ask about situations that might come up in which using the legs is a good strategy. What should your client avoid saying because they know it will frustrate the other person? What might the other person say to your client that could upset them, and how will they react?

Being the message

The most profound coaching on communication focuses on the messages that the client sends with every interaction. Here, you coach clients about how they show up as a leader—or don't—every minute of every day. When we think of communicating powerfully, some people tend to think first about the big, huge motivational speeches, such as in Braveheart, Independence Day, or MacArthur. At the same time, we all know that most communication is nonverbal. Even here, though, we can expand on what communication really means. True, authentic communication means that the leader is the message. People look to the leader for clues about what kinds of things are tolerated and not tolerated, what gets rewarded and what gets ignored or punished, and how things should get done. In this context, the leader is the message. Everything the leader does is the message—far beyond their facial expressions, gestures, and voice tone, although those are important too.

This opens up the opportunity to coach the client if you notice they are not being the message they want to be in any of the following areas:

- Body posture. Do they slouch, stand up straight, walk with confidence, or walk like Eeyore in Winnie the Pooh?

- Facial cues and expressions. Do they show confidence, look angry, look depressed, or look happy and full of possibilities?

- Hand gestures. Do they show nervous twitches, touch their face, hide their hands in their pockets, or gesture with confidence to accentuate their points?

- Dress, hair, accessories, and even hygiene. These all send messages about how your clients think about themselves, their job, and others.

- How they listen. Are they distracted? Do they interrupt? Are they always judging? Are they listening in ways that say they are there to help or in ways that say they already know the answer and are arrogant?

- How they spend their time and with whom. Do they spend more time with their best performers or worst performers? Research shows that the best managers spend the most time with their top performers, which sends a message and also allows your client to work with the people most likely to help them succeed.

- Where they allocate resources and where they don't. We send strong messages based on the projects we approve, those we don't, and those we commit to only halfheartedly. We also send messages through how long we take to make decisions about allocating resources—whether we make rash decisions or are stuck in analysis paralysis, taking too long to decide or being wishy-washy.

- How they react under stress. Does your client get angry, run away, blame, or handle stress with resilience and confidence?

- How they reward success. Is your client stingy? Or are they so generous that people are not hungry and take big rewards for granted, even for insignificant achievements?

- How they react to risk-taking that doesn't work out. Do they punish it, use it as a teachable moment, ignore it, etc.?

- When they give up on an idea or initiative. When do they cave on quality, new ideas, new products, closing a big deal, or ethics? This sends messages to others about when they should quit or cave in.

- When they celebrate success. There are many ways to celebrate success, from a pat on the back to bonuses, awards, and big parties. Different people respond differently. Some like public recognition. Some like private. Some love thatches to acknowledge success. Others prefer cash.

- When they assert themselves and when they don't. People watch your client to see when they take a stand and when they back away.

- How they show they appreciate their employees or members of their team.

- How they show they trust their employees or members of their team.

- How well they know their employees or members of their team.

- How willing they are to go the extra mile.

- How willing they are to be human or vulnerable.

- Their sense of humor.

- Their level of passion.

- When they take personal risks and go out on a limb for an idea, employee, or colleague. Do they support your employees and peers, or do they hold back? Your clients have to be politically savvy, but are they team players?

- How hard do they fight for their ideas while still balancing relationships and results?

- Where they sit in meetings.

- When they do and don't keep their word. Breaking promises, such as coming late for meetings, sends a strong message about character, commitment, and self-perception. So do your clients respond if they have to break a promise. Do they make a flimsy excuse, blame others, or apologize and take full responsibility for their error?

- When they avoid conflict.

- When they push so hard that they come across as inappropriately aggressive.

- What is their orientation to customer service and satisfaction? How often do they talk about the customer? I worked with a CEO who would leave a meeting if the customer wasn't mentioned in the first couple of minutes. He was sending a message about the main priority of his company.

- What is their orientation to quality? Where do they cave on quality? How often do they raise the bar?

- Where do they tolerate low productivity? This sends strong messages about standards.

- What about making financial targets? Your client sets the tone about achieving goals.

The above list is not comprehensive, but it makes the point. Your client sends messages in many ways. As a coach, you can help your clients develop awareness about how they show up as a leader, the messages they send, and how they can be more consistent and intentional.

Influence Others

Leaders get great ideas, sell great ideas, and make great ideas happen. Selling great ideas requires two skills. First, your coaching clients have to know the politics of getting the idea accepted. Once they know whether or not their idea even has a chance and that the battle is worth fighting, they can influence the right people one-on-one to get on their side. Working with clients on their influence is one of the most practical and valuable benefits you can provide as a coach. You can help people become more aware of what it will take to get their ideas to happen and then help them develop the insights and skills to increase the odds of success.

Stakeholder analysis and the politics of getting an idea accepted

Stakeholder analysis is an approach to helping your clients discover if the idea even has a chance to succeed and, if it does, what it will take to get enough people on their side to ensure they can move ahead with it. As a coach, you can help your client get a bird's eye view of the politics of the idea. There are two ways to do this. The first is to create a table that has four columns. An example follows. In the first column, ask your client to list each stakeholder's name.

Next, the client scores each stakeholder based on how much power that person holds specifically in relationship to this decision. A 1 is very little power, and a 3 is lots of power. If the person's power score is a 0, he or she shouldn't be on this grid right now. Remember to coach your client to focus on the person's power in relationship to this decision and not overall in the organization. Power tends to shift based on the issue being discussed.

Third, coach your client to rate the stakeholder's opinion of the idea, from -3 all the way to +3. No 0 is possible here. If your client isn't sure, the client should count the person as a -1. A score of -3 means the stakeholder absolutely hates the idea. The person feels threatened by it and will do whatever it takes to defeat it. A +3 means the opposite: the person totally loves the idea and will go out of his or her way to support it. A +1 means he or she is mildly supportive, while a -1 means he or she is mildly against it. A +2 means he or she supports the idea, and a +2 means he or she really doesn't like the idea.

Often your clients won't know the answer to these questions. That's where you can coach them to get more information either by speaking directly to the stakeholder or by asking others what they think. This approach prevents the person from going full to push on an idea before testing it out a bit to get the general feel of it.

Once the client has filled out the grid, they can multiply out the Power score times the Opinion score and put that in the total column. The score will either be positive or negative, depending on whether the stakeholder has a positive or negative opinion of the idea. If the score is positive, write it down in green. If the score is negative, write it down in red.

Now you and the client have a good color representation of how things stand in relation to the idea. Coach the client to have insights about who supports the idea, who doesn't, how much overall support for the idea exists, whether or not it makes sense to pursue the idea at this time, and what to do next.

Stakeholder Grid

NAME	POWER IN RELATIONSHIP TO DECISION (1, 2, 3)	X OPINION OF IDEA (-3, -2, -1, +1, +2, +3)	= TOTAL

Next, you and your client can map out the grid in organization chart form to get an even better look at the politics of the idea. The process is shown below:

- Draw a traditional organization chart, except:

  * The box size is relative to power in relation to the decision. A person with a Power score of 3 will have a box three times bigger than someone with a Power score of 1.

  * The color of the box is red or green depending on the opinion score.

- Review the organization chart with your client. What does the client notice about the support, or lack thereof, for this idea?

- Help clients assess if they have enough people on their side to win or if this is not a battle worth starting.

- Work with clients to determine a strategy to get enough people on their side to win.
  * Who do they have to influence?
  * Who supports their idea and can influence others?
  * Who do they have to isolate?

- Coach the client to develop a one-on-one influence strategy for each key stakeholder.

Coaching on one-on-one influence conversations

Influence happens one person at a time. In addition to working with your client to map out the politics of an idea, you can also coach people to be more effective in one-on-one influence conversations. Here is a process to do that.

Choose a goal. Many leaders and managers go into high-stakes conversations without a clear goal. You can coach your client to make sure they choose a goal that is specific and measurable. What does your client want the other person to say, think, feel, or do differently, by when? For instance, suppose your client wants Mike to have a better attitude in his job. If your client told this to Mike, he would probably say, "But I do have a good attitude. I show up every day for work and do what I need to do." Now suppose your client tells Mike that he should come to team meetings on time, speak positively about team initiatives, and stop rolling his eyes when people suggest ideas. Now there is something we can measure and even videotape. It is specific and clear, and there is nowhere to hide. Mike either agrees to do it and he does it, or he doesn't.

Assess the situation. After clients choose a goal, coach them to assess the situation. They can develop the best approach to achieve their goal. Coaching questions to ask include the following:

- How is the other person likely to react when you tell them what you want from them?

- What are the other person's motivations in this situation?

- Why will the other person agree with you? In other words, what's in it for them?

- Why will the other person resist?

- What are facts that matter to the other person that would influence them?

- What are things you control (e.g., time, advice, credit, visibility, ability to give more authority) that you can offer the other person if they agree?

- What questions do you have to ask the other person to understand more about their motivation and what can influence them to do what you want?

Plan the approach. After assessing the situation, you can coach the client to develop an approach that will work best in this situation. You might review the different styles of communicating from the previous chapter. For instance, your client can use the left brain to use facts and logic if they want to convince the other person that an idea makes sense. They can use the gut if they have to assert or negotiate and if they care about getting the other person's compliance more than his or her commitment. They can come from the heart if they want to involve the other person and secure their commitment, and if they want to have the other person feel aligned and excited, they can use a combination of spirit and vision and ways of communicating using the right brain. Coach the client on some of the following questions:

- How will you open the conversation?

- How do you expect the other person will react, and how will you respond?

- What objections will the other person raise, and how will you address those?

- How can you avoid having the conversation go in the wrong direction, for instance, by having the other person get angry or too emotional to focus? What will you do if things do go wrong (e.g., find a way to take a break and then get back together)?

- What else do you have to think about to make sure the conversation is successful?

Role play. Role play is almost a must-do when coaching people to have high-stakes or influence conversations. As discussed in the chapter about role play, this is a time when the coach can be quite valuable. A process for role play during influence conversations is as follows:

- Ask the client about how you should play the role of the person being influenced.

- Let clients take a couple of minutes to say everything they really want to say uncensored. Let them have fun and get all the nasty stuff, if any, out of their system.

- Ask the client to practice their opening. Stop and ask what they liked and didn't and what they will do differently next time. Offer your own advice if needed.

- Practice again until the opening is solid.

- Ask the client to practice answering objections. Stop and ask what worked and didn't and what the client will do differently. Offer your own advice as needed. Keep practicing.

- Try different styles: more facts via the left brain, negotiation via the gut, asking questions and listening to secure commitment via the heart, sharing a vision, and appealing to common values and experiences via the spirit.

- Capture lessons learned, and coach the client until they feel they really have it down.

Be sure to follow up after the client has their meeting. There are no guarantees in influence conversations. After the conversation happens, you can coach the client to learn what they can do better and also to decide what to do next in case they don't achieve their influence goal the first time.

Note: Another component of influence is the strength of our network of relationships. A future chapter discusses how to coach your clients to build a strong network.

Manage Time and Overcome Overwhelm

Time is the most precious asset anyone has. When executives, managers, and up-and-coming talent don't have enough time to do everything they want or need to do, they can start to feel overwhelmed. The coach can help people get back in control and spend their time in the most productive and strategic way. The following process is a simple approach to working with clients who feel overwhelmed or that they are juggling too many priorities and responsibilities.

Clients track their time for a week. Have clients track their time, preferably in 15-minute intervals, for about a week. If needed, the client can track in 30-minute or 60-minute intervals. Create a simple tracking sheet for the client that shows the time intervals and a blank space for the client to track what they do during those intervals.

Evaluate the client's use of time. Start by asking the client what they noticed about how they used their time. What ideas do they already have to be more productive and in control of their time? Then ask the client to highlight areas where:

- They were not focused on something of strategic importance to the organization.
- They could have delegated the activity to someone else.

- The activity didn't need to be done at all.

- The activity was a time waster, for instance, a longer than required lunch.

- The activity didn't need to be done as perfectly as the client did it.

- They could benefit from training to be more efficient, for example, when using a particular technology or process.

- The client tolerated unnecessary interruptions.

- They notice anything else about their use of time.

Work with the client to design an ideal day and week. You can do this in many ways, depending on the client's thinking style. Examples include:

- You and the client take out their online calendar and design the ideal day and week.

- Create a pie graph that shows how major chunks of the client's time are allocated now and how the client wants time to be allocated in the future. A pie graph is helpful when clients also want to reduce the number of hours they spend at the office. The current state could be a large pie graph, and the future state could be a smaller pie graph representing fewer hours worked. Bar graphs can also work, with bands representing different uses of time.

- Redo the activity tracking to represent how the client wants to spend time.

It will be hard to complete this work if clients are not grounded in their most important initiatives and priorities. If you discover that the client is not sure of these, coach them so that they are.

Coach clients to achieve their ideal day and week. Start with general active inquiry to get the client's own ideas. From there, you can more specific questions to help the client get where they want to be:

- What boundaries do you need to set and with whom? Note that this conversation can lead into influence coaching.

- What are your top three priorities? How will you allocate more time to these?

- How can you delegate some of your less strategic activities to others?

- What can you do to reduce the number of meetings you attend?

- What technologies can help you be more productive?

- How can you use a gatekeeper, such as an administrative assistant, to make you less accessible?

- How can you schedule specific activities that you have to do in your calendar so that you are not interrupted except for emergencies?

- How can you schedule in more time for you to recharge so that you can get more done in less time.

- What will you stop doing?

- What will you do less well?

- What limiting beliefs might be making it hard for you to set boundaries or get things done more efficiently?

- How can you set specific times to manage email and texts rather than constantly checking?

- How can you reduce interruptions?

- How can you create more consistent processes that run without you?

- How can you eliminate the need to fight frequent fires by fixing the root cause of the issue?

- How can you prioritize your activities every week and day to be sure you get the most important tasks done first?

The results of this coaching can be profound. I have witnessed executives and managers do this work and get their lives back. They have more time to be with family, enjoy a personal life, focus on what really matters in work and life, and find ways to avoid burning out.

Think Comprehensively About an Issue

A coach can be a great resource to make sure a leader or manager is thinking thoroughly about an issue. A client of mine shared an interesting observation: "I have 15 six-sigma black belts in this organization that can calculate statistics on a variety of quality issues to the thousandth decimal point. However, none of them think practically about how to translate their knowledge to sound, practical solutions." Coaching can help leaders and managers come up with creative, yet practical resolutions to top issues.

First, the coach can work with the client to define the problem accurately. A problem has a current state that isn't acceptable, a clear end state that is acceptable, and a deadline to get there. For instance, "Improve revenues by 25% within six months."

Second, the coach can ask questions that challenge the client to look at the issue from a variety of different perspectives:

- Logical perspectives. Here, a well-trained coach can bring out tried-and-true tools, such as fish bone diagrams and other root cause analyses; six-sigma tools; scenario planning; strategic thinking tools, such as the SWOT analysis or McKinsey 7s framework; systems thinking archetypes; Pareto analyses; and process flow diagrams to help the client think clearly about the issue. Even if coaches don't have training in these tools, they can still challenge clients about their reasoning and logic. They can ask the client about the pros and cons of moving forward with an idea, look at risks, and explore creative alternatives.

- Creative brainstorming. The coach can work with the client to come up with new ideas through creative brainstorming exercises. Some managers rush to solutions and don't consider creative alternatives. The coach can encourage the client to slow down, take a step back, and consider a variety of options.

- Political considerations and stakeholder perspectives. The coach can challenge the client to look at how the issue is perceived by different stakeholders and what that might mean for decisions about moving forward. He can ask how different people involved in the issue perceive the issues, where they have common ground, where they might resist, and how best to accommodate the stakeholders that really matter.

- Shorter- and longer-term views. The coach and client can explore short- and long-term implications of different approaches to resolving the issue.

- Different filters to evaluate alternatives. What if the client looks at the issue financially? Operationally? Technologically? Strategically? Environmentally? Ethically?

- Devil's advocate. The coach can play the role of the devil's advocate and - with the client's permission - try to poke holes in the client's logic.

- Implementation and action planning. How will the issue play out in practical terms? Who is accountable for doing what, and by when? Who should be part of the implementation team? What contingency plans are in place when things go wrong?

Develop Leadership Presence

A common request is "How can I develop leadership presence?" That's a great question because the phrase "leadership presence" could mean almost anything. Take a minute to think about some people you know who need more leadership presence. What would you say are the behaviors, attitudes, and conversations they need to be having? My guess is that if you think of enough people your answers will be all over the map. The most efficacious approach to helping a client develop leadership presence is by using any or all of the tools you already have at your disposal by reading this far in the book:

- Conduct a 360-degree verbal assessment to discover the client's biggest gaps in leadership development.

- Choose a specific behavior that will help the client have more impact. Watch out for general behaviors, such as "have more confidence." Instead, choose a very specific behavior that shows confidence (e.g., walking tall, making eye contact, speaking with more direct phrasing). Create a behavioral coaching process to make the new behavior a habit. When the client succeeds, choose another behavior.

- Use perceptual coaching to help the client overcome any perceptual blocks and improve. Two common limiting beliefs that managers and executives have and that relate to leadership presence are that conflict is bad and they need to be liked.

- Coach them on their communication skills so that they achieve the impact they want to have.

- Help them get better at having influence conversations.

- Coach them to use their time in ways that match how the people perceived as leaders or up-and-coming leaders in the organization use their time.

- Challenge them to think comprehensively about the top issues they have to resolve.

- From there, you can help them build a strong power base of professional relationships, engage their teams, and develop the organization.

Coaching and the Personal Realms

Once clients trust you, they are likely to open up about personal issues outside of work and career that are troubling them. This can show up in a few ways:

- They open up about a specific issue, for instance, a fight with their spouse, frustration over a child's behavioral problem, or concerns about a recent doctor's visit.

- They tell you that life feels out of balance, and they want to find a better work/life flow.

- There is a specific realm in their personal life that they want to explore, such as how to get more involved in the community.

- Sometimes, they want to take an overall look at the major aspects of their lives.

When a client comes to me with these issues, I make it clear that I'm not an expert in these realms, but I can certainly listen and try to ask powerful questions to help them see new possibilities. If it seems that an expert would be better suited to address their challenges, or if it is clear that they need a licensed mental health professional (e.g., in cases of substance abuse, threats to hurt themselves or others, or depression), then I am ready with referrals.

Remember that the fundamental coaching process and conversations can be extremely valuable to a client in almost any situation. The act of listening, asking questions, and letting the client process issues on their own can help clients relieve stress, identify a new course of action, and make their lives better. In addition, the coaching methodologies of helping a client influence others, resolve conflict, change behaviors, shift perceptions, and make the best use of their time among others all apply to personal realms as well as to work and career.

One way to start is by asking the client which aspects of life concern them. Then you can ask questions to help the client come up with ideas, actions, and commitments to improve or find more time for these.

If you have a client that wants to improve overall work/life flow or look at major areas of life, a starting point might be to discuss various points in life, including:

- Health

- Nutrition

- Fitness

- Romance and intimacy

- Relationship with children

- Relationship with spouse or significant other

- Relationship with parents

- Relationship with extended family

- Friends

- Budget and spending

- Savings and investments

- Knowledge

- Hobbies

- Personal time

- The arts

- Vacation

- Adventure
- Community and civic involvement
- Philanthropy or charity
- Possessions/luxuries
- Personal growth and development
- Spirituality
- Relaxation
- Sleep

Ask the client to highlight which areas satisfy them the most, those they have complaints or concerns about, and those that really do not interest them. For each area of concern, ask:

- What can you do in this realm to get more energy, be more balanced, and recharge?
- What can you stop doing to shed behaviors that waste your time and energy or that lead to problems?
- What are specific action steps you will take and by when?
- When a client wants to explore a specific realm beyond the above questions, lines of inquiry include:
- What is your overall vision for success and fulfillment in this area in the next one, three, five, and even ten years?
- What is your mission or the "Why?" behind why this area is important to you?
- How do you define success?
- What will you start doing and by when?
- What will you stop doing and by when?

- What will you stop doing in other areas to make more time in this area?

- What else is important to think about and do to achieve your vision?

- What are immediate next steps?

A fascinating aspect of coaching is that clients hire us for one thing and then sometimes want to talk about other things. By being open to providing coaching in the personal realms without crossing the boundaries into therapy or clinical work, you can bring significant value. At a minimum, you can serve as a sounding board for major issues outside of work, including those that might be distracting them from effective performance on the job.

Part Five

COACHING SITUATIONS: STRONG RELATIONSHIPS

Overview

Now that we have covered a few topics related to individual effectiveness, we can move to coaching topics that help leaders and managers strengthen relationships to be even more effective. The topics covered in this section include the following:

- Improve one's power base of professional relationships.
- Engage and mobilize employees.
- Manage up.
- Resolve a conflict.
- Foster collaboration
- Build a great team.

From there, we can explore ways that coaching can move organizational initiatives forward.

Improve One's Power Base of Professional Relationships

Relationships are one of the most important currencies that leaders and managers have. Their power base allows them to make things happen, learn about opportunities before they are posted publicly, and gain access to resources and information that others don't have. Some leaders and managers build their base of professional relationships proactively. Other do this intuitively without thinking about it, and still others have a blind spot when it comes to constantly nurturing and strengthening their professional relationships.

The coach can help in any of these situations by reviewing the client's power base and developing ways to strengthen it. Here are three coaching exercises you can do with your clients, especially those you think can benefit from a review of their power base.

Their organizational power map. Have the client list the most important people in their power base inside the organization. Include employees, colleagues, senior leaders, and any other relevant roles (e.g., outside vendors and advisors). The client should categorize each person in two ways: quality of the relationship and the power the other person has in the organization. Rank the quality of the relationship on a scale of -2 to +2.

- A +2 means that the other person is committed to your client's development and will even take personal risks to support your client's career and success.

- A +1 means that the other person is supportive but won't take personal risks.

- A score of 0 means that the other person is neutral, neither supportive nor unsupportive. It can also mean that they don't know your client well.

- A score of -1 means that the other person is antagonistic toward your client. They generally don't like your client, although they won't go out of that person's way to thwart the individual's career or success.

- A score of -2 is bad news. These are people who are nemeses or foils to your client. For whatever reason, they really want to see the client fail.

Second, rate the power that the other person has in the organization overall. We know that title and power don't always go together. Rate each person on a scale of 1 to 3 in terms of their informal power in the organization regardless of title. A score of 1 represents low power, and a 3 represents high power. Now your client can draw an organization power chart, which is similar to the exercise in the chapter about influence. In this kind of chart, the size of each person's box is proportional to how much power they have. Someone with a power score of 3 has a box three times larger than someone with a power score of 1.

Next, color the border lines of each box according to the quality of the relationship. A +2 gets a double green line. A +1 gets a single green line. A score of 0 gets a yellow line. A -1 gets a single red line. A -2 gets a double red line. This map gives your clients a graphical look at their own power in the organization. After you coach them to have insights about their power, you can work with them on strategies to improve their relationships.

The best way to improve a relationship is usually by improving performance. More subtle strategies will be required at other times, such as asking for advice, developing approaches to help the other person succeed, and getting more visibility by asking to be on initiatives that the other person is leading or involved with in some way. For relationships that are not working, your client might need to think about ways to make amends for past incidents that caused a rift, have a conversation to resolve the conflict, get others to intervene, or find a way to work around the other person. All of these rely on the coach working with the client to understand the other person's motivations, values, personal and professional goals, ways of thinking and making decisions, and communication style. Clients might also have some overall insights about how they show up in the organization, including attitudes and behaviors to change.

Industry and functional power base. If appropriate, you can work with your clients to think about their relationships outside the organization. How can they be more visible in their industry or profession, for instance, by getting involved in professional associations or reaching out to experts in the field?

Power base into the future. The most profound coaching about power base is coaching clients to think about what their power base needs to look like in the future to achieve their overall vision for career success. This kind of coaching is profound because clients will often realize they are or are not showing up as effectively today as they would like. They can identify new behaviors, skills, experiences, and attitudes they need to have to get where they want to be.

The first step in this kind of coaching is for clients to share their vision for their career. What do they want their career to look like in the next five, ten, and even twenty years?

Second, coach clients on who will have to know them and support them for them to achieve their vision. Don't let clients limit their thinking. Challenge them to think about key industry luminaries, opinion leaders, and even legends in the field.

Third, have clients imagine and then tell the story about how they met each of these individuals and developed a strong relationship with them. In other words, the client writes the story as if the relationship had already developed. Sometimes meeting major opinion leaders takes a long time, lots of experience, and a bit of luck. Sometimes, however, we can develop these types of relationships by being active on a nonprofit board, taking on a leadership role in an industry association, or even through a hobby (e.g., religious organization, team tennis league, or a social club). Challenge the client to think creatively.

The final piece of this coaching is to ask clients what they need to change now about how they carry themselves, their attitudes, their behaviors, their skills, and their experiences so that they attract the types of people they want in their future power base. For some clients, this kind of coaching can be an invaluable wake-up call. They realize they haven't been showing up the way they need to in order to attract key people to their professional network. Suddenly, coaching about power base becomes coaching about leadership presence and ways of being.

Engage and Mobilize Employees

Lack of employee engagement is a multibillion dollar problem, with the costs including turnover of top talent, reduced productivity, and absenteeism. According to Gallup's annual employee engagement survey, engagement scores worldwide show lower than desirable levels of engagement and, more disturbing, surprising levels of active disengagement. You can coach managers to be more effective at engaging and mobilizing their teams.

The key to this type of coaching is to get away from blanket generalizations about the manager's overall style or about engaging a monolithic "them." Engagement happens one employee at a time. Therefore, the crucial first step in coaching clients to better engage their team is to list each employee. That opens up the opportunity to develop a strategy for each employee that reports to the client.

For managers that have a huge span of control, with dozens and dozens of direct reports, you can focus first on three types of employees: those that are taking most of the manager's time, those that frustrate the manager the most, and those that are high potentials and need to remain satisfied in their roles. For each employee, the coach and client can discuss the following:

Get to know the employee. What are their talents? What is their communication style? What are their values? How high can they go in the organization, and how high do they want to go? What are their personal goals? By knowing the answers to these questions, your client can have insights about how best to engage the employee. Some employees want to keep moving up, and some don't. Some are happy to work all hours of the day, while others need to be superproductive during normal work hours to get home and take care of their family. Some employees like in-person meetings, while others are more comfortable texting results.

Occasionally, clients will complain that they don't know the answers to these questions. That's a great opportunity for them to sit down with the employee and find out. Another complaint is "I don't have time to get to know my employees." Challenge the client to list any other responsibilities that are more important than engaging employees. Also, the client can do this work over time, for instance, by focusing on a plan for one employee every couple of days.

Set clear expectations with the employee. Managers set the tone in their area of responsibility and get what they tolerate. At the same time, some employees are left wondering how they are doing, waiting for the dreaded annual performance review to find out. Top-performing managers take time to give regular feedback. Sometimes the feedback is about a specific issue, and sometimes it is about overall performance Many managers don't give feedback properly. You can coach your client to be sure stated expectations include the following:

- What they like about the employee's performance.

- What they don't like, if anything.

- What they want the employee to do differently, if anything (sometimes the message is "Keep it up!").

- What they can do for the employee if the employee improves.

- What might happen if the employee doesn't improve (Note: negative incentives should be used sparingly and only when the employee shows a repeated pattern of poor performance).

- Ask "How can I support you in making this change?"

The message can range from "You are doing great and should keep it up" to "I need you to make some major improvements."

Coach clients to customize their leadership style to the employee. Some managers are one-trick ponies when it comes to leading. They use the same approach regardless of the employee's performance and ability to move up in the organization. You can help such managers customize their approach to each employee. Options include the following:

- For poor performers, remove them from the organization.

- For poor performers who have talents that could be useful in a different role, redeploy them.

- For employees who aren't performing well and you can't remove or redeploy, there is no choice but to look over their shoulder and micromanage until you can make a change, especially if they are in a crucial role.

- For employees who have a great attitude and really want to move up but aren't yet ready or aren't performing well, give them some training and oversight to help them develop.

- For employees who used to be performing well but their attitude has slipped (e.g., something is going on at home, or they are frustrated at work for any number of reasons), have a heart-to-heart discussion to find out what happened and what they need to get back on track.

- For employees who are doing fine and are not ready to or interested in making a move, check results, ask how you can support them, and acknowledge them for their good work. Make sure they stay engaged.

- For top performers who are almost ready to move up in the organization or take on more responsibility, become a mentor and guide them to take on more responsibility.

Develop ways to recognize and reward employees for their contributions, if appropriate. Many managers are so busy that sometimes they forget that we all appreciate being recognized. Some employees appreciate a pat on the back in private and would be mortified by a public display. Meanwhile, others relish public recognition. Some respond best to a bonus check. Others would be fine with a humorous certificate or trophy. The key is to coach the client to figure out what works best for the specific employee.

Send a complete set of messages to help employees know they are important in the organization. Employees want to know that what they are doing matters and has purpose. They also want to know how they fit into the overall story of where the organization has been and where it is going. A full range of messages includes the following:

- where we have been
- where we are going
- why what we are doing matters, and why what you are doing matters
- our values
- our top strategic initiatives and how your role fits in
- our top performance indicators/metrics as well as yours and how they fit in
- the employee's specific role and how it fits into our vision, mission, and strategy
- what support do you need from me?

Develop the employee. At many organizations, professional development planning is at best an afterthought. It is something managers and employees do to satisfy Human Resources but without much follow-through. In such organizations, you have a great opportunity to coach your client to take a stand for the professional development of each employee. Hold the client accountable for sitting down with each employee, developing a plan for ongoing development with them, and making available the time, experiences, and resources needed for the employee to implement the plan.

Note that the number one way employees develop is through work experience and challenging assignments that help the employee grow. After that come relationships with key people in the organization. Training and development are a distant third. Coach clients to work with each employee to develop a practical plan that will help each member of their team grow.

The final and most important place to coach your clients is on the question "Have you earned the right to lead?" Managers tend to blame their employees first for lack of performance without exploring their own leadership. By conducting a 360-degree verbal assessment of your client's employees, you can find out what your client can do better to earn the right to lead. Typical examples of opportunities to improve are shown below:

- being more positive
- taking a personal interest in each employee
- going first as a leader instead of asking employees to go first
- keeping their word and doing what they say they will do
- respecting employees
- trusting employees to do the job
- avoiding both micromanagement and abdication
- modeling the values and behaviors they expect to see in employees
- setting a tone of excellence

- asking employees for input
- listening
- eliminating nasty behaviors that can destroy motivation (e.g., publicly criticizing, reacting poorly under stress).

One way to have your client identify the behaviors of managers who have earned the right to lead is by asking them about the behaviors of the best manager they ever had. Then ask the client to compare their own leadership style to that of each manager. Coaching on employee engagement can help managers improve productivity, keep and develop top talent, and ultimately have more people on the team to allow them to grow in the organization. Everybody wins with this type of coaching!

Manage Up

Our relationship with our manager is critical to our success, but many executives and leaders do not have as strong a relationship as they would like with their managers. You can coach them to improve that relationship. (If you are coaching somebody who happens to report to you, you can use the framework in this chapter to help them understand how best to improve their relationship with you. At the same time, see the chapter about engaging and mobilizing employees so that the process goes both ways.) The process is simple and applies to improving almost any professional relationship.

First, coach the client to get an in-depth understanding of the manager:

- How do they define success in their role?

- What are their most important priorities and initiatives?

- What are their professional aspirations?

- What are their goals for personal success and fulfillment?

- What is their communication style?

- What are their values?

- What drives and motivates them?

- How do they make decisions (e.g., based on financials, politics, technology, cutting-edge ideas, relationships)?

- What is their tolerance to risk?

- What are their pet peeves, including things to not say or do?

Second, work with clients to assess their current relationship with the manager:

- What does the manager expect your client to achieve?

- What are up to five things they must do well to meet the manager's expectations?

- How would their manager say they are performing?

- How does the manager expect your client to communicate about progress and issues?

- How well would the manager say your client is communicating?

- How well does the manager trust and have confidence in your client?

- How would the manager say your client adapts to their own communication style?

- How committed is your client to helping their manager succeed?

- What past issues, if any, might be causing conflict and need to be cleared up?

- What are the strengths and weaknesses of the relationships?

Third, develop ideas to improve the relationship:

- What is their vision for how the relationship with their manager can be?

- How can they improve their performance, if applicable?

- What does your client need to ask the manager to find out about how they are performing?

- What else does your client need to discuss with their manager, for instance, to clear up past issues or learn more about the manager's expectations?

- How can they help their manager look better in the organization?

- What can they do to help their manager avoid looking bad in the organization?

- What can they do to give their manager more time?

- What can they do to reduce the hassles and headaches their manager experiences?

- How can they help their manager be more successful and achieve their professional and personal goals?

- What judgments do they have to discard about their manager in order to strengthen the relationship?

- What can they do to communicate progress and issues more effectively to their manager?

- What requests do they have to make of their manager but without coming across as entitled?

- What, if anything, can they do to improve their manager's trust and confidence in them?

- How can they build more of a personal relationship with their manager within the limits of what's appropriate?

- How can they do a better job communicating their value to their manager and organization but without being obnoxious about it?

Given your client's answers and insights about the above, develop an action plan that pulls everything together and gets your client into action. If there is a high-stakes conversation your client needs to have, remember the value of role play.

Resolve a Conflict

Executives and managers often struggle with conflicts at work. Sometimes these conflicts are appropriate, based on tensions that naturally exist between different functions and the need for collaboration. However, when conflicts become personal or unproductive and your client is stuck, you can coach them about ways to resolve the conflict.

The first area of inquiry for resolving a conflict is to discover how willing your client is to do what is needed to resolve the conflict. How flexible are they willing to be? What are they willing to do differently or give up? How responsible are they willing to be for the impact they might be having on the other person?

Some people prefer to be self-righteous and stubborn more than they want to resolve the conflict. Your client might want to win at all costs. They might want to see the other person suffer, even if it means hurting results and perhaps their reputation. By starting out with a discussion about how willing the client really is to resolve the conflict, you can get a sense of how successful your coaching will be. Also, by starting here, you can remind the client that they said they were willing to resolve the conflict during times when the other person digs in their heels.

If the client is willing to resolve the conflict, the coaching can follow along these lines:

Understand the other person's position. What is their point of view about the conflict? What motivates them in this situation? What are incentives and pressures that will make this person willing to give ground? What are reasons that might appeal to them? What information does your client need to find out about their position, and who can they ask? What else about the other person's world is important to know?

Understand your client's position. What is the end game? What would it look like if the conflict were resolved? Where are they willing to be flexible? Where are they not willing to compromise? What requests can they make of the other person? Where do they have to make amends for past incidents that caused friction and perhaps resentment? Remember that if the client isn't willing to change anything then the conflict will continue.

Evaluate each party's styles. Sometimes conflicts emerge when two people have very different styles. Ask your client how they might have to adapt to the way the other person things, speaks, or behaves. For instance, suppose that your client focuses on technology and cutting-edge concepts when making decisions, but the other person focuses on financial performance. Challenge the client to consider how the other person is thinking about the situation and how they might adapt to that approach. Similarly, if the other person speaks quickly and gets to the bottom line but your client thinks methodically and needs to talk things out in detail, perhaps your client can learn to adapt more to the other person's communication style.

Find common ground. What do both parties have in common? What are their mutual goals? What are their shared values? Where do they overlap in their vision for what's possible for their organizations? How does this common ground provide openings to resolve the conflict?

With the assessments conducted so far, coach your client to develop the best approach to resolve the conflict. There are many ways to approach someone to resolve the conflict: listen and understand their needs to develop a collaborative solution, make amends for past issues, start a negotiation with give and take, appeal to shared values and a vision for future success, get a trusted third party (perhaps you) to mediate, find someone the other person respects and who can influence the other person to be more flexible, and approach the other person with reasons that will persuade them to move forward in more productive and mutually beneficial ways.

Anticipate objections that the other person will raise and how to handle them.

Consider what might go wrong and how your client can excuse themselves from the meeting before things spiral downhill. If new information emerges or the other person gets angry, the smartest strategy is to take a break, reconsider the approach, and reconvene after everyone has cooled down. Help your clients think about what they will do if the meeting starts to go poorly and they can't think of a way to get it going again. Also, coach your clients about what not to say because the other person will react poorly as well as how they will keep their own cool if the other person says or does something that is inflammatory.

Role play, if appropriate. Once again, role play can serve as an important tool to help your client prepare for a high-stakes meeting with the other party.

The above coaching plan addresses a conflict between your client and another person. What if your client manages a team that has many conflicts? In that case, you can coach your client to look at what they are tolerating. What are they doing, or not doing, to allow these conflicts to happen? How can they get involved to set expectations about the tone of the team? How might they have to change roles and responsibilities? How can they coach team members to resolve their own conflicts?

Foster Collaboration Inside and Outside the Organization

An issue in some organizations is that there are silos among functions and business units that prevent people from working collaboratively, effectively, and efficiently with each other. For instance, in many health systems, managers complain that it is hard to quickly communicate with other units without going up their own chain of command, down the other unit's chain of command, and back. This "horseshoe effect" wastes time and prevents nimble action to help improve patient care and satisfaction. Similarly, I recently worked with a business of seven profit centers built through acquisitions. The heads of each profit center had never met each other despite an overall strategic priority to bring together the different units into one coherent operation.

At the same time, some business leaders have the opportunity to form collaborations outside their organizations to their benefit. Examples include alliances to co-market products, collaborations to serve mutual customers, and initiatives to co-develop new technologies.

You can coach leaders and managers to foster collaboration. This work can enable their organization to innovate better, improve working relationships, increase understanding of different areas of the organization, and build stronger teams. By coaching clients to form collaborations outside the organization, you can help them form new alliances and relationships that can improve their organizations.

Explore the individual's skills, behaviors, and attitudes about collaboration

The first step in helping clients foster collaboration is looking at the individual and their attitudes and orientations about collaboration. Some managers and leaders are not natural collaborators. You might discover this during a 360-degree verbal assessment or based on some attributes on an off-the-shelf profile (e.g., a combination of low accommodation or manageability with high independence scores). Perhaps the client will share that they are not comfortable collaborating or have never had a successful collaboration, and that will allow you to explore new approaches. Questions to ask might include:

- How do you define effective collaboration?
- What behaviors are required for effective collaboration?
- What beliefs are required to collaborate successfully?
- What beliefs do you have about collaboration?
- What beliefs do you have that support your ability to collaborate?
- What beliefs do you have that might hinder it?
- What talents do you have that help you to collaborate?
- What behaviors do you have that might hinder collaboration?
- What would others say you do well when you collaborate? What areas would they suggest you can improve?
- How well do you receive feedback from others when collaborating?
- How effectively do you influence and negotiate with others during collaboration?
- What are some things we can work on together to help you better develop the skills and attitudes for collaborating even better?

Depending on what you find out from the above inquiry, you might move on, or you might coach the client on new skills, behaviors, and attitudes.

Identify areas that can benefit from improved collaboration

Next, coach the client on areas within the organization that could benefit from improved collaboration. Ask the client for areas that they know can collaborate better and how they can facilitate this improvement. To be more rigorous in the approach, you can ask the client to assess how well every area in the organization collaborates with their own area and opportunities to improve. If your client leads several areas or is the CEO, you can use a round-robin process and assess how well each area collaborates with each other area, benefits of improving collaboration among various areas, and how to make that happen.

If the client is more interested in fostering collaboration with entities and individuals outside their own organization, you can brainstorm about potential new collaborations as well as existing collaborations that can be improved.

An important line of questioning for each current and potential collaboration is about how much mutual value exists. Two entities will only collaborate if they each perceive value. Therefore, you can explore the value your client receives by collaborating and their perception of how much value the other party receives. If the other party doesn't think they will get value by collaborating, the client either has to move on or find a way to change their thinking and help them see value.

You can also ask some high-level questions, adapting them based on whether this is a new or existing collaboration:

- What is the value to them of collaborating with you?
- What is the value to you of collaborating with them?
- What are the overall benefits of a collaboration?

- What are the potential risks/downsides? How can these be addressed?
- What is in scope with how you collaborate together?
- What is out of scope?
- What are the possible ways to collaborate or improve collaboration?

Help the client develop a strategy to improve or develop the collaboration

Once the client has identified areas for new or improved collaboration, you can coach the client about how to make progress. Use active inquiry to help the client:

- **Assess the overall opportunity in more detail.** What would an ideal collaboration look like? What are possible ways to make it happen?

- **Understand the other party and what their needs might be.** Who are the key people involved? What drives them? What do they want in this situation? Where might they be willing to be flexible during a negotiation? Where will they not be willing to compromise or give in?

- **Help the client shape their influence and negotiation strategy.** What requests will they make? What are they willing to give in return for these requests? What objections can they anticipate? How will they address these objections?

- **Determine how to measure success.** What metrics will be used? Who will track these metrics and how?

- **Create a communication plan.** How will both parties in the collaboration communicate to discuss progress, resolve issues, and maintain the working relationship? Who else needs to be informed?

- **Develop the overall action plan.**

Build a Great Team

Leading teams causes frustration for many managers and executives. Many reasons account for this dilemma, from lack of a clear goal to unclear roles, personality conflicts, unrealistic timelines and budgets, poor communication, and having gaps in the talent needed to succeed. As a coach, you can help the team leader and members of the team discover what's working well on their teams and what can be better. You can have many different discussions with your clients about their team. In fact, so many books about teams are on the market that you can even buy your favorite book about teams and use it as a guide. Get a copy for your clients, have them read it, and coach them through whatever framework the book uses. In my own coaching, the questions I ask the client include the following:

- What's the specific and measurable goal for the team? Knowing the outcome not only gives the client clarity about how to get there but also serves as a great question to ask when the team gets frustrated. By getting back in touch with the overarching goal and what that makes possible, team members often get back to the work at hand and put conflicts aside.

- What are the roles you need on the team to achieve the goal?

- How will you recruit for the talent you need?

- What are the team values?

- What are the rules of the road about how team members will work together and create a productive environment?

- How do team members know what is expected of them?

- How do team members get feedback about how they are doing and advice about getting better?

- How will team members come together to get to know one another, build chemistry, and come to trust each person on the team?

- What's the plan of action?

- What are the risks, and how will these be prevented and mitigated?

- How can the team get some early wins?

- How often will the team meet to update each other on progress and clear up issues?

- How can the leader ensure there is open, honest communication on the team?

- How will the leader set the tone for a productive team environment?

- How will the leader and team members acknowledge successes and contributions?

- How will the leader and team members make sure that setbacks are discussed openly, in the spirit of learning, so that members can move forward from them and get back on track?

- What motivational strategies work best for each team member, given his or her unique style, aspirations, and drivers?

- How are new people integrated onto the team to make sure they have a smooth transition?

- When people have to leave the team, how is their knowledge captured so that no momentum is lost?

- How can the team come together from time to time to discuss how the team is working and commit to getting even better?

The coach can also play other roles to help the team get better. First, the coach can interview team members from time to time to conduct a 360-degree review of the team. The starting questions are as follows:

- What is the team doing well?
- What is one thing it can do better?
- What other advice do you have to make the team more productive?

From there, the coach can ask team members to assess their individual performance on the team and perhaps also give candid feedback to other members of the team.

A second role for the coach can be as a facilitator. When the team comes together to discuss progress, the coach can step in to review the results of the 360-degree review and also conduct some exercises to improve communication. For instance, the coach can pass out index cards to each team member, one card for each member of the team. Each team member can then give feedback to each member of the team by writing a team member's name on a card and then noting up to three things that the person is doing well and one request for that person to help the team do even better. The cards are passed out to each team member so that each person gets feedback and advice from everybody else. The facilitator can then ask team members to share one new commitment they will make to help the team get better.

Another way the coach can help in a facilitative role is by resolving challenges and conflicts that are coming up on the team. In some cases, my clients ask me to lead entire team retreats over the course of a weekend.

Finally, the coach can also provide training about what makes an effective team. One way to do this is by giving everyone a book about teams to read and having them discuss the contents in the context of their specific team challenges.

Part Six

COACHING SITUATIONS: SUPPORTING ORGANIZATIONAL INITIATIVES

Overview

We have provided examples of coaching to help improve individual performance and to address issues involving relationships and communication with others. Now we can focus on ways that coaching can accelerate and enable major organizational initiatives. This section includes discussions of coaching to:

- Plan strategy.
- Lead change.
- Develop a pipeline of leaders and plan for succession.
- Improve employee engagement throughout the organization.
- Create a culture of service excellence.
- Integrate mergers effectively.
- Develop the board of directors.
- Create a high-performance culture.
- Execute more effectively up, down, and across the organization.

In these situations, coaching can have impact as a stand-alone solution. At the same time, savvy leaders know to combine a variety of approaches in any major initiative. Training, facilitation, consulting, incentives, data-driven assessments, new roles and responsibilities, providing sufficient resources, and hiring people with skills not found in the organization can all be components to make sure an organization-wide priority succeeds.

Plan Strategy

Traditionally, leaders hire a consulting firm when the organization struggles developing a strategy to move forward more successfully, but consulting firms have significant disadvantages. They cost a fortune. The consulting process feels invasive, with a bunch of people in dark suits swooping into headquarters even if they have almost no management or industry experience. Once the process is over, the consultants disappear, and the organization has to implement their recommendations, many of which turn out to be a house of cards. Most importantly, it seems disrespectful to the employees of the organization when a company essentially outsources its brain power.

Coaching is a more efficient approach for developing a strategy. A coaching process respects the experience, knowledge, and wisdom of the organization's employees. It relies on leadership to get a conversation going in the organization and make the difficult choices required to set direction. The coach can ask tough questions, keep people on task, serve as a sounding board, speak up when leadership wavers, and assist with implementation support.

In the strategic coaching process I use, the coach guides the client through three phases. While one-on-one and group coaching can help leaders create strategy, this process usually includes a series of strategic retreats, one for each phase. Key executives and managers can come together to discuss the issues, provide input, and get clarity. In between each meeting, the coach and participants conduct research, get input from employees, and collaborate on ideas.

Before the process begins, the client answers questions about the scope of the strategic plan and how it will be completed:

- How far out does the plan go?
- Who is involved as a core part of the team that develops strategy?
- Who provides input, information, and advice?
- When must the strategic plan be completed?
- What is the process to get it reviewed and approved?

How are decisions made? For instance, does a single leader decide based on input, or does a leadership group achieve consensus together? Once these details are clear, the first phase of the coaching seeks clarity about the big-picture strategic questions that every organization needs to answer:

- What is the mission of the organization?
- What is the vision?
- What are the core values?
- Who are our customers, and who should they be?
- What is our best positioning in the market?
- Which products, services, and solutions best serve our customers?
- Who are our competitors, and how do we stay ahead of them?
- What do we do best now, and what should we do best?
- What are our strengths and weaknesses?
- What opportunities and threats do we face?
- How do we build on our strengths and shore up our weaknesses to be ready for the opportunities and protect against threats?

During this phase, it is not essential to dot every "i" and cross every "t." Rather, the conversations uncover potential strategic priorities. By the end of the first phase, the coach and client should have a list of initiatives that could be a focus for the company. Typical examples include improve quality, dominate a particular market, improve innovation, roll out a new product line, test a variety of new products and see which one the market wants, expand into a new market, develop new leadership, and improve process efficiency. Of course, the organization needs to add specifics to these very general ideas.

The second phase of the process reduces the list of potential priorities from many to no more than three. It also results in a tagline or a simple statement that summarizes the strategy so that every employee understands it. Examples include "Beat Google," "Expand internationally," and "Zero Errors!" In this phase, the coach and client develop a process to focus on the few initiatives that will have the most impact on the organization. One way to complete this process is to assign a champion to each potential priority. The champion's task is to create the case for why their priority should be the top strategic priority for the organization. The coach can work with this person to create the case, if needed. The case must include the rationale for the idea, metrics for success, along with what it will take to implement it—from an action plan and risk assessment to the required budget.

During this second phase, which usually culminates in a retreat so that leadership can debate ideas together, each champion makes the case for their assigned priority. Then the participants discuss and rank each priority. A simple voting exercise can take the pulse of the group and discover how much agreement or disagreement exists about direction. Almost every time I have done this kind of exercise a few strategic initiatives tend to receive most of the support. The coach can serve as a facilitator to help the group make progress.

By the end of this phase, the group now has a succinct list of priorities along with a tagline that describes the overall theme or purpose of the strategic direction. Now the process moves to the third phase, which is preparing to implement. One of the biggest complaints leaders have about strategic planning is that the organization takes forever to come up with a strategy and never implements anything. The coach can be especially valuable during this phase of the process.

First, the coach can confirm that the organization has a workable action plan, which includes promises for funding and providing other resources, what the organization will stop doing to free up employees' time, how people will communicate about progress and stay on track, new roles and responsibilities, new compensation and incentives, and new reporting relationship, as appropriate. The coach can serve as a sounding board and devil's advocate to make sure the plan has integrity.

Second, the coach can help resolve issues that come up during implementation. In some cases, the coach can work with leaders to press through unanticipated challenges that come up with almost any new initiative. At the same time, conflicts often arise during implementation, for instance, because a particular executive doesn't want to give up a project or resources that are no longer relevant to the new strategy. In other cases, leaders waver when it comes time to release required resources, setting up employees for failure and frustration. It is tempting for many leaders to avoid these issues and just pile new priorities onto old ones or tell employees to get it done regardless of resources available. The coach can help the organization work through these challenges.

Third, the coach can be a resource to periodically review the strategy and confirm that it still makes sense. Markets change quickly, and organizations need to be always ready to pivot. When new information throws the current strategy into question, the coach can simply ask, "Do you want to do the plan we agreed on, or has new information come up that suggests we should go back to the drawing board and rethink the strategy?" In this way, the coach can make sure that leadership communicates transparently and honestly and keeps the organization informed and aligned.

Throughout the three-phase strategic planning process, the coach can play an important role. The coach can coach leadership through key strategic questions. The coach can help bring together the people with knowledge so that they provide input into the strategy. The coach can support the champions of the potential strategic priorities to make the best case possible for their potential initiatives. The coach can help make sure the overall action plan has organizational support and is realistic. The coach can follow up after the strategic planning process is done to make sure that implementation goes as smoothly as possible and that communication is effective.

Finally, the coach can work with leadership to review the strategic plan and determine when it is time to tweak it or even go back to the drawing board. Shown below is a typical flow for a strategic planning process using the coaching model:

Prework

Coach and client agree on the scope and process for developing the strategic plan, including who is involved.

Phase I: Big-Picture Strategic Questions

- The coach interviews key leaders involved in the process to get their input about the big-picture strategic questions. Prior to the interviews, leaders are expected to get input from their employees and other experts, including advisors, customers, and other constituents.
- The coach synthesizes the interviews to determine where the leadership has consensus and where the leadership has significant disagreements or lack of clarity.
- Coach and client develop an agenda for the first retreat.
- Coach facilitates the first retreat. As the group discusses the big-picture strategic issues, participants are encouraged to identify potential priorities. A scribe tracks these on flip charts.

- At the end of the meeting, the priorities are consolidated where possible to avoid overlap and eliminate purely tactical ideas. A champion is assigned to each remaining priority to develop the best possible business case.

Phase II: Agree on Strategic Priorities

- The coach works with the champions to refine the business case, as appropriate.

- A second retreat is held. During this retreat, each champion makes the case for their assigned strategic priority. The group debates the merits of each priority. A voting exercise takes the pulse of the group. The coach can serve as a facilitator to help the group reach consensus, or the leader can make the final decision about which priorities will be the focus of the strategic plan.

- The coach works with the group to develop an overall message for the organization that succinctly communicates the theme of the strategic plan.

- The champions of the remaining initiatives for the plan are tasked with finalizing an implementation plan for the initiatives. The plan must address how to track progress, required resources and milestones for their release, risk mitigation, how to free up employees to make room for the new initiative, new reward and reporting structures, and any other issues that must be resolved to successfully implement.

Phase III: Implementation

- The coach meets with the champions to help finalize the implementation plan. The coach can ask tough questions to make sure that nothing stands in the way of implementation.

- The leadership team meets to review and agree on the implementation plan. During this time, they commit to releasing resources when required.

- The team creates a communication plan, including a plan about how often they will meet to discuss strategy and clear up issues.

- The coach works with leadership to resolve issues that might come up during the implementation process.

Lead Change

Coaching can be an excellent tool to help leaders and managers in your organization accelerate change. Numerous issues come up to hinder change initiatives. Some can be addressed with the fundamental coaching conversation of active inquiry. Others relate to issues we have already covered, such as influencing others, engaging employees, communicating powerfully, and resolving conflict.

At the same time, you can take your clients through a process to help them have insights about what parts of the change process are working well and which need a plan for improvement. Lines of inquiry include the following:

Assess the organization's readiness for change. Which parts of the organization are ready? Which are not? Who will support the change, and why? Who will resist, and why? Who will have a wait and see attitude?

Anticipate resistance. For those people that will resist the change, what is the strategy to deal with them? What are ways to convince them that the change makes sense? What would be a strategy to isolate, neutralize, or remove them? What are the triggers to put the action plan into place?

Anticipate momentum. For those people that will support the change, how can you leverage them to gain momentum? What roles can they play to lead the change? Who can they influence to get more people on board?

Set clear goals and a vision for change. How will your client know that the change initiative is complete? What metrics define success? What will be possible? What will people be saying and feeling?

Create the case for change. What's the core message to convince people in the organization that the change makes sense? How can supporters spread the case for change without going far astray from the core message?

Go first. Leaders go first during change. How can your clients demonstrate their commitment to the change and model new behaviors and habits? What sacrifices can the leader and others at the top make before asking others to sacrifice?

Set the path for change. What's the plan? Who does what and by when? What are contingencies in case things don't go as planned?

Create teams, if appropriate. What teams can work on specific pieces of the change initiative? Who leads each team? Who participates on each team? How will you make sure these teams are a priority? What will you take off people's plates so they can participate fully?

Provide appropriate support and incentives. What support will people need during the change process? What resources? What training? What political cover? What incentives and rewards? Who will provide this and by when?

Track progress. How will progress be tracked and communicated? Who will compare progress to the plan and make midcourse corrections as needed?

Get quick wins. What is a process to get some initial momentum going by getting some quick wins? How can employees present their ideas for quick wins and have them implemented without bureaucracy?

Develop, sell, and implement ideas. For performance improvement, teams of employees are often the ones who redesign processes and come up with long-term solutions. How can your client make sure there is an easy path for employees to present ideas, have them vetted, and then turn to implementation?

Communicate, communicate, and communicate. What is the plan to communicate progress and other crucial information to the organization? Note that the most effective ways are also the most time consuming—walking the halls, asking how things are going, and having conversations to address people's fears about the process.

Handle setbacks and resistance. During challenging change initiatives, it is not uncommon for the coach and client to spend most of their time on things that are not going well. The coach can play an essential role in making sure the client has a safe, objective person to talk to about what's not working and how to keep moving forward.

Keep setting the tone. Coach the client to set expectations and keep people motivated and on track during the change process. The leader has to continue to go first and set the example.

Celebrate results. How will results be acknowledged and celebrated? How will key contributors be acknowledged for what they are doing to support the change?

As with any significant organizational priority, leading change succeeds when supported by a variety of approaches. Coaching is only one. At the same time, coaching provides a sounding board for leaders to work through complex, often frustrating issues. It is lonely at the top, especially when it comes to change. Coaches give leaders a safe place to vent, test out ideas, and get a source of support.

Develop a Pipeline of Leaders and Plan for Succession

How you coach a business owner, CEO, executive, or manager about succession planning depends on how much of the process is in their control. For some clients, you might focus only on developing potential replacements for their role. For others, you might cover the full range of issues to bake succession planning into the fabric of the organization. Even if your focus with a client is narrow, I suggest that you work with as many leaders as possible in the organization to make sure succession planning is treated as an ongoing, essential process that needs to be baked into the fabric of the organization. Otherwise, the organization will be less likely to grow, attract top talent, and - for for-profit organizations - attain its highest-possible valuation. Also, leaders and managers will not have the leverage they need to focus on strategic issues rather than constantly fighting fires and immediate crises.

Shown below are examples of coaching conversations you can have with your clients about succession planning, depending on the scope of their responsibilities and control. Note that you might have to shift from coach to consultant to facilitator. However, the coaching role is especially powerful because it respects the client's own knowledge and experience.

Use active inquiry to understand what the client means by succession planning. Succession planning means different things to different people, depending on their title and what they want to achieve. Take time to understand what succession planning means for your client. What is a good outcome of a succession plan? At the same time, challenge the client to think about succession planning as a crucial organizational process that should be part of its culture, not just a one-time event to replace a key employee.

Define the future talent needs and roles for the organization. A quarterback throws the ball where the receiver will be, not where he is now. Similarly, organizations need to think about the talent and roles it will need into the future. Coach the client to consider the organization's strategy, future direction, and the types of talent and roles it will need as it evolves.

Plan out the future organization chart(s). A powerful coaching exercise is to have the client map out the current organization chart and then organization charts one, three, and five years into the future. This exercise helps the client see where the organization is, where it needs to go, and what it will take to get there. Based on these charts, work with the client to answer these questions:

- What gaps and risks in key personnel does the client notice in the organization today?

- Who are the top performers who can keep developing and help the organization grow? If the client plays multiple roles, what do clients have to do to delegate more or hire new resources so that they can focus on their most strategic role?

- Looking into the future, what are milestones when the organization will make strategic new hires? Who are the people who need to be prepared to develop and advance into new roles? If your clients are CEOs playing multiple roles, when will they cede those roles to employees so that they can focus on being a true CEO and not a jack-of-all-trades?

Become a talent magnet. Succession planning requires a pipeline of leaders, and that pipeline starts with recruiting. What does the organization need to do so that top talent flocks to it when new jobs open up?

Manage performance to be able to identify top performers. What does the client see as strengths and weaknesses in the organization that affect performance? How are top performers and high-potential employees identified? How are expectations set? How do employees receive ongoing feedback about what they are doing well and can be doing better? How well does management do the job of setting a tone where consistent, high standards are required?

Have a sound professional development planning process to help talent grow. Many organizations have a professional development planning process in name only. Employees fill out an annual form from Human Resources detailing a plan for them to develop professionally, but there is no follow-up. Challenge your clients to develop a development planning process for their organization or for their employees that has teeth, including incentives for both manager and employee when a plan is implemented. What would this kind of process look like at the organization? What role does the manager play? What role does the employee play? What is expected of each party? How will the organization support a strong professional development planning effort? Remember that the top ways people develop in organizations is through challenging work experience and getting to know key people; professional development does not require a massive investment in training programs.

Develop career paths and career plans so that top talent can advance. How does a high-potential employee advance in the organization? For each role that involves leaders and potential leaders, what are potential career paths? If the organization doesn't have clear career paths, what does it have to do to develop them?

Optimize retention strategies to keep top performers. What are compensation packages, incentives, and engagement strategies to keep top performers? How can managers improve their ability to engage top talent so that involuntary turnover of top talent is the lowest in the industry?

Address flight risks. Management should meet every six months to identify high-potential employees that might be thinking of leaving. It can develop strategies to keep key people. Many organizations are blindsided when a top performer decides to leave, and this is inexcusable. Organizations that care about succession planning develop managers who are aware of the attitudes and aspirations of their key people. Coach your client to consider possible flight risks and how to keep good employees engaged and motivated.

Identify roles that need a succession plan. Coach your client to take a look at the current and future organization charts (done previously) and identify the key roles that need a succession plan.

Identify internal people who can fill key roles. In large organizations, succession planning best practice means that each executive has three possible successors, not just one or two. Coach the client to think hard about who can fill key roles and what it will take to get them ready.

Identify roles that will require external hires. Some roles cannot be developed from within, especially newer roles that require specialized technical knowledge. The coach can challenge the client to confirm that an external hire really is required and where to find the talent required.

Develop and test candidates. Finally, after all of the above has been completed, coach and client can develop an action plan to develop and test potential candidates for key roles.

Succession planning is complex and requires a serious commitment, but overlooking this process is much more costly than waiting until the last minute to try to replace someone who leaves a key position. As a coach, you can hold executives and managers accountable for completing a comprehensive succession planning process.

Improve Employee Engagement Throughout the Organization

A previous chapter discussed an approach for coaching managers to be better at engaging their people. This chapter lays out a framework for implementing a comprehensive approach to improving engagement throughout an organization. Coaching plays an important part in this approach but is only one part.

Make the goal of improving engagement a strategic priority. Some organizations have so many programs going on that they treat each one superficially. Improving engagement, as with most other important initiatives, requires focus. If senior leadership doesn't make engagement an area of focus and then get behind it, the organization will not be successful.

Get data with a robust and reliable engagement assessment tool. Measurement is the crux of any change initiative, and engagement is no exception.

Set an overall organizational target for engagement. An overall score gives the organization a target to shoot for and celebrate when they achieve it. The score can be an absolute total or the organization's percentile ranking compared with benchmarks.

Set targets for each manager to improve their specific engagement score. A robust assessment tool breaks out engagement by each manager. This allows the organization to focus on managers that need to make significant improvements. It also makes it possible to give each manager a target to improve engagement and reward managers who succeed.

Look at specific drivers of engagement at the organization and focus there. Many engagement assessments survey the organization to discover what drives engagement at each specific organization. Examples can include how involved employees are in decision-making, whether or not the job provides autonomy, and how much feedback employees receive about their performance.

Train managers on best practices in employee engagement and specifically the most important drivers of engagement. Once data has been collected, the organization can train managers on the key factors in engaging employees and also on how to focus on the most important drivers based on the assessment.

Hold managers accountable for creating and implementing an action plan. Based on their individual engagement scores and what they learned during the training, managers create an action plan and submit it. Achieving this action plan and improving their scores becomes the basis of a portion of their performance review and compensation.

Base a portion of the manager's performance review and compensation on improving engagement scores. If the organization is serious about improving engagement, it has to provide incentives and pressures, which includes putting managers who do a poor job of engaging employees on a probationary period and removing them if they cannot improve their scores.

Put structures in place to give managers more time to engage employees. For instance, one organization realized that managers spent so much time in meetings that they didn't have much time left to meet with and engage employees. They made certain days meeting free and also launched an initiative to eliminate standing meetings that were not productive.

Train internal coaches to work with managers on improving engagement. Coaching reinforces training because it is an ongoing process that looks at real-time events. See the earlier chapter that described a process to coach managers about engaging their employees.

Coach managers who can have the most impact on engagement scores. Few organizations have the resources to coach every manager. The organization can focus on those managers who have the greatest opportunities to improve. Also, group coaching can make the process more efficient.

Senior leadership models the appropriate behaviors. A common frustration among middle managers is that senior leadership doesn't model the behaviors they are expected to demonstrate. For instance, one organization I worked with had respect as one of its core values. One day a senior leader was ruthlessly critical of a middle manager during a major meeting, humiliating him in front of hundreds of colleagues. This leader clearly failed to model the value of respect and never apologized. Employees talk about this incident a year later as an example of senior leadership not modeling the behaviors they want to see and of being hypocrites.

Continue to track engagement scores. Ongoing measurement is required to make sure there is progress and to make midcourse corrections if not.

As you can see, coaching plays an important role in an initiative to improve engagement in an organization. This chapter shows the need for other activities to reinforce coaching and make sure the organization achieves its desired goals. The approach mapped out here applies to almost any other major organizational initiative.

Service Excellence

Providing outstanding service remains a challenge for many companies and their leadership. I was surprised when the president of a $750 million company told me that his strategy was to focus on serving customers with consistency and excellence, and yet he had no processes in place to measure customer satisfaction. In the smaller business market, many business owners start their businesses with great service and then seem to grow tired of providing the same level of service after a year or two. As their interest in providing great service wanes, so does their customer base.

Coaching is a wonderful approach for helping clients improve service. Unlike consulting, which makes lots of recommendations that the client may or may not ever implement, you can coach clients to take responsibility for improving their service and creating a culture of service excellence. You can make sure that clients follow through and create improvements that last.

An approach to coaching clients to improve service includes the following lines of inquiry:

General inquiry. Start with some general questions: What does service excellence mean to you and your organization? What do you already know are issues? What works well? Discuss what you want the organization to do differently in terms of delivering consistently excellent service. What becomes possible if you make these changes?

Do reconnaissance. Work with the client to implement a plan to learn about the service experience customers have with the organization as well as the competition's performance.

Set metrics to define what service excellence means and track results. You can't improve what you don't measure. Also, without metrics, you won't know whether or not the coaching is working. Which metrics does the organization use now? Which metrics will it use in the future? Who is responsible for tracking these metrics? How will results, progress, and issues be communicated?

Examine the values and culture of the organization. Which values support service excellence? What are specific examples of how employees live these values? What are examples where employees fall short of the values? How well does leadership model these values? What new values might be needed?

Standardize where it makes sense. Standardization can help ensure that each customer has a consistent experience. Work with the client to list customer interactions that they can standardize. For instance, a restaurant can set, monitor, and implement standards for how quickly a new customer is greeted, seated, drink order taken, drinks delivered, meal order taken, meal order delivered, specific times to check in, and time frames for the bill to be delivered and payment taken. What can be standardized? What is the standard? Who is responsible for overseeing this standard? How will it be measured?

Evaluate all customer interactions. Have the client list every single interaction that customers have with the company and employees. Rate each interaction, and come up with ideas to improve it. Ideally, the client identifies every customer process and every single potential interaction within each process. Examples include answering the phone, employee attire, cleanliness of the facility, signage, selection of products, ease of finding products, ease of buying, ease of getting help, convenience of hours and days of operation, location, contacting the company, following up with customers, handling complaints, answering emails, greeting a new customer, thanking a customer for the order, refund policy, and many more.

Give employees the authority to resolve issues. Companies known for their service anticipate that about 20 percent of customer requests/ needs won't be covered under standard procedures. They train employees on a variety of situations and give them authority to handle these and make the customer happy. Coach your client to write an overall statement of principle authorizing what employees can and can't do to satisfy customers. What are specific situations that come up? What are employees authorized to do? When do they need a supervisor? What training is required? What types of employees need to be recruited to be able to meet the challenge of responding on the spot?

Focus on the best customers. By studying the most profitable, loyal, and satisfied customers, the client can do two things. First, they can find ways to keep those customers satisfied and loyal. Second, they will have insights about the customers that are the best fit for the company's service model and market to other customers who might share their characteristics.

Build in magic moments. Disney theme parks are famous for building magic moments into the customer's experience. For instance, when a child has a birthday, they get a pin to wear. Every character knows to give a special happy birthday wish when they see the child. Restaurants in the park serve special cupcakes and sing a song. Challenge your client to identify opportunities to create magic moments specific to their customers. How can employees go the extra mile?

Implement employee recruiting, engagement, reward, and development strategies that support service excellence. Happy, engaged employees are one of the biggest factors in creating a culture of service excellence. Coach the client on how to recruit employees that are passionate about service, engage them, reward them, and develop them professionally so that they have opportunities with the organization. See the section in this book about employee engagement. In addition, coach the client to research other companies and best practices that might apply to their own organization.

Consider technology that can improve service. Some technologies improve service, while others hurt it. The best example of the latter is the call answering software that forces people to press buttons for what seems like hours before—if ever—reaching a live person. Some technologies, however, standardize the customer's experience—making ordering easier, processing orders faster, and reducing errors. Each industry has specific technologies that your client can identify and research. Examples include point of sale ordering, customer relationship management software, website user interfaces for each order, and software that automates and speeds up paperwork.

Set clear expectations. Ultimately, your client is responsible for creating a culture of service excellence. Part of this role requires your client to set clear expectations. For each key to good service in the organization, what does your client expect from managers and employees? Who oversees the area? How will success be measured? What feedback does your client need to give, and to whom, to raise the bar? What is your client tolerating that they need to stop tolerating?

Set the tone and model key behaviors. Beyond setting expectations, leaders set the tone. Challenge your client to evaluate how well they model customer service and set the tone for others. What is one thing your client can do to set a stronger tone? What about each leader and manager in the organization? See the section of the book about creating a high-performance culture. The approach described there uses the metaphor of a chocolate fountain and works well when the client wants to create a culture of service excellence. The idea is that culture starts at the top with the behaviors that leaders model and flows down, just like one of those fancy chocolate fountains that we see at weddings and other big events.

Create an action plan to prioritize issues. The above work is detailed. In fact, it raises an important point about coaching: We often want transformation to come about in flashes of emotion and catharsis for our client. In reality, transformation is more often the result of very detailed work, in this case going through each process, customer interaction, employee engagement strategy, and key leadership behaviors, and improving what is not working. Therefore, a good final step is to summarize the top service issues to address, the plan and cost to address them, and prioritize the list. The top priorities are usually initiatives that have the most impact or small wins that generate enthusiasm and momentum.

Mergers

Most mergers between two companies fail. One of the biggest reasons is that the cultures of the two entities are so different that they never quite come together. As a result, the merger doesn't achieve the financial, strategic, or operational benefits that the shareholders and investment bankers anticipated.

You can coach clients to help them be more successful during mergers. The process ideally starts before the merger is consummated so that you can help the client assess whether the merger will even succeed or at least consider everything required to improve the chances of a good outcome. However, you can also get involved after the merger to help bring both cultures together.

An approach includes:

Define success and go/no-go. Start by defining the overall vision for what becomes possible with the merger. What are the key reasons the merger makes sense? How is strategic success defined? Financial success? Operational success? Cultural success? What are the specific metrics and milestones? What resources are required? How likely is it that all these metrics will be achieved? What are the risks, and how can they be addressed? What else needs to happen to achieve success?

Financial assessment. Work with the client to identify all the potential benefits, negatives, and risks of a merger financially: sales gains, cost savings, net profit gains, improvement in the business model, valuation gains, assets acquired, and anything else. What actions would be required to maximize financial success?

Strategic assessment. Repeat the above approach but this time with a strategic filter. What is the strategic fit with what each entity does best? How will the merger help improve market share? Increase power over suppliers? Improve competitive positioning? Give power over customers? Add new technology or intellectual property? Enter new markets? Enable new products? Acquire top talent? Block a competitor from advancing? How does the merger build on strengths, shore up weaknesses, allow the new entity to pursue new opportunities, and protect against external threats?

Operational assessment. Next, consider the merger from an operational standpoint. How will various functions, processes, and units be integrated? Who will lead the integrated operation? Consider marketing, sales, distribution, product development, manufacturing, financial operations, human resources, information technology, executive administration, facilities, plant and equipment, procurement, and compensation systems. What is the overall vision and plan for integration?

Cultural assessment. Finally, work with the client to consider cultural issues. The above areas are usually well thought out before a merger. Culture is the one area that isn't assessed enough. What are the similarities and differences in culture between the two entities? Where is there a positive fit? Where are there areas of concern? For instance, how would the client characterize each entity in terms of bureaucracy vs. agility, risk tolerance, team vs. individual perspective, transactional vs. relational, intimacy of relationship with customers, types of employees that are most valued, compensation expectations, collaboration, competition vs. cooperation, centralization vs. decentralization, control vs. autonomy, which behaviors get rewarded, relationship to change, career aspirations of employees, primary motivations of the people in each entity, core values, pace of work, commitment to quality and service, commitment to innovation, commitment to consistency, expectations about work ethic and time spent working each day, and expectations about commitment. Challenge the client to imagine the merged entity and how easy it will be for people from both parts of the new organization to come together and work well.

Prepare for turnover and retain key people. People often leave after a merger because they don't want to deal with the friction of integrating two entities. Coach the client to consider possible flight risks and the impact if these people were to leave. What are ways to keep these people? What is the succession plan to replace them if needed? Who are key people that the client wants to be sure to retain? What's the best strategy, including paying a retention bonus, to keep them?

Set a positive tone. Leadership sets the tone in any merger. Work with the client on their own attitudes and behaviors to set a positive tone. Then coach the client on expectations to set with their leadership and management team. Have the client consider each member of the executive team. Which behaviors and attitudes do they need to model? Which should they stop, for instance, talking negatively about the merger to their people? What is their specific accountability to help the merger succeed? What are their most likely challenges and risks? What is their plan to mitigate these risks? Who are key employees that they need to engage during the process, and how will they do that? How will they lead during perceived negative changes, such as layoffs? What messages do they need to send to demonstrate confidence and clarify about the future? How will they be measured? What are their key milestones and timing?

Oversee the integration. For each area that requires integration, how will success be measured? What are the milestones and timing? Who is accountable as the leader? If there is an integration team, who is on it? How is progress communicated? What are key issues that are already known and need to be handled? How will conflicts be resolved?

Communicate progress. What are the key messages to communicate? Who does it? Through which medium? To whom? How often? Starting when? Note here that the most effective form of communication is face-to-face interactions between leadership and employees. It is more personal, which is needed and desired during stressful times, such as mergers.

Identify translators. Translators are employees who go first to learn about the other culture. They help bridge gaps and possible misunderstandings between each entity. They act like anthropologists, although with a more practical orientation. For instance, in any two entities, the same words might mean different things. The terms "strategy," "project plan," "progress report," and "career path" might mean different things to an informational technology firm than they do to a strategic management consulting firm. If these firms merge, there could be challenges until people from both entities understand each other's meaning. Coach your client to identify pioneers who can serve as translators by working on combined teams, learning the languages of both parties, and being a bridge to help employees from each entity work together more effectively.

Share strengths and knowledge. Coach the client to think about ways to share key strengths and knowledge between the merged entities. How will new knowledge be captured? Who does it? How can each entity learn about the other, for instance, by having managers meet with each other and report about what they do well and what they have to offer?

Build relationships. A merger will be more successful when people from each entity get to know each other and build trust. Who are the key people in each entity that should meet each other? What is the plan to come together?

Manage the drama. Mergers are a Petri dish for drama—people complaining, resisting, and sowing seeds of discontent. Coach your client to anticipate people and areas that will be most likely to resist the merger and cause drama. How will the resistance show up? What is the best way to neutralize these people or get them on board? At the same time, sometimes these same people have legitimate issues, and it can be valuable to listen to them. Are the reasons for their resistance logical? How can these issues be dealt with so that the merger goes more smoothly?

Build on what works and celebrate results. Finally, as the merger progresses, there will be successes. Coach your client on the best ways to communicate, celebrate, and build on or even replicate these positive events

Mergers are a special case of change leadership as well as building a high-performance culture. As you work with your client on the above issues, review the sections of this book about coaching through change and building a strong culture. You might find other lines of inquiry that could also help your client through this very challenging process.

Board Development and Effectiveness

Boards of directors, especially nonprofit boards, often need help, as conflicts are common. Board members may not fully understand their roles and responsibilities. The composition of the board may not support the organization's strategic priorities. Leadership may want to upgrade the board. Some board members may not carry their weight. The board may not agree on strategic direction.

You can coach leaders to discuss these issues, whether through one-on-one coaching or facilitated retreats.

Begin with inquiry and assessment

As always, start with active inquiry. Understand the client's viewpoint of what the board does well and what it could be doing better.

In addition, the coach can serve as a consultant and interview individual board members, asking for their perceptions about their own performance on the board and the board's performance as a whole. This will help uncover whether they believe they are doing more or less than their share and also uncover strengths and weaknesses of the board in general.

From there, you can help the client break down the issues by looking at specific board members and specific roles of a best-practice board. You can help the client move from generalities to specific issues. Finally, you and the client can determine how to recruit the best mix of board members while developing existing board members to perform even better.

Assess each board member

One way to assess each member of the board is by asking the following questions:

- How would you rate this person's commitment to the board?
- How well do they help with fund-raising, both through their own contributions and by raising money through others?
- How much time do they devote to the board compared with expectations and what other board members are doing?
- How strong are their status and connections in the community to help attract resources and positive attention to the board?
- What else do you expect from this member, and how are they doing?
- What do they do especially well?
- What can they do better?
- Who will communicate this feedback and these expectations to the board member and by when?

Assess the board by key competencies

Next, you can work with your client and perhaps the board as a whole to evaluate the board's performance in the following areas:

- Being a steward of the mission and values of the organization.
- Developing and overseeing strategic planning.
- Making sure the organization is fiscally responsible and healthy.
- Confirming that the board is on top of legal, regulatory, and compliance issues.
- Reviewing the leadership of the organization and making sure that a succession plan is in place for both paid and volunteer leaders.

- Organizing itself well, including getting agendas out on time, having good attendance, and running meetings efficiently.

- Recruiting new members to the board, orienting them so that they can perform, and constantly strengthening the composition of the board while also meeting their standards for diversity.

- Respecting boundaries, for instance, by not imposing on the staff or getting too involved in operations.

- Making decisions efficiently, effectively, and transparently.

One issue that leaders wrestle with is what it means to have a diverse board, which usually means that the board reflects the makeup of its key constituents. It can also mean having a diverse set of perspectives and ideas. Some boards like to use a diversity grid to look at the current board composition and discuss diversity. For instance, you can list each board member going down the grid and then have key criteria for diversity going across. Criteria usually include gender, race, geography, income, generation, special skills, and sometimes sexual preference (if relevant to the organization's mission). Work with your client to develop the criteria that make the most sense to the organization, emphasizing the types of people that will help the organization achieve its mission and priorities. This assessment helps pave the way for new board members to recruit.

In parallel, coach the client to explore a second grid that lists each strategic priority of the organization and how well each board member can support that priority. This will uncover whether or not the board has enough people to help the organization execute its strategic plan.

Upgrade the board's capacity and membership

Once these assessments have been completed, your client should be able to determine how to do the following:

- *Improve the abilities of the current board.* What does your client have to do to improve the current board's understanding of their roles and responsibilities, and give them the education and training they need to be successful as board members? What are the areas where the present board is weakest, and how can it address these issues? Where does the client need to do to set stronger expectations with and give more frequent and specific feedback to board members about their roles and performance? Who is on the board that shouldn't be, and how will your client manage this issue?

- ***Recruit new membership to strengthen the board.*** What types of talents, skills, and characteristics does the board need because it doesn't have them now and can't develop them with present members? Answers here can range from people with more financial knowledge or other specialized skills and those with more connections and status in the community to people who match a certain criteria related to diversity and those who have the time and abilities to lead committees or key parts of the strategic plan. Once your client knows the types of people they want, they can move to brainstorming about how to identify and recruit them. You can coach them on who they know, who they know who knows lots of people, and organizations (such as local and online services that match board members to organizations) they can contact.

It is important to start with the "what"—talents, skills, and attributes—before moving to the "who." If you let the client start with who should be on the board, you often end up with a list of friends and an insular board made up of a clique based on shared history or popularity.

Create an action plan

Finally, you can coach your client to create an action and accountability plan to tie all the above decisions together into a coherent action plan, with goals, metrics, deadlines, and specific responsibilities to make sure it happens.

All this work can be done through one-on-one coaching, coaching a small subset of the board, such as the executive committee, and/or leading the board as a whole through a board development retreat. If the board is especially dysfunctional, a smart course of action is to work with a small group of board members who "get it" and develop a plan to involve and influence the rest of the board afterward. Avoid leading a board retreat until you have interviewed board members to get a clear sense of how aligned and effective the board is as a whole. In general, it is a good practice to interview board members one by one before deciding the best course of action to assist the board.

Create a High-Performance Culture

Creating a high-performance culture is a lot like the flow of chocolate down one of those fancy multilayered chocolate fountains you see at weddings. Pure chocolate starts at the top, flows to the next level, and then the next level until it reaches the bottom. In organizations, we want to see the top model the culture, set expectations for the next level to do the same, all the way to the bottom—just like the chocolate fountain. Unfortunately, in many organizations, some layers of the chocolate fountain have something flowing that looks a bit like chocolate but doesn't smell or taste anything like chocolate. The coach's job is to help leadership develop consistent habits, messages, and performance throughout the organization—to make sure the chocolate is pure up, down, and across.

The process of coaching for a high-performance culture is simple. In fact, if you can coach one leader effectively, you can help an organization change its culture. The process involves starting at the top, coaching the top leader or leaders, and then coaching people in each successive layer to spread and reinforce the culture change. Notice that this process is much simpler than the inauthentic and ineffective way that far too many organizations role out culture change. Many organizations make one of three mistakes:

Senior leadership team goes on a luxury retreat somewhere exotic. While swimming and playing golf, they come to an epiphany about how the culture needs to be. Then they come home and expect employees to make the change. Naturally, employees are cynical and resentful because leadership is dumping the hard work on them.

Senior leadership hires a marketing firm to create all sorts of fanfare about the new culture. This turns the culture change into yet another expensive program that never seems to work. Employees see a lot of sizzle but very little substance.

Senior leadership borrows a culture from a successful organization. They adopt the Toyota Way, the Ritz Way, the Disney Way, or whichever company's way seems to be capturing the business world's admiration at the moment. Unsurprisingly, the full culture never seems to translate, and senior leadership looks as if they are attracted to easy answers instead of the hard work of real change.

True culture change requires serious work from those at the top. The top leaders need to take a realistic look at how they are contributing to the current culture, how they are showing up as leaders, what they are tolerating, and changes they need to make to their own attitudes and behaviors. Most senior leaders don't want to bother with this kind of work. It makes them feel vulnerable and is just plain difficult.

If you are lucky enough, however, to be working with leaders who understand the amount of work, introspection, and courage required to really change a culture, you can help them accelerate the change with coaching. Again, the process is simple - if your client is coachable and willing to go through it:

Define the new culture. Coach clients on what they want the new culture to be. Also, what do they like and not like about the current culture?

Get specific by defining performance metrics. Culture is a fuzzy term, often described with descriptive words. Help your client get specific. If the client creates a new culture, how will performance change? What metrics can track success? For instance, when Paul O'Neill took over as CEO of Alcoa, he set a goal to be one of the safest companies in the world.

Similarly, I worked with an executive who wanted his nonprofit organization to be more entrepreneurial, but when we interviewed employees about this change, they had no idea what it meant to be entrepreneurial. The client had to define specific metrics so that everyone understood. In this case, the organization set targets for how much of the organization's revenues should come from grants and fees from the general public as opposed to from government funding.

Get even more specific by defining key habits expected throughout the organization. A culture expresses itself through the habits and behaviors of its people. What new behaviors does your client expect from employees at all levels? Using Paul O'Neill as an example, he set the expectation that when any injury happened at Alcoa, a line of communication would notify each layer of management and then tell him, even if it meant waking him up in the middle of the night. Also, a team would form to make sure that whatever caused the injury never happened again. (You can read more about what O'Neill did in Charles Duhigg's *The Power of Habit*.)

In the case of the nonprofit organization, the leader realized that he needed more of his program managers to start writing grant proposals and also to start charging the general public for the organization's programs rather than offering them for free.

Work first with the top leader or a small group of leaders to model those habits and set expectations. Culture change starts at the top. Too often senior leaders expect the layers below to make changes first. That only creates cynical employees. Coach your clients to model the behaviors they want to see and also start setting new expectations to their direct reports. Behavioral coaching, described in a previous chapter, can be effective here.

Coach the top leader(s) to communicate the culture change to the next level. Once your clients start making changes to their own leadership, their direct reports should start to notice. As soon as the changes have become habits, leaders can communicate their vision for the new culture and performance expectations to their team. This process usually moves ahead through a combination of one-on-one and team meetings. Your client gives specific feedback to each employee during the one-on-one meetings, while team meetings give your client the opportunity to send a consistent message to everyone and get a dialogue going.

Repeat the process of modeling the new behaviors and habits and then moving to the next level and so on. Now you, or a colleague, can coach each member of the client's team to start modeling new habits. Again, behavioral coaching works well here. Once this layer of the organization models the new behaviors, leaders can communicate their expectations to their direct reports, and the process repeats. The chocolate fountain metaphor works well because you and the client work with each level in the organization to ensure consistency and success.

As soon as your clients start making changes to their behavior, culture change can roll out rapidly, but if the client encounters resistance from one or more leaders or managers, you can use active inquiry to develop a plan to help your client handle the challenges.

Why Can't We Execute Effectively?

A common frustration of leaders and managers is that their organization doesn't execute effectively. They can't get things done on time, under budget, with the desired quality. Alternatively, they can't figure out how to solve problems or how to innovate faster than the competition. These complaints present another great opportunity for coaching. As always, the place to begin is with inquiry to better define the problem. Is it an issue with an individual or with a group of individuals who can't seem to execute? Is a team struggling? Is a particular initiative being derailed? Does the entire organization seem to have a culture that keeps things from getting done?

Once the coach knows, they can refine the discussion with the client. For instance, if the issue involves a specific individual who can't seem to execute, the coach can work with them to help them improve. The issue can be one of many:

- limiting perceptions that prevent the person from getting things done, such as a belief that perfection is required

- a behavioral issue, such as procrastination, that causes the person to be late or sloppy with key deliverables

- issues with time management and focusing on the most important priorities

- poor relationships up, down, or across the organization that makes it hard to get things done through other people

- lack of planning or project management skills

- gaps in influence and communication skills

- failure to set high expectations and a strong tone with colleagues and employees

- understanding the conversations that move things forward toward results rather than staying stuck with the status quo

Alternatively, a team might have issues executing. In this case, the coach can work with the team leader and team members to resolve issues. A previous chapter outlined an approach for working with teams, and coaching conversations typically focus on the following:

- setting clear goals

- recruiting the right talents and skills

- having clear roles

- setting clear expectations and holding people accountable for achieving them

- communicating effectively among members and with stakeholders outside the team

- building strong relationships and chemistry so that the team knows each other, cares for each other, and trusts one another

- measuring and tracking key performance indicators

- finding ways to get small victories and gain momentum

- knowing how to have conversations to clear up conflicts and setbacks

Finally, if the entire organization seems to have issues executing, the coach needs to work with senior leadership. Areas of inquiry can include the following:

- how to change the culture with new behaviors, habits, and disciplines

- new roles that might be required

- reducing the number of initiatives to a manageable number
- rewards and incentives that will motivate people
- the ability of management to engage and mobilize teams
- whether or not sufficient resources are made available for success
- whether or not the right people are being recruited
- how people are developed
- which processes need to be redesigned
- how supportive and effective senior leadership is when employees present ideas, when tough decisions need to be made, and when initiatives hit roadblocks

The above issues are only some of the challenges that come up. A coach can help leaders define the problem so that it can be addressed, focus on the root causes of the problem, and find solutions without jumping too quickly to generalizations or superficial conclusions.

Part Seven

CAREER COACHING

Overview

Many coaches focus on helping people plan their careers, find new opportunities, and succeed in new roles. Managers and internal coaches work with employees to create development plans to progress in their careers as well as overall career plans within the organization. External coaches work with professionals in all walks of life to clarify a career vision and make it happen.

For external coaches, the trouble with this focus is that it is hard to generate ongoing business from the same client. In this sense, career coaching is a bit like being a car dealer that only sells new cars. People typically buy a new car every few years. By the time they are ready for their next car, they have probably forgotten about the dealership that sold them the last one.

This issue can be handled in two ways. One is to do the same thing that car dealers do and add a service center. This brings in ongoing revenue after a customer buys a new car. In other words, instead of focusing on career coaching only, it makes sense to be able to offer leadership and executive coaching to clients after they launch a new career or land a new position. The client considers you to be a resource for a variety of issues. You become a trusted advisor who happens to offer career coaching in addition to many other solutions.

A second way is to find a gatekeeper that can supply a healthy flow of clients. For instance, form an alliance with a recruiting firm to help candidates succeed in their new roles and offer outplacement coaching to organizations with employees that have been displaced. Similarly, connect with a university to provide career coaching to students; you might even find a niche, such as coaching athletes or other students who have a hard time getting to the career office during regular hours.

In this part of the book, we cover the key areas of career coaching, including:

- Initial planning
- Creating the career plan
- Personal branding
- Managing transitions
- Finding the new opportunity
- Success in a new role

We also discuss creating career coaching packages for your clientele.

Initial Planning

For most clients, the starting point for career coaching is identifying the sweet spot among three domains:

One: The client's dreams, aspirations, and passion. These define the client's ideal career.

Two: The client as a product. The client's talents, skills, achievements, and values determine how the client shows up as a product in the marketplace.

Three: What the marketplace wants. The market determines the opportunities for your clients to find a fit with their passion, talents, skills, and values.

Your coaching should help clients find a fit among their dreams and aspirations, talents, and what the market wants. If your client has talents and a dream but there is no demand for or interest in what they can do, then essentially your client has a hobby.

If your client has dreams to enter an in-demand field but lacks the necessary talents and skills to succeed, they won't be successful until they develop new skills.

If your client has the talents in a specific area and the marketplace wants what they can do but they lack the passion or aspiration to succeed, they won't be very happy and probably won't be successful either.

It is not easy to find a fit among all three of these areas. It requires a commitment to do lots of research and learning, while maintaining the attitudes needed for success. It also requires flexibility on the part of your client because a perfect match is rare. If your clients take time now to learn about the opportunities that come closest to meeting these three aspects of a successful career, they will set themselves apart from the vast majority of people in the workforce today. Let's explore each of these areas.

One: The client's dreams, aspirations, and passion

Key coaching questions and approaches to explore this area include:

- What are your dreams for your life after your current role?
- What makes you passionate?
- What do you love?
- What motivates you?
- What would the perfect life look like for you in your next role?
- What would be the perfect life for you five years from now? Ten years?
- What kinds of opportunities will give you the kind of life and career you want to have?
- What is most important to you about working? What would motivate you to love going to work?
- What do you like doing for fun?
- Which issues in the world give you a sense of urgency?
- What are some of the most valuable life experiences you have had that might influence what you want to do next?
- What is most important about your career?
- What is your dream job, and what would make that job attractive?
- What do you enjoy doing most at work? Least?

- From where you are today in your career, what is the path to your dream job?

- What areas excite you to learn, grow, and develop as a professional?

- What are your key motivators in a job and in your career?

- Describe the kinds of people with whom you want to work.

- Describe the ideal company or organization for you. What size is it? What kind of culture does it have? What are its values? What types of products or services might it offer?

- What do you like to read? What topics are most interesting to you? How might your answer point you to your ideal career?

- What kinds of current events capture your attention?

- What kinds of television shows and movies do you enjoy?

- If you read about business, which industries appeal most to you?

- Which organizations do you respect and admire the most?

- What kinds of companies do you spend money on?

- What is your ideal environment for being productive and getting results?

- What is your ideal work setting?

- What kind of life do you NOT want? Which industries and types of companies are not a good fit for you?

Imagine that you are 65 years old, fulfilled and satisfied, looking back on what you did during a great career. What were some of the things you did? What contributions did you make to others? How did you help your customers or constituents? How did you make a difference in your community? What achievements make you the proudest? What kinds of jobs did you have? What kinds of companies did you work for? What was your favorite work experience? What was your greatest challenge at work? Which work experience do you remember most fondly? What did you learn along the way? What kind of education did you have?

What kinds of limiting beliefs might be holding you back from describing the life and career you really want (e.g., I am too old, I don't have the education, this will take too long, I might look stupid)?

As you lead your clients through these questions, don't let them limit themselves based on past experiences, self-talk, or perceptions that hold them back. Challenge them to see the world as one of abundance, not scarcity—even in tough economic times—and that resources come naturally to people with dreams and passion.

Consider the following quote from W.H. Murray, leader of the Scottish Himalayan Expedition:

> *"Until one is committed, there is hesitancy, the chance to draw back, always ineffectiveness. Concerning all acts of initiative (and creation) there is one elementary truth, the ignorance of which kills countless ideas and splendid plans: That the moment one definitely commits oneself, the Providence moves too. All sorts of things occur to help one that would never otherwise have occurred. A whole stream of events issues from the decision, raising in one's favor all manner of unforeseen incidents and meetings and material assistance, which no man could have dreamed would have come is way. I have learned a deep respect for one of Goethe's couplets:*
> *'Whatever you can do, or dream you can, begin it.*
> *Boldness has genius, power and magic in it.'"*

Two: The client as a product

After your clients have a sense of their dreams, you can coach them to define who they are as a product in the marketplace. Ask your client: How well do you know your product, which is YOU? Most people spend more time planning their annual vacation than they do assessing who they are and creating their plan to move ahead in the world.

Suggest that your clients take some time to thoroughly assess who they are. Have them understand their accomplishments and how they get results, acknowledge their strengths and weaknesses, think about the types of people they admire and abhor, and get clear about their most important personal values.

Use the following approach to get started on this process. See also the future chapter about coaching your clients to develop a strong personal brand.

Portfolio of accomplishments. Ask the client to list five accomplishments that have significance for them. For each accomplishment, answer the following questions:

- What happened (the story)?
- What did you do, how did you do it, and what was your contribution?
- What was the result?
- What was your experience while you were achieving this accomplishment?
- What were your emotions throughout this process?
- What was important about this accomplishment?
- What did you learn?
- How did this experience affect you and your life?
- What is the pattern for how you go about accomplishing something that matters to you?
- How can you strengthen your strategy for and approach to getting results?

The client's development. A study by Selection Research International of more than 400,000 employees revealed that a company can double or triple effectiveness and productivity by exercising strengths, talents, and passions. Your clients should determine what they do well and how to take these assets into the professional world. Questions to ask in this area include:

- What are your strengths as a professional?

- How do you leverage your strengths?

- What are your weaknesses as a professional?

- How do you hedge your weaknesses?

- What gives you the most trouble at work? What is easy for you at work?

- What do others see as your weaknesses or opportunities to improve?

- What kind of feedback have you had about opportunities to improve?

- What have you done about that feedback? What will you do?

- What have you done to improve your capability as a professional? What will you do?

- How do you prefer to be managed? How do you prefer not to be managed? Examples?

- How are you most likely to fail as a professional? What can you do to prevent that from happening?

- What do you want your colleagues to say about you? Why?

- What do you want your direct reports to say about you? Why?

- What is the best way to build a successful working relationship with you?

- What is the best way to build an unsuccessful relationship with you?

- How do your answers to the above questions point to areas where you can develop your skills?

Models. An effective approach in many coaching situations is to take the client out of the picture by having them take the perspective of other people. In career coaching, it can be valuable to have the client think about people they admire and people they don't. This can lead to insights about who the client is as a product and what they have to do to continue their development.

Ask the client to list three people they like, admire, and respect as professionals. For each person, have the client describe exactly what they like, admire, and respect. Then repeat the process with three people the client finds challenging to like, admire, and respect. Based on this exercise, ask clients to compare themselves with these people, pointing out similarities and differences. What insights does the exercise open up about the client's next steps in their development and career?

Working style. The client's working style is part of who they are as a product and can also shed light on the opportunities that would be best for them to seek.

- How would you characterize the way you work most productively?

- What are your feelings about working in teams vs. alone?

- Which types of teams are most satisfying to you?

- What matters most to you when working with or building a successful team?

- What matters most when you build a successful working relationship?

- What matters most for you to perform at your peak?

- What matters most when working on or managing a successful project?

- What is most important to you when you are leading others? How would you describe your leadership and communication styles?

- How do you solve problems?

- How do you tend to participate in meetings?

- What types of meetings excite you and frustrate you?

- How do you lead meetings when that is your role?

- What is your approach for communicating results, issues, and requests for resources?

- How would you best describe how you make decisions (e.g., intuitive, analytical, political, technical, financial, outcomes driven)?

- What else is important to describe your working style?

- How do your answers to these questions point to the types of opportunities you are best suited to pursue?

Core values. Knowing our core values is crucial to finding a good fit in almost anything we do in life. Your clients should know their core values as well as the values they don't like. Coach your client to define their core values. Have them define each and give examples. Have them describe a violation of each of these values.

As a coach, you can give your client a list of values to jog ideas; an online search for "examples of values" will provide you with a list. Challenge the client to choose the values that authentically fit. Clients shouldn't do this exercise out of a sense of guilt of what others have told them they should do. For instance, if wealth is important to a client and compassion isn't, the client should choose wealth as a value. Your clients have to be truthful only to themselves and to what inspires them.

If your client has trouble honing in on just five core values, you can do an exercise to help them. Start with a big list of generic values, and then work with the client to narrow it down. From the list you provide, first have the client circle all the values they feel are important. Next, have the client highlight only ten of them. Finally, from the list of ten, challenge the client to select the five values on which they will never compromise.

Leadership and personality style. As part of your coaching process, your clients should assess their leadership and communication style. A number of tools are available to understand one's natural management and leadership behaviors as well as assessments to help clients identify careers that might be the best fit for them. The more objective information and feedback your clients can get about who they are, the more they can understand their strengths and find opportunities that best match their personality and values.

There are hundreds of assessment tools. Some are simple, and some are complex. Some are costly, and some require a very small investment. Top assessment tools for career coaching include:

Profiles International. Profiles offers a suite of robust assessment tools. The ProfileXT gives a client a look at how they compare with others on a variety of dimensions. The assessment includes thinking styles, such as verbal and numerical thinking, and behavioral traits that include energy level, sociability, decisiveness, objective judgment, manageability, accommodating, and more. It also tells the client their top three career interests.

Myers-Briggs Type Career Assessment. This is a popular tool that helps clients categorize and describe themselves along four orientations: how they take in or perceive information, how they make decisions and judgments, their energy orientation, and their extraverted orientation.

Holland Psychological Assessment Resources Trio. Holland classifies jobs into three groups: job categories, interest clusters, and work personality environments. The assessment identifies different work personalities, which in turn can help your clients identify jobs that are a good fit. Work personalities include realistic, investigative, artistic, social, enterprising, and conventional (these personalities can be remembered using the acronym RIASEC).

The Gallup Organization's Strengths Assessment. This tool helps clients identify strengths so that they can build on them and apply them to their career.

Edgar Schein's Career Anchors Assessments. Career Anchors is an industry standard, research-backed program that enables participants to identify their career anchors—perceived areas of competence, motives, and values related to work choices. Developed by MIT professor Edgar Schein, Career Anchors is an affordable tool for anyone planning or in the process of a career transition. Anchors include entrepreneurial creativity, autonomy/independence, lifestyle, pure challenge, technical/functional competence, service/dedication to a cause, and security/stability.

PDP's ProScan. The ProScan survey tells a person what their natural personality is, how they perceive how others see them, and in what ways they need to adapt their natural personality to the current situation. The survey gives clients a detailed way for people to know who they are and identify stress points in their lives that might be robbing them of focus.

Taylor Protocols. Taylor Protocols finds one's innate values, based on a set of four core values: power, knowledge, love, and wisdom.

The Self-Directed Search (SDS) Occupations Finder from Psychological Assessment Resources. This tool is most effective for people relatively new to the workforce. The participant fills in a survey and gets a code that reveals occupations that best fit their profile.

DiSC. DiSC is a widely used assessment created by William Marston. DiSC tells the client which of four primary personality drivers best apply to them: dominance; influence; steadiness or stability; and compliant, conscientious, or cautious.

Other companies to explore include the Center for Creative Leadership, Leadership Challenge, and Leadership Circle.

The data and specific recommendations from these tools become powerful guidelines for your clients to discover where their talents and passions can best fit in the world of business and leadership. This fit is critical to one's long-term happiness and success. Research has proven that individuals who are in a job they love, making use of their talents and strengths, are more likely to achieve levels of personal and financial success than others.

The reports generated by these assessments also have value for ongoing one-to-one coaching. You and the client can refer back to them as new situations and challenges come up.

Unique selling proposition. Once your clients know about their achievements, talents, development, and values, they can craft a unique selling proposition (USP) that sets them apart as a product, offers value to others, and helps them find a niche. A USP defines who your client is and why they are better than other people competing for the same position or role. Another buzzword for USP is "value proposition" or the value that your client brings to others.

Your clients can't be everything to everyone. Each person is unique, and your clients will find successful fulfillment more easily if they can articulate what makes them unique and valuable. Each of us has special gifts and talents. When your clients really understand what they do best and truly motivates and inspires them, it becomes their niche; it becomes who they are. When they can truly leverage their gifts, getting up and going to work is easy. It's not like going to work at all. Your clients will have more fun and contribute at a much higher level.

Have your clients evaluate their unique selling proposition by answering these questions:

- What are your top three talents that you like to use?

- How can you use these talents to help get results for others?

- What kind of world would we live in if everyone could benefit from your talents?

- How can you apply your answers to the above questions and the work you have done so far to your dream position?

For instance, the USP used by a consultant might be: "I use my speaking and facilitation skills, as well as my passion for working with leaders, to help elite performers in the healthcare industry enjoy a fulfilling career and get great results in and out of their health systems."

Similarly, an entrepreneur who now runs a chain of successful restaurants decided that her USP is "To use my ability to motivate and build great teams to create consistent, excellent results in business."

A former basketball player discovered that he loved music. He took this passion, along with his natural talent for discovering musical talent, to start up a series of Internet-based radio stations playing alternative music for niche audiences. A biochemical engineer declared, "I will use my chemical engineering knowledge and passion for the food industry to make innovation in the chocolate industry."

Note that your clients will have to constantly refine their stated USP to apply to the specific field or industry where they are passionate about working. For instance, if your client happens to be a great speaker, that person can use that talent in many different fields, e.g., teaching, television broadcasting, radio talk shows, acting, motivational speaking, corporate training, and even announcing. If your clients can narrow down their dream niche, they can come up with even more powerful language to describe how they are different from and better than the competition. Once your clients have a sense of their dream future and a niche to fill, they have to figure out where actual opportunities exist in the marketplace for their talents. Be aware, though, that in an actual coaching relationship, this work usually happens with the client and coach toggling back among the different areas. As you move among these areas, new areas for exploration come up, and it becomes more likely that the client will have clarity.

The marketplace

The market is always right. The career marketplace gives your clients cold, hard, objective feedback about whether or not their passions and talents are in demand and what they might have to do to have more opportunities.

Coach your clients about the best way they can get information and advice from prospective employers. Examples include:

- Read trade journals.

- Visit industry association websites.

- Visit company websites.

- Get annual reports and investment analysis for publicly traded companies.

- Read general business publications to keep up with overall trends.

- Attend industry conferences, especially those with recruiting booths.

- Most importantly and best of all, ask for information interviews from contacts on LinkedIn, through networking with current colleagues, through alumni networks, and any other means possible.

This process often leads directly to job offers for your client. For instance, I worked with a graduate of a leading engineering program. He didn't like the opportunities that came through the traditional recruiting process during his senior year and sought out a coach. He listed eight companies that he thought would be great employers, along with how he could bring them value.

Even though this individual grew up during the rise of social media and even though he was highly intelligent, he did not know how to research the market and discover what opportunities existed in his desired niche. He didn't know how to use LinkedIn. He hadn't explored his vast alumni database. He didn't know how to craft a short email requesting an information meeting.

Therefore, the coaching focused on introducing him to these tools and basic skills. We got on LinkedIn together and identified people that might be willing to do an informational interview. We logged in to his alumni database and found more people. We worked on crafting a short and sweet email that asked for an informational meeting. We role-played the questions he might ask.

As a result of this work, he uncovered a number of opportunities at these companies and, as he got more information, at other companies in his niche.

Similarly, I worked with a more seasoned executive who wanted to do something more significant and exciting than he was experiencing in his current leadership role. Due to a two-year deferred compensation package, he didn't want to make any immediate moves, but he did want to explore. We developed a plan that worked with his busy schedule to contact people in some new industries that interested him, to smaller companies in his industry that he felt would be more dynamic, to opportunities to serve on the boards of local nonprofits, and even to a division in his current company. He also explored executive education programs at business schools. With a measured pace, reaching out to a couple of people every week, the client developed renewed energy while developing new contacts and learning about numerous opportunities.

Exploring the marketplace is the final leg in the three-legged stool of career planning for your clients. As a coach, your role is to make sure your clients identify how they will research the market and follow up with them so that they feel accountable to take action and build momentum.

Creating the Career Plan

An effective way to synthesize the work you do with your clients during the planning phase is to create a concise career plan, ideally on no more than one or two pages. Shown below is an example of a template for a career plan. A few things set this career plan apart:

- It is short and concise.
- It starts by challenging the client to identify where they will excel in their career and the value they bring to others. This forces the client to think about their value proposition right up front.
- Instead of having a single linear career track, it encourages the client to identify a number of possible pathways. The client can prepare and be ready when opportunity comes up.
- It includes specific action steps so that the client proactively develops new skills and relevant behaviors.

Instant Career Plan

Date	

The area of expertise where I will excel or "spike"

The specific, measurable value I bring to others

My vision of what I want to achieve in my career

The top three to five values that guide my career

The one to three most advantageous possible next steps in my career

	What (or Who)	By When
The top one to three assignments, projects, or achievements I need in order to develop expertise and my track record		
The top one to three key skills or knowledge I need to acquire		
The top five mentors, industry leaders, functional experts, and other key people I need to know and who I don't know now		
Any specific formal education and training that will help me achieve my career vision		
Other action steps that will help me achieve my career goals, vision, and next steps		
Top 3 immediate next steps		

Personal Branding

Sometimes clients are comfortable in their career and want to strengthen how others perceive them. In other words, they want coaching about their personal brand. This type of coaching brings value to employees at all levels in an organization as well as to independent professionals and business owners.

In the past, we used to work for a company for life and didn't need a brand. We found a job after school and plugged away until retirement. Today, life is more complex. We have to switch jobs many times and may even spend time as a solo professional. Each individual must craft their own personal brand to stand out and succeed in a more chaotic, cluttered economy.

Consider the following celebrities and what makes them compelling as a personal brand:

- Why does Judge Judy get $45 million per year and dwarf the ratings of other daytime court shows?

- What was it about Barack Obama's brand during the 2008 election that helped him defeat the Clintons and then-established Senator McCain?

- What makes Martha Stewart so popular, even after a jail sentence?

- Why did Steve Jobs of Apple become such an icon? What about Richard Branson of Virgin Air? Bill Gates of Microsoft?

- Why is Michael Jordan still getting fantastic endorsement deals years after his professional basketball playing days are over?

- What do you think of when you consider the following talk show hosts: Jimmy Fallon, Oprah, Ellen DeGeneres, and Conan O'Brien?

- Why did Donald Trump get a television series and book deals and run a campaign for president of the United States when he isn't the wealthiest or most successful businessman by a long shot? Why does the Trump name command such respect with certain groups?

- Why did Andre Agassi get the most lucrative endorsement deals during the time he played tennis, even though Pete Sampras won far more titles and matches than he did?

All of the above people have created a personal brand with the following characteristics:

- **They are unique.** That is, no one else is like them, and we recognize them instantly. For instance, Judge Judy is famous for her bluntness, toughness, and efficiency in the courtroom as well as for her insistence on personal responsibility.

- **They are consistent.** Their personalities don't change. They provide us with a consistent experience, even as they continue to surprise us with new initiatives and developments. Even pop star Madonna, who changes her image every few years, has become known for consistency in reinventing herself.

- **They are memorable.** The word "brand" has roots in the branding iron that would permanently imprint a mark on cattle. Personal brands imprint an image in our minds.

- **They bring value.** A brand without value makes a person famous for being famous or an empty suit without substance. Your clients also have to be excellent at what they do so that others see substance, value, and relevance. Remarkably, some celebrities still create value with their name even if they haven't done much more than put out a sex tape, such as Paris Hilton (who managed to get television shows and put out numerous products after her tape was released) and Kim Kardashian (who also got a television show and continues to earn income for appearances and modeling). However, those instances are rare. True substance makes a brand compelling, relevant, and valuable.

- **They are trustworthy.** A brand is like a promise. If you break it, the value of your brand plummets. Consider the wealth that Tiger Woods lost when his scandal broke. The same happened as Mel Gibson unraveled with each new racist, sexist, and violent rant. When steroid use was exposed in Major League Baseball, many great players lost their reputations, endorsements, and their seemingly guaranteed entry into the Hall of Fame. You can recover trust sometimes, but it takes a very long time. Michael Jordan came back after his gambling scandal. Martha Stewart seems to have recovered after her insider trading sentence. It is best to never break the brand promise in the first place! Remain trustworthy.

Your clients need to have the above five characteristics to have a successful brand, and you can help them. Below is a step-by-step process to help your clients establish their personal brand. By using this process, you can attract clients (they want to know that you have a proprietary process) and guide them to results.

One: Assess the client's current brand.

Two: Identify the client's talents.

Three: Which values does the client stand for?

Four: Create a mission.

Five: Define the client's value and to whom.

Six: Make sure the value is unique.

Seven: Make sure the brand has impact.

Eight: Provide proof to back up the brand's promise.

Nine: Create messaging that compels.

Ten: Create the image that goes with the message.

Eleven: Orchestrate a consistent experience.

Twelve: Get visible.

Now let's go through each in depth.

One: Assess the client's current brand. To assess the client's current brand, have them (or you can do this for them if the client wishes) go to ten to fifteen of their colleagues and answer the following questions. If you do this assessment on behalf of your client, keep the answers confidential so that the exercise is safe. In other words, tell participants that you will share trends but not tell the client specific things that were said by specific individuals. Here are the questions to ask:

- What are up to three adjectives that best describe this person?

- What are up to three adjectives that would NOT describe this person?

- What are up to three talents this person has or up to three things that this person does exceptionally well?

- What is most unique about this person?

- What else about this person stands out?

- What is one thing that this person can do to have a stronger personal brand?

- What other advice do you have for this person?

Make sure that you ask the client to answer these questions too. Often your clients will not have an accurate perception of how they come across. Comparing your client's answers to objective data will help them see the truth.

Once you have collected the above data, compile it. Look for common themes. Then ask the client the following questions:

- What was different about how others see you and how you see yourself?
- If you had to define your brand now, what words would you use?
- What do you like and dislike about your current brand?
- How does your current brand match up to the definitions of a strong brand mentioned earlier—unique, consistent, memorable, valuable, and trustworthy?
- Do you like how others see you and want to build on what they said, or do you need to remake how you come across so that you change how people see you? If you need to remake yourself, what behaviors, attitudes, and talents do you need to develop?
- What other insights do you have after this assessment?

You will use the above exercise during the remaining steps in the process.

Two: Identify the client's talents. A brand has to have substance. During this phase of the process, ask your client to identify their unique talents, strengths, and gifts. If your client were the Michael Jordan of something, what would it be?

It might be that they have to continue to develop their talents to become the best. That's fine. Work with your clients to create a development plan, which is an action plan to improve professionally.

Three: Which values does the client stand for? A personal brand is strongest when it includes a core set of values. We respect and admire people who stand for something and are authentic about their stand. The previous chapter outlined a process to help uncover the client's core values. Use that exercise during this step in the branding process.

Four: Create the client's mission. A mission defines a person's purpose. Some people wrestle with their purpose for years and years. Your clients don't have to because you can use a simple process to help them come up with at least the start of a mission statement in about ten minutes.

Here is how it works:

First, ask the client to describe up to three talents or gifts that they have and like to use. This should be easy because you did this earlier. Make sure the talents are nouns (e.g., organizational skills, sense of humor, ability to relate to people). List them here:

A. _____

B. _____

C. _____

Second, ask the client to describe up to three ways that they express the above talents or gifts. They should write each example as a gerund, or a verb ending in "ing" (e.g., speaking, organizing, analyzing, setting direction, building relationships). List them here:

D. _____

E. _____

F. _____

Finally, ask the client to describe, in no more than five to ten words, their vision of an ideal world. They should fill in this sentence:

"An ideal world is one in which all people experience . . ." (e.g., peace, abundance, joy, adventure). Label what the client writes here as "G."

Now put it all together into the client's mission statement:

"I will use my [A], [B], and [C]
by [D], [E], and [F]
to create a world in which all people [G]."

The first time around the above paragraph might not make much sense. Work with your client to refine it until they love it. Some people find this exercise extremely powerful and gain a tremendous sense of clarity after completing it.

On the other hand, some people shrug after completing this exercise and don't come up with much of interest. That's okay too. If that happens, encourage your clients to keep thinking about their unique talents and the contribution to the world they want to make with those talents.

Five: Define the client's value and to whom. In this step of the process, your client needs to come to understand why they are valuable to others. Why would anyone pay them money? Why should anyone care about them?

A good value statement follows this format:

"I help X get Y."

"X" is a specific group of people, such as an industry, geographic area, demographic group (e.g., Millenials), or psychographic group (e.g., motorcycle riders, fundamental Christians, owners of faith-based businesses). "Y" is the benefit that your client offers. The more specific you can make it, the better. For instance:

- I help golfers improve their drive distance by 20%.

- I help stay-at-home moms become mompreneurs and earn a great living while taking care of their children.

- I help companies use big data to get insights that beat the competition.

- I help companies that produce consumer packaged goods launch new products successfully.

Six: Make it unique. Value is important. Unique value is priceless. What makes your client unique? Alternatively, if the client is still developing their skills, what do they need to do to become unique?

We covered this concept in the previous chapter and can build on that work here. To discover your client's uniqueness (aka Unique Selling Proposition, or USP), you have to fill in the following sentence:

Unlike other "Zs," I . . .

"Z" is your client's profession or area of expertise. For instance:

- Unlike other engineering graduates, I have three summers of experience working with some of the top engineering firms in the state.

- Unlike other attorneys, I have successfully prosecuted more than 500 drug cases.

- Unlike other strategic consultants, I have a 3-part methodology that guarantees your strategy will actually get executed.

- Unlike other golf professionals, I can document that my average client improves their game by 5 strokes after only one month.

There are some common themes in an effective statement of uniqueness:

- A proven approach to solving a problem that is more efficient and effective.

- Achievements, credentials, or awards that no one else can beat.

- More breadth or depth of experience than anyone else.

- Something that the market values and that your client does best (e.g., provide the most personal assistance, be the most responsive, be the toughest negotiator, be the hardest working).

- For business owners and independent professionals, an ironclad guarantee, or at least a pledge, can be a great way to stand out.

At the same time, make sure your client starts to embody the "Wow!" factor. Anybody can be good or fine. You want your clients to be extraordinary—outrageously excellent. You want them to stand out as the best of the best. For instance, there are many attorneys. All attorneys are highly educated. All attorneys pass the bar exam. What makes one attorney stand out from the pack? The answer depends on the attorney but should include their record of success, creative ways they have won cases or helped their clients when no one else could, their distinguished client list, their passion for the law, who they know, their team of experts, where they socialize, and how they contribute in the community.

Seven: Make sure the brand has impact. A strong brand has impact. Otherwise, it isn't memorable. Ask your client the following questions:

- What do you want people to say about you after they meet or work with you?

- What are effective and positive attributes that you already have that we can build on to make you even more memorable in your market?

- What are attributes that you might not have now but can develop to make you more memorable and have more impact?

- How do you want to come across to others in the market so that they remember you favorably and talk about you to others who might be seeking people with your qualifications?

- What will someone experience while working with you?

Your clients don't have to be charismatic to stand out. In some cases, charisma can hurt, especially if it comes across as being forced, but they do need to define the impact they will have on others. Make sure this impact aligns with the clients' mission, values, and uniqueness.

Depending on your client's area of expertise, examples of impact could include:

Personable
Authentic
Knowledgeable
Brilliant
Energetic
Enthusiastic
Salt of the Earth
Tough
Compassionate
Caring
Prosperous
Trustworthy
Competitive
Humorous
Humble
Spiritual
Bold
Adventurous
Innovative
Supportive
Loyal

Rebellious
Contrarian
Risk taking
Conservative
Seasoned
Passionate
Meticulous

Take the time needed to define with your client the impact they want to have every time they interact with others.

Eight: Provide proof to back up the brand's promise. A strong brand has both sizzle and substance. Your client needs to back up the sizzle of the brand with substance in the form of proof. Proof includes:

- Specific results and achievements
- Credentials
- Third-party testimonials, especially from respected opinion leaders
- Interviews with your client in the media
- Articles and books your client has published
- Awards
- Case studies that document past results
- The client's network of supporters
- Samples of the client's work (e.g., a writing sample for authors, music samples for singers)

If you are working with inexperienced clients, they may need some time to continue to build proof, but you can help them use finesse to be successful. That's because of the concept of social proof. People tend to give credibility to what they read in the media, to third-party opinion leaders, and to what lots of people say.

For instance, here is an easy way to quickly get dozens of testimonials for your client: Have your client give a speech at a local organization. Pass out a feedback sheet to each participant that asks, "What was the one thing you found most valuable in this presentation?" The sheet should also ask for permission to use the participant's name. After the speech, your client will have dozens of testimonials.

Similarly, your client can gain instant credibility by joining the right organizations. Love him or hate him, Donald Trump did this when he first started out in New York City. He joined one of the city's most prestigious social clubs. He could rub elbows with the movers and shakers in the city and build his network and reputation. According to the rules of social proof, he became someone based in part on the credibility of the people with whom he socialized. Your clients can do the same by getting involved on the boards of prominent community organizations and nonprofits, joining the right country and social clubs, and volunteering for leadership roles in places where their target audience takes notice.

Nine: Create messaging that compels. Your clients need up to four messages to support their brand. If you and your clients have done the work so far, they already have much of this in place. Now you need to work with them to organize it.

First, they need a quick hook that rapidly tells people the bottom line about who they are. You already created this with the format, "I help 'X' get 'Y.'"

Second, clients who are independent professionals should have a compelling tagline that instantly positions them. For instance, a comedian in my town focuses exclusively on jokes about the construction industry. He brands himself as "The Construction Comic." A personal injury attorney in town brands himself as "For the people." An etiquette trainer is the "Etiquette Mom." Jay Conrad Levinson established himself as "The Guerrilla Marketing Guru." This part of your work requires creativity. Sit down with your client, get out a white board, and brainstorm as many ideas as you can. Eliminate the ideas that aren't so strong, and refine the ones that are. Then have your client ask some trusted colleagues for honest feedback about which of the remaining taglines are most compelling and authentic.

Third, your clients need at least one Walk on Water or WOW story. Help them to develop a 30-second story about their greatest, most amazing achievement. This is a story they can use anytime as proof that they bring value.

Finally, your clients should have a complete marketing message that embodies much of the work already done. Coach them to define:

- The problem they solve and for whom
- The benefits they provide
- How they realize those benefits
- Their unique edge or USP
- Proof that their claims are accurate

A marketing message can also include a call to action for times when they want another person to take action. For instance, a solo professional might invite people to read an executive brief about a topic of interest.

Your clients will use the above messages in all their marketing collateral, so take as much time as required to make sure they are thrilled with the output. Please don't put too much pressure on yourself to create this material alone. You are the coach, not the copywriter. Your job is to ask great questions to get the client thinking about who they are and how they can express it in a way that is most memorable and impactful. Insist that your clients take an active role in participating and contributing.

Ten: Create the image that goes with the message. Once you have defined the brand in words, your clients need to create the image that goes with the message. They need to "become" the brand. For instance:

- How should the client dress?

- What should the client's hair and makeup look like?

- What accessories should the client have (think about Paris Hilton's dog Tinker Bell as one outrageous example)?

- Does the client need to change their physical shape and health to match their brand (e.g., can you be a fitness guru if you are obese)?

- Does the client need some etiquette lessons?

- For solo professionals, what logo best represents the client's firm?

- What marketing collateral does the client need (biography, resume, speaker's sheet, business card, website, articles)?

- What groups and associations should the client join to meet decision makers and build their network?

- What alliances should the client form (e.g., with complementary professionals in the industry, similar professionals in other industries, opinion leaders)?

- What skills does the client need to build (e.g., public speaking, writing, leadership)?

Eleven: Orchestrate a consistent experience. A brand requires consistency to be memorable and powerful. Your clients must be the brand, especially when they are out in public. That's why it is important for them to pick a brand that is authentic for them; otherwise, they will be putting on an act and will not come across as real, not to mention the stress they will feel trying to be somebody they are not.

Everything your clients say or do, everyone in their network of contacts, everywhere they go, every organization they join, every customer or client with whom they work—everything—should match the brand.

Disney and The Ritz are the most brilliant companies at creating a consistent experience. Disney is fanatic about the details in their theme parks. Every single interaction with a character or cast member is choreographed and polished down to the millisecond. Anytime a customer comes into contact with one of their employees, Disney has trained that employee to give a consistent, positive experience every time. Their cast members know how to keep the park clean, manage long lines on rides, empathize with a frustrated parent, be polite and friendly no matter how annoying the guest, deal with a child who is pulling Pluto's tail, give directions, take a fast-food order, process a ticket, and usher people out of the park at closing time.

The Ritz does the same thing, with extensive training of every single employee. Employees do whatever it takes to please a customer, down to creating a custom dish at one of their restaurants when the items on the menu aren't enough. They know the minute details of formal dining, responding immediately to customer needs, and going out of their way to personalize the guest's time at one of their properties.

Ask your client to describe all the different moments when they interact with a constituent—whether a client, manager, direct report, or someone in the community. Challenge the client to define how the constituent will experience each moment. What behaviors will your client need to put into place habitually to make sure that each constituent has that experience every time?

Role-play each interaction with the client and try to throw them some curve balls by being somewhat obnoxious or asking tough questions. Be sure to warn the client that you will be doing this, so they don't fire you on the spot. Keep working on each interaction until you are confident that your client is polished, consistent, and as extraordinary as Disney and The Ritz.

This work can also turn into a behavioral coaching process because the client might need to develop new habits.

Twelve: Get visible. A brand doesn't matter if no one sees it. Getting visible should be one of your client's top priorities.

One's networking is the primary way to get visible. Coach your clients to build their power bases by meeting with people in their networks and asking for new connections.

Second, online marketing, especially social marketing, is a key way for people to build a brand. Your client should be active in the social media platforms that are most relevant to their career and industry. LinkedIn is a must, and your client should have a strong profile, connections, and activity in various LinkedIn groups.

Finally, your client can get visible in numerous manual ways, from leadership roles in their community and industry to activities that allow them to meet socially with decision-makers.

Work with your clients to create their plan to get, and stay, visible.

Final Note: If there were a step thirteen in this process, it would be to work with your clients to assess, improve, and even reinvent their brands from time to time. Make sure your clients are living up to the promised value in their brands and also have brands that stay relevant in changing times.

Managing Transitions

Some career coaching clients need to find a new job by necessity and not by choice. Others experience burnout and quit their jobs because they can't stand another day working in their current positions. You need to know how to help these clients navigate their transition.

We all experience a number of transitions in life: from high school to college, leaving home, getting married, becoming a parent, experiencing the loss of a loved one, and career setbacks.

Being laid off or forced to find new employment can be extremely challenging. The questions for your clients are:

- How are you going to adapt to this transition?
- How will you take control of this transition and really do something special in the next phase of your career and life?

A career transition will test and reveal a client's character, perhaps like no other challenge they have faced. Your clients are going to need a winning attitude. They are going to need to know who they are and their core values. They are going to have to be humble and call on friends, family, and their network for support.

There are three models that you might share with clients to help them navigate their transition.

The first is what might be called the transition roller-coaster. In this model, clients experience a jolt of some sort, one that leads them down to the bottom of a metaphorical emotional roller-coaster. Then they develop and implement a plan to move back up to new heights, regain confidence, and achieve their vision for their career. There are seven phases in this process:

- The shock that comes when the client experiences the end of their current situation.

- The feelings of anger, sadness, and/or fear the client may feel when they realize that they have lost their status and the worry about what comes next.

- The bottom comes when the client's emotions reach their nadir. Call this phase "The Pits." Things feel as bad as they are going to feel. Here, the coach has to be careful that the client doesn't turn to substance abuse or reckless behaviors to cope with their feelings, and that the client doesn't exhibit signs of clinical depression. If you have any concerns, immediately refer the client to a licensed health professional.

- The client makes a choice to start crawling back up the slope. Here, the client makes a conscious decision to take control and take action. They start the planning process and take steps to find productive opportunities for the next part of their life. Note that some people are quite vulnerable in this phase. Most cases of suicide happen just as someone begins to improve and move up from The Pits. Clients have to have support, especially as they experience setbacks or need guidance. Again, be prepared to refer them to a licensed health professional or other expert if they exhibit signs of hurting themselves or others, substance abuse, or clinical depression.

- The client implements their plan.

- The client taps into their natural confidence and feelings of self-worth to do what it takes to conduct a successful career search.

- The client achieves their short-term vision and is back on the path to long-term career success. Of course, the long-term stage of the process might not happen for a while and will likely come only after other ups, downs, and transitions. If clients do the work of knowing themselves, keep learning and developing, and are proactive in pursuing opportunities, the odds of reaching this phase are excellent.

Second, William Bridge's work on transitions make an important contribution. His primary insight is that transitions don't have a beginning, a middle, and an end. Instead, they start with an ending and end with a beginning. His three stages of a transition:

Ending, Losing, Letting Go. The ending phase is about helping the client do what they have to do to say good-bye to the past and let go. They have to give proper respect to the past and to their achievements to date, accept and acknowledge the many difficult emotions they will feel, and define what they are really leaving behind and what they aren't.

The Neutral Zone. Once the client lets go, they enter the Neutral Zone, a period that seems suspended between what is and what will be. This phase is a vulnerable time and feels a lot like the journey through the desert that Moses and the Jews made in *Exodus*. Forward movement seems to have stopped and the client can't see the end point. If they are not careful, they can fall back into old habits and patterns and wallow in self-pity. At the same time, this period can be extremely creative. The client can uncover new possibilities and move ahead.

New Beginnings. The client emerges into the final phase almost as a new person. They shed their old identity and take on a new identity and behaviors. They see new opportunities and possibilities for themselves, have new attitudes, and take on new actions.

The third framework that might help the coach is Dr. Elisabeth Kubler-Ross's five stages of grief. While often applied to the death of a loved one, these stages apply to the loss of anything precious to us.

- *Stage One: Denial and isolation.* The client might deny that any kind of loss has happened and also withdraw from their network.

- *Stage Two: Anger.* Clients might become furious with themselves or others for the loss, even if nothing could have been done to stop it.

- *Stage Three: Bargaining.* Now the client tries to strike a deal, usually with a higher being, asking, "If I do this, will you let me play again?"

- *Stage Four: Depression.* The client fees angry, sad, and numb. This is "The Pits."

- *Stage Five: Acceptance.* The client's anger, sadness, and mourning begin to fade, and they simply accept the reality of what they have lost. They begin to crawl back up and live again.

Not everyone, though, goes through these phases at the same rate or even in the same order.

One thing that each of the above frameworks suggests is that your client should feel entitled to take time out to deal with the transition. Encourage your client, if they have the resources, to take some time to honor their feelings and go through the process needed to grieve. Clients also have an opportunity to use transitions as a chance to explore and find new possibilities. Don't let your client stay in the denial stage, in which they downplay the transition. If your client has done some good planning before having to make the transition, they will be well prepared to move on once the reality of the transition hits.

As you work with clients, explain to them the above frameworks and get a sense of where they are in the process. Listen and be a source of support. Use active and appreciative inquiry to go where the client wants to go. Don't be preachy.

One exercise that can work with some clients is to have them focus on the strengths and resources that can help them build momentum. Challenge your clients to come up with a list of twenty-two things that will keep them moving ahead. Of course, "twenty-two" is an arbitrary number; the idea is for your client to list as many items as possible. Questions to ask include:

- What options are available to you to process the change at your pace?
- Who supports you?
- What talents do you have?
- What resources are at your disposal?
- When have you gone through a transition successfully before, and what did you do to be successful?
- Whom do you admire, and what would they do in this situation?
- What is a small step you can take now to get some momentum?
- Whom can you go to for advice?
- Whom do you know who knows lots of people and can make introductions for you?
- Where can you go to learn new skills to make you more valuable?
- What requests do you need to make to others?

You can also do the opposite exercise with your clients. Challenge them to come up with a list of twenty-two things that stand in the way of success, whether limiting perceptions or external factors. Then work with clients to understand which are real barriers and which are perceived. From there, coach clients about ways to reframe or address each of these challenges. The roller-coaster of emotions will be less brutal if your clients make this list disappear so that they can do their career search tenaciously.

Finding the New Opportunity

By now, your clients have done some assessment and planning. They have an idea about what they want to do. They've made the transition in their mind. Now it is time for action. It is time to seize the opportunity that comes closest to matching their aspirations, talents, and what the market demands.

To have doors open for them so that they land the situation they want, they need to take care of the nuts and bolts of getting their name into the marketplace, becoming a candidate, and closing the deal.

Therefore, this part of your clients' journey involves these steps:

- Making sure their finances are in order
- Setting aside enough time to do justice to the search
- Developing compelling marketing collateral, from a 30-second speech to LinkedIn profile, resume, cover letter, and references
- Leveraging their network
- Honing their interview skills
- Following up on opportunities
- When offered a job, negotiating the terms appropriately

Finances

A client with resources in the bank and little debt has a lot more time to find a new job and wait for their terms than a client who is living from paycheck to paycheck and has considerable debt. As a career coach, you might feel awkward asking your clients about their personal financial situations, but this is an important area of inquiry.

Ask your clients to lay out their liquid and nonliquid assets, debt, and monthly expenses. Find out their monthly burn rate, or cash they spend each month; and their fume date, the date on which they will run out of cash if they are not earning an income. The fume date might have a few milestones, starting with regular savings, then loss of the emergency fund, then loss of retirement savings. If a client doesn't have resources on hand, they probably shouldn't quit their job or start a new business and should instead work on living frugally, paying down debt, and setting up cash reserves.

Set a goal with your clients who are still employed to start saving as much as they can, cutting out all necessary expenses, and trying to put as much as possible in the bank for the upcoming search.

Ideally, your client should have at least six to twelve months of cash reserves saved up, noting that in dire financial times it can take even highly educated and skilled workers up to three years to find work.

If your client does not have lots of reserves, your job as a coach is to challenge them about how flexible they are willing to be. Would they rather be proud and employed or take care of their family? What are they willing to give up in terms of salary, benefits, and title? Some clients are too proud and end up going broke after passing up acceptable opportunities.

Setting aside enough time to do the search

Challenge your clients to take the job search more seriously than they would a full-time job. I have been in seminars with job seekers and asked participants to total the amount of time they actually spent networking, researching jobs, going on informational interviews, and so on. Rarely does the time add up to even 20 hours per week.

Job seeking needs to be at least a full-time endeavor. During every session with clients who are actively seeking opportunities, ask them to tally up how much time they actually spend seeking a position. If they aren't spending the time required, they may need some honest and tough talk from you.

Developing compelling marketing collateral

A good portion of career coaching is about marketing, and marketing eventually comes down to collateral.

First, coach your clients on a 30-second pitch. They need to be able to answer one of the hardest questions to answer: "Tell me about yourself." The answer should tell the other person about their unique value, passion, and track record. For instance:

> "I have a decade of experience increasing sales for technology companies. I'm passionate about helping young companies reach the next level of sales, and most recently I increased sales at a start-up by 125%, or $5 million, before we were acquired."

> "I'm a seasoned Human Resources leader in the legal industry, and my forte is connecting HR to a company's strategic plan. For instance, at XYZ Law Firm, I implemented a leadership development program that improved billings by $10 million by developing our highest potential associates in business development and team leadership skills. I also have outstanding knowledge of the benefits area and have reduced costs while expanding benefits for two different legal practices."

Videotape your client giving their pitch. Spend the time needed to help them gain confidence and develop a compelling pitch that will get a prospective employer, or someone connected to employers, interested. Remember that you don't have to be a guru to help them. Record the client, and start by asking them what they thought they did well and what needs to improve. They usually know.

Make sure your client also has the other aspects of their message down pat, as described in earlier chapters, from the Walk on Water example to "I help X get Y."

The client also needs to develop a strong LinkedIn profile, resume, cover letter, and references. I recommend that you form alliances with experts in these areas and outsource this work to them. You can be a sounding board to make sure these pieces of collateral send the right message, but it is hard to keep up with the latest fashions and styles. For instance, in the past ten years, accepted resume formats have changed dramatically, along with the need to identify and use keywords that catch the attention of automated systems. Another reason to outsource this work is that you want to be at the highest strategic level when working with executives, leaders, and managers. By outsourcing the tactical work, you maintain the highest strategic ground. If career coaching will be a staple of the services you offer, form alliances with the top LinkedIn profile and resume writers by searching online. If you disagree with this advice and want to do the work yourself, take a course that will teach you the most up-to-date approaches.

Leveraging the network

The client's network is the number one way they will land a new position, usually before the position is posted publicly. This book covers building a power base in depth elsewhere, and here we customize that to the job search.

First, if your client has recently left a position, they have a window of time when people will open doors for them. Their connections are still fresh, and colleagues are more likely to want to help. This is good news for your client because most jobs are not found via online ads but rather through existing connections and networking. The key for your client is that they take advantage of this window of opportunity sooner rather than later.

Of course, one's network will open doors but won't guarantee success. Your client still has to set themselves apart as the best candidate for the position(s) they want.

Shown below are some steps for you to coach your client so that they leverage their network:

- **Identify the top people the client knows who can open doors.** The key to networking is meeting one person and having that person either identify an opportunity or, more likely, agree to make connections with other people. If your client can get two introductions from each person they know, their network will continue to grow.

- **Coach the client about the outcome they want from the conversation, and role-play the conversation with them.** Generally, your client will have one of three different outcomes when they contact people in their network, which means they might be setting up three different types of meetings. Regardless of the outcome they seek, tell your clients to ALWAYS ask for the names of other people to talk to. Again, have them set a goal of getting two contact names after every meeting so that the well never runs dry.

  First, if your client is still trying to decide what to do, they might set up meetings to get advice about how to best use their talents and about opportunities that will best take advantage of what they do well. In this kind of meeting, your client asks for feedback about their strengths and weaknesses and what the contact would do in their situation. They can also ask for introductions to people who can help them in their continued search.

  Second, if your client has ideas about what to do and wants to know more, they should set up informational interviews to learn about specific industries, companies, or job functions. Here, they contact an insider who works in an industry or company that interests them. During this kind of meeting, your client asks questions to understand what it takes to succeed, what the work is like, and strategies to get into that particular field. At the same time, the client should not be shy about asking if the contact knows about any opportunities currently open. Often, informational interviews uncover opportunities before they are announced to the public. If a well-placed contact likes your client, they might even create a position for them to get them on board!

Finally, your client's most common meeting will be to ask their contacts for introductions to people who can help open doors or give them more information about a particular field or company. In these meetings, your client's goal is to get introductions to other people. They should tell the contact what they are trying to achieve and ask them who they know that might be able to help. They should either ask for people who might meet with them for an informational interview or ask if the contact knows anybody looking for someone with their talents and interests. Be sure to coach your clients to ask how they can help the contact in return. Remind your client to always be a giver, and doors will always be open.

- **Use social media and directories, especially LinkedIn, alumni directories, association directories, and any other directories where the client is active.** Such sites as LinkedIn make it possible to find connections anywhere in the world that might be able to help. Coach your client to get active on LinkedIn by joining groups, posting discussions, participating in discussions, posting articles on Pulse, and contacting people who have shared interests.

  The rule with online media and directories is: Start online and then connect offline. Anyone can click the "accept" button to get a new connection online. Only the savvy networkers follow up to schedule a phone call. Coach your client to develop a concise message that requests a networking meeting, including how your client can bring value to the other person.

- **Coach the client to ask the contact for the best way to follow up with any introductions.** Sometimes the contact will be willing to make an introduction, and sometimes they will give your client the other person's contact information and tell them to reach out directly, using the contact's name as a reference. Sometimes a phone call or email is best, and sometimes your client will need to write a letter requesting a meeting. Make sure that your client asks the contact to tell them which approach makes them feel most comfortable and has the best chance of success.

- **Coach the client to send a thank-you note to the initial contact within twenty-four hours, thanking them for their time, information, and any connections they made for them.** Handwritten notes are important because nobody expects them anymore. If someone is especially helpful, coach the client to send an appropriate gift.

- **Make sure the client tells the initial contact what happened.** Remind your clients that their contacts are taking a risk by opening up their networks. It is important that your clients follow up to let their contacts know how subsequent meetings went and whether or not they produced results.

- **Remind the client to send a handwritten thank-you note within twenty-four hours to anyone they meet during this process.**

- **Repeat until the client achieves their ultimate goal.** Have your clients keep building their networks. Challenge them to set specific goals to encourage them to keep asking for more contacts. Encourage them: "Keep following up with people who have helped you to let them know how your search is going. Keep asking for help. Keep thanking people and being gracious, and keep asking how you can help them in return. Once you land a position, let everyone know, and thank them for the continued help and support. Be ready and open to help others in return when they are going through the same thing."

Help your clients hone their interview skills

When your client gets invited to an interview, they need to be prepared. Ideally, they have already spent time researching the industry and the company. They have visited the website and read recent news releases. They have done an Internet search to learn more about the company. They have had some informational interviews with executives in the industry. If the company is publicly traded, they have read its annual report and recent news releases; they also know the current stock price.

In preparing for the interview, have your clients think about the image they want to convey. They are one of many people applying for the position. If they were an executive in their previous role, have them assume that their former status will no longer be particularly helpful. You want your client to present themselves as professional, confident (but with the ego in check), competent, positive, enthusiastic, and as someone others want to have on their team.

In some cases, you may need to coach your client about what to wear to the interview. Clothing will be a big part of the image the client presents. Advise your client to dress for the job they want, not the job they used to have (if significantly different). If your client is applying for a leadership position, they should plan on wearing a conservative suit, preferably a solid color, with conservative, well-shined shoes.

Make sure your client's suit fits properly. Have them try it on a few days before the interview in case it needs some alterations. I've known more than a few people who found to their dismay on interview day that they had gained a few pounds and their suit no longer buttoned at the waist! (In some cases, you may even advise clients to get on a diet/workout plan to get back into shape and look more attractive to employers. It sounds superficial, but life is not fair, and attractive candidates are more likely to make a favorable impression.)

Your client's hair should be neat and professional. Remind them to avoid wearing too much cologne, aftershave, or perfume. Many workplaces today have scent-free policies due to allergies and complaints from employees. They should avoid wearing lots of jewelry too.

Today, some corporations, especially start-ups and companies in technology hubs, such as Silicon Valley, allow business-casual and even casual dress. Some high-tech companies' personnel instantly distrust people in suits. Your client should confirm with the human resources representative how executives at the company dress, and then dress just a bit more formally than they do. It is better by a long shot to be a bit overdressed at an interview than underdressed.

During the interview process, your client will likely be invited out to a meal. It is important that they employ proper business meal etiquette. Below are some tips to give your clients about dining with prospective employers. Some of these tips might seem obvious to you, but you haven't seen how some of your colleagues eat. You might even dedicate one coaching session to a meal out with your client to make sure they employ proper etiquette. (A great ancillary service as a coach is to offer business etiquette courses by aligning with a local etiquette expert.)

Advice for dining out with a prospective employer:

- If you can, check out the restaurant's menu ahead of time. You'll then already know what to order and can appear decisive when ordering.

- Treat your server with respect, even if you don't get exactly what you order.

- Use "please" and "thank you" to your host, server, and anyone else at the table.

- Start with the salad fork, which is on the far left. The fork to the right of that and closest to your plate is your entrée fork.

- Your dessert spoon and dessert fork are above your plate.

- Here is how to remember where your bread and water glass go: Make an "O" with the index finger and thumb of both hands, and hold your hands up so that you are looking at the backs of your hands. Notice that your left hand makes a "b," which stands for "bread." So bread goes on the left side. Your right hand makes a "d," which stands for drink. Drinks go on the right side. Simple!

- Your napkin goes in your lap when everyone sits down.

- Keep your elbows off the table.

- Sit up straight, just like your mother told you again and again and again.

- Don't talk with your mouth full, and make sure you keep your mouth closed when you are chewing.

- Order foods that won't make a mess. Avoid pasta with sauce, ribs, huge sandwiches, juicy burgers, whole crabs or lobster, and chicken on the bone. Order foods that you can cut into small pieces.

- Order a reasonably priced entrée, not the most expensive item (unless the host insists on a special item they absolutely love and want you to try).

- If you have soup, move the spoon away from you to gather up the liquid. That's not only polite but avoids spills.

- Eat your dinner roll by breaking a piece off and eating that piece. Don't bite a chunk out of the roll.

- For items you need to cut, such as a steak, cut a single piece, put down your knife, and eat that piece. Then cut the next piece. Don't cut the whole steak into small pieces at one time.

- If you need to leave the table, excuse yourself, and place your napkin on your seat.

- When you are done with your food, put your fork and knife at four o'clock on your plate, with the fork upside down. This will tell the server that you are done.

- Avoid alcohol. You want to stay sharp. Plus, don't you have enough stress as is without worrying about getting a buzz?

- Participate in the conversation. Listen, show interest, be enthusiastic, and relax.

- Let your prospective employer/host pick up the bill and the tip. That is the expectation.

- Thank your host for the meal and compliment something you liked about the restaurant they chose.

Now we get to the interview itself. Here is advice to tell your clients to follow. Of course, you will conduct role-play mock interviews with them, preferably videotaping them so they can see how they come across.

First, be aware of your body posture. Make sure you have a firm handshake. Make eye contact. Stay actively engaged in the interview (you are one of many candidates; this is not an interview with a reporter or a meeting with your agent).

Listen for your interviewer's voice patterns, body posture, and how they sit. Try to subtly mirror these behaviors without imitating them. For instance, if your interviewer speaks quickly and in short sentences, try to do the same. If they speak slowly and tend to ramble, make sure your own cadence slows down to match theirs. If your interviewer leans forward or crosses their legs, you might do the same, but don't cross your arms during the interview or lean back in too relaxed a fashion; these types of gestures show that you are closed or lack interest.

Shown below are some common interview questions that you and your client should rehearse. Assign your client the task of reading the questions and writing down how they would answer them. Then work with your client to hone their answers (per the guide that follows). A number of books provide advice about answering tough interview questions, including *Knock 'Em Dead*.

Keep adding your own tough questions to the list. As with resumes, interview approaches often change. For instance, it used to be fashionable for technology and consulting firms to test candidates with IQ-style questions, such as "Why are manhole covers round?" Now firms focus more on finding people with unique skills and talents they can bring to the job as well as having the right values and character.

Role-play mock interviews with your client. Record them. As always with role-play, let the client tell you what they thought they did well and what they can do better. Keep your own constructive suggestions to a minimum so that you don't overwhelm the client. Stay positive and encouraging, and be patient.

Common Interview Questions:

- Tell me about yourself.

- What are your strengths and weaknesses?

- How are you going to make the transition from your previous position to this one?

- What are your goals three to five years from now?

- Why are you interested in this position?

- How would you compare your previous job with this one?

- Describe a time when you disagreed with your boss and what you did about it.

- What are your pet peeves?

- Tell me about a time when you felt anger on the job.

- How did your previous boss get the best performance out of you?

- Tell me about how you have worked with a diverse group of people with different backgrounds and interests from yours?

- What is the most foolhardy decision you have made or thing you have done at a previous job?

- What do you know about this industry (and company)?

- What would you say will be key to success in this role?

- Three years from now, once you are established in this position, how will you cope with change?

- What results have you achieved in similar roles?

- How did you get those results?

- How would you teach someone to get similar results?

- What would your previous boss/colleagues say about you?

- What would your boss/colleagues NOT say about you?

- What are your qualifications for this role?

- Tell me about a time when you had difficulties getting along with others.

- Tell me about a time when you managed conflict.

- Tell me about a time when you influenced someone to do something they didn't initially want to do.

- Tell me about what makes a great salesperson.

- What are your salary expectations?

- Your resume doesn't reflect experience in this industry. How can I assess you when most people applying for this position have previous work experience in the industry?

- How long do you think it will take for you to get up to speed and show results?

- Describe your ideal job.

- Describe your ideal work environment.

- Have you ever been fired?

- What questions do you have about our company or this position?

Comments on Common Interview Questions for Your Clients:

Tell me about yourself.

This may be the first question you hear, and the employer doesn't want a twenty-minute autobiography. Instead, connect your top achievements and talents to the job for which you are applying. Focus especially on results and contributions you have made.

What are your strengths and weaknesses?

Pick the three strengths that are most applicable to the job. Don't spend too much time on weaknesses; pick one attribute from early in your career and how you learned from it and improved.

If pressed about a weakness, don't disclose anything too personal, and don't gloss over the question by being glib or saying you don't have a weakness. Perhaps pick a situation and explain how you learned from it: "I can be impatient when others don't deliver according to my expectations. I'm careful to balance results and relationships, and I've gotten much better at finding the right mix of pushing and being constructive when there is pressure to get results against a tight time frame and within a tight budget."

How are you going to make the transition from your previous position to this one?

You want to show that you have been preparing for some time for the transition. Your time in that other industry was productive and rewarding, and now you are looking forward to new challenges.

What are your goals three to five years from now?

Employers want to be sure you aren't going to milk the company for new skills and then leave for new opportunities. Frame this answer in the context of how you hope to learn and grow in the position and move up in the company when you are ready.

Why are you interested in this position?

Be prepared to show enthusiasm. Focus especially on how your talents, skills, and passions will help you get results.

How would you compare your previous job with this one?

Talk about attributes from your previous role that connect to the current job and company culture.

Describe a time when you disagreed with your boss and what you did about it.

The interviewer wants to know how you deal with conflict. Your answer should show how you resolved differences with maturity and professionalism.

What are your pet peeves?

The interviewer is probing to see if you are eccentric or difficult to manage. Talk about one or two blind spots you don't like in others (e.g., people who avoid accountability). Show that you deal with these issues not by complaining but by being a positive example and encouraging people to give their best.

Tell me about a time when you felt anger on the job.

Anger management is a big issue in the work force. Deflect this question by mentioning that you may get intense and focused and you might get frustrated sometimes but without feeling angry. Note that you manage your frustration through calm communication and dialogue.

How did your previous boss get the best performance out of you?

The interviewer wants to be sure you are not high maintenance and also check the fit between you and your prospective new boss. Give a simple answer that talks about your self-motivation and that you respond best to bosses who are fair and treat people with respect.

Tell me about how you have worked with a diverse group of people with different backgrounds and interests from yours.

Diversity is another hot button in many organizations. Talk about your travels, the different experiences and backgrounds of your colleagues, and how you have built teams made up of very different personalities and backgrounds.

What is the most foolhardy decision you have made or thing you have done at a previous job?

This question can make people squirm. Be clear that you haven't made foolhardy decisions. You have developed strong judgment in work and your personal life. If you are pressed for an example, use something from long ago that ended up working out favorably for you.

If you have had some sort of scandal associated with you (e.g., embarrassing photos in the media), don't bring up that issue unless the interviewer mentions it. Then talk about what you learned from this experience in ways that cast you as someone who learns from mistakes—not as someone who was a victim of the situation (e.g., the media).

What do you know about this industry (and company)?

Before your interview, you need to have researched the industry and company thoroughly through Google, annual reports, visiting stores (if any), checking out the products, doing informational interviews, and reading relevant books. You should talk about the research you have done. Limit your answer to three key points that you discovered, and connect those points to your talents and how you can contribute.

Side note: Make sure your client checks the company's stock price and trends if it is a publicly traded company. Interviewers have been known to ask.

What would you say will be key to success in this role?

From your research, you should tie your talents to the requirements of this job. Focus on the abilities you have to achieve success. Be sure to ask the interviewer what they think will be key to success, and then show how you meet those criteria.

Three years from now, once you are established in this position, how will you cope with change?

The workforce changes quickly. The employer wants to know that you are resilient and open to continuous learning and change. Talk about how you have coped with change in previous roles and projects.

What would your previous boss/colleagues say about you?

Emphasize the same talents and skills that are required for success in this job. More importantly, focus on the results and contributions you have made.

What would your boss/colleagues NOT say about you?

This is an interesting question that can throw you for a loop if you are not prepared. Emphasize some negative qualities that you do not have

What are your qualifications for this role?

If you have done your research, you know what the job entails. You should connect your talents to the job. Even better, focus on how you can get results and contribute in this position. Employers are focused on results and want to know the outcomes you can achieve and the value you can bring to the company.

Tell me about a time when you had difficulties getting along with others

Discuss the way that you join and build a team. In other words, focus on how you build relationships up front so that you establish an environment for dialogue when things don't go smoothly.

Tell me about a time when you managed conflict.

Talk about times when you were calm, spoke honestly, listened, and engaged in dialogue with somebody else to achieve a mutually beneficial outcome.

If you have experienced a "bad apple" in your company who violated your organization's values, you might talk about how you met with this person and convinced them to change their behavior.

Tell me about a time when you influenced someone to do something they didn't initially want to do.

Influence is a key skill in most jobs. Focus on how you determined what was in it for the other person, listened to their concerns, and got the outcome you wanted. Keep your example focused on a work or team situation.

Tell me about what makes a great salesperson.

The interviewer is testing your knowledge of the position in question (sales in this case; the same question applies to any position you might be seeking). Your research should uncover a list of talents and skills required in the position. Talk about the top three to five attributes. Make sure to include attitude and behaviors.

What are your salary expectations?

This can be tricky for someone who has just come from a high-paying job and expects to be offered a lower-paying job. Your employer is concerned that they can't pay anything near your expectations.

Let the employer know that you are making a transition in the workforce and are more interested in learning, contributing, and building a foundation for a career.

If they ask about your expectations, play dumb. Ask them about the range. Tell them that you really mean it when you say that you are looking to build a foundation with a great company and team, and that salary is secondary right now.

Your resume doesn't reflect experience in this industry. How can I assess you when most people applying for this position have previous work experience in the industry?

Talk about your research, informational interviews, and any other inquiries you have made to acquire background in the industry. Then discuss the extremely high standards required of you in your previous role and that you have learned many skills that most successful leaders have, e.g., relationship building, teamwork, work ethic, discipline, and a passion for success. You are smart and can get up the learning curve quickly in terms of industry content, but you also have skills/talents that can't be trained!

How long do you think it will take for you to get up to speed and show results?

Focus here on your attitude and willingness to learn quickly. Let the interviewer know that you are results driven and will do what it takes to get up the learning curve as fast as possible. You might also ask a bit about how the company plans to orient you to the position, if appropriate. If you have been in a situation before where you have had to hit the ground running, talk about the rapid results you achieved.

Describe your ideal job.

Focus on how your ideal job fits pretty closely to this job.

Describe your ideal work environment.

Make sure you know the work environment at this company so that you can tailor this answer to the culture of the company. There should be a good fit if you have done your homework!

Have you ever been fired?

If you have been fired, never blame other people or speak disparagingly about past colleagues or managers. Don't dwell on this question if you have been fired. Just give the facts and talk about lessons learned. Don't lie because the truth usually comes out, and if you lie during the interview, you will be fired when the truth is uncovered.

What questions do you have about our company or this position?

Great questions include:

- What will a typical day be like in this position?
- Why is this position open? Why did the previous person leave?
- What are the specific metrics by which my performance will be measured? What would be an outstanding job in this position?
- What kind of training is provided?
- What is the leadership style of my prospective boss?
- How do you see my background contributing to this company?
- How does this company review and reward performance?
- What are the biggest challenges you see facing the company right now?
- How would you describe the company culture?
- How does the company intend to grow in the next three to five years?
- What are the specific strategic goals of the company?
- What is the employee turnover rate, and what are the top reasons why employees leave?
- What do you like most and least about working here?
- What do you see as the main competitive advantage of the company?
- What do you see as the main competitive weakness of the company?
- How do you think frontline employees feel about upper management?
- What are the biggest changes facing the company right now and in the next couple of years?
- What would you change about the company?

Especially important: How well you do in every interview will be the direct result of how much time you spend practicing the interview with someone. Remember to arrive early, get in a relaxed frame of mind, and review your company research notes before the interview. Most interviewers make a decision about you within the first sixty seconds of the interview, so especially work on that first impression.

Finally, coach the client to follow up with a thank-you letter. After each interview, it is important for your client to follow up with a follow-up letter and/or email. You never know when your client's path will cross again with the interviewer's. In business, the world is small, and people in the same industry tend to know each other. Even if your client didn't care for the company or person after the interview, they should still follow up.

Tips for your client about sending a follow-up letter:

- Send out your thank-you letters no later than twenty-four hours after your interview has ended. If the employer is Internet savvy (and most are!), send out an email thank-you within two hours after you return from the interview. You can also use simple, elegant thank-you cards from your local discount store.

- Keep your audience in mind. Address the issues and concerns that were mentioned during the interview.

- Use the thank-you letter as a follow-up "sales" letter in which you restate your reasons for wanting the position and remind the interviewer why you're qualified.

- Mention anything of importance that your interviewer might have neglected to ask in person.

- If you're only writing a few sentences, send a handwritten note. Otherwise, send a typed, formatted letter.

- Thank everyone who contributed to your job search.

- If you decide after the interview that you don't want the job after all, write a respectful note withdrawing your application.

- Choose your words carefully when using email. Email creates an instant written record, so don't let the speed and the ease of sending it blind you to not knowing that you will be judged on what you've said and how you've said it.

- An effective business habit to form is to let someone you trust preview your letter before you send it.

Negotiation when offered a job

If your client follows the advice you have taught them so far, eventually they will get a job offer. Congratulate them heartily when this happens. Now comes the time for your client to negotiate terms of employment.

There are two secrets to a successful negotiation. First, your client has to know who they are and what they really want out of the position. If they make the job about ego and status, they may end up disappointed, especially in a tough economy when people may have to lower their expectations about salary and glamour. Instead, if your client views the job as yet another stepping stone and learning experience, then they can afford to be more flexible in exchange for valuable experience.

Second, the primary way to improve one's negotiating position is with leverage. If your client has other opportunities, they can ask for more than they could if they only had one job offer.

My suggestion is to advise clients to focus first on a job that comes close to meeting their passion and talents and worry about the terms secondarily. If your client finds the right position, they will succeed and be able to name their own terms soon enough.

Some coaching questions for your clients include:

Key Performance Indicators, or KPIs. Before taking the job, confirm how you will be measured and evaluated. Make sure you can achieve these metrics.

Signing bonus. What kind of signing bonus can they offer to get you on board?

Salary. What is the salary range? Are you at the lower or upper end of the range? What is your potential salary increase and over what time frame? (Be sure your client has checked out pay scales online so that they are armed with data.)

Bonus. What kind of bonus can you achieve and based on what results? Note that in some firms, such as investment banks, bonuses based on performance can be in the many millions of dollars and amount to far more than the salary.

Stock options. Some publicly traded companies provide stock options. Make sure your client understands when the stock options vest (i.e., become yours), how long before they expire (and are worthless if they don't exercise them), the strike price of the option (i.e., the price at which they can purchase company stock), and what the company's stock has to do for the option to be worth money. Refer your client to a financial advisor for details about any option packages and get their advice.

Commission. For sales positions, your clients need to know exactly how the commission structure works. When do you get your commission? Does the commission percent change over time and then reset? Do you get commissions every time a particular customer buys, forever, or only on the first sale? What happens if you leave the company?

Draw. If your client is in a sales job, you might get a draw from the company while they build a client or customer base. Be careful! Sometimes a draw is a loan the company can collect if the employee leaves or doesn't succeed. You don't want your client to end up as an indentured servant to the company.

Vacation. How much vacation time do you get? Starting when? How does vacation time increase over time?

Benefits. What kind of health insurance do you get? What is covered and what isn't? What is the deductible? What kind of life insurance do you get? What kind of 401(k) or other retirement plan does the company offer?

Career options. How is your career path expected to unfold in the company? What is the opportunity to grow?

Training allowance. How much, and what kind of training do you get? How many conferences and seminars can you attend?

Expense allowance. What can and can't you expense when you travel on behalf of the company? Some companies are very stingy when it comes to per diem meal allowances, hotel allowances, and car rental.

Title. What will be your job title?

Ability to work from home and work hours. Can you telecommute? How often? What kind of flexibility do you have in work hours?

Termination. If you leave the job or are fired or laid off, what are your ongoing obligations? Advise your client to get an attorney and be very careful about signing an extended non-compete clause that prohibits them from working for another company in the industry for a long period of time. Also, make sure the company puts its severance policy in writing up front, or your clients may find themselves laid off with no severance.

Separation package. At almost any management level that your client may enter, it is increasingly common for medium to larger companies to provide a "guarantee of pay" and perhaps some limited benefits if someday they ask them to leave the firm for any reason.

Most importantly, conduct active inquiry with your client about the terms that are most important to them. Work with your client on influence and negotiation strategies to get the best possible deal. As always, role-play is a great way to ensure that your client negotiates with a proper balance of getting what they want, preserving relationships, and not coming across as obnoxious or arrogant.

Success In a New Role

By coaching clients to succeed in a new role, you set yourself up to coach clients about a range of leadership issues. This type of coaching is an effective segue from career coaching to executive and leadership coaching.

The first ninety days of a new role are important. During this time, the employee makes an initial impression, one that can last a long time. For instance, one of my clients approached his new executive role with the same style he used in his previous company, one with a culture that rewarded aggressive, competitive behavior. Unfortunately, the new company was more collaborative. Even though this executive realized his mistake and adapted within a few months, it took years for his reputation to fully recover.

Shown below are some of the lines of inquiry that work well when coaching a client to succeed in their new role. In many instances, it will be too soon for your client to know the answers. If that is the case, coach your client about whom to ask to find out. For instance, if the manager doesn't know much about the manager, they can ask colleagues who have a successful relationship or set up a meeting with the manager to get a sense of their style and requirements.

Clarify success. What does the formal job description say about key performance metrics? As important, what are the unspoken requirements of the job? What does the client's manager expect? What are the unspoken rules about how to get the job done? What are the political issues that require delicate navigation?

Help one's manager to be successful. What is the client's manager trying to achieve? What are their professional aspirations? What are their personal aspirations? What is the manager's communication style? How does the manager like to get updates, and how often? What are the manager's pet peeves? What are things to NOT do when working with this manager? What is the best way to give the manager more time, eliminate hassles, and be successful?

Get to know the team. I recently completed a 360-degree assessment for an executive in a new role. One of the comments that kept coming up from his colleagues was that this executive was trusting his team too much and needed to do a better job assessing who was in the right role and who wasn't. The job of getting to know and assessing the team can be challenging when someone starts a new job. However, you can coach your client to set up meetings to get to know their team, start to set expectations, learn as much as possible about how to support the team and bring value, and develop initial impressions about who gets results and who doesn't. In one case, this meant traveling to different offices and shadowing a direct report for a week at a time to really understand each team member's style and capabilities. After getting to know the team, the client will likely benefit from coaching about how to bring the team together and engage them.

Learn the culture and fit in. It is dangerous to be an outlier or be perceived as eccentric, especially in organizations with strong cultures. What is the culture of the organization? Which behaviors exemplify this culture? Which behaviors are shunned? What are the values of the organization, and how are these expressed? Which values and behaviors are never tolerated? What are the informal ways that things get done in the organization? Who are people that best embody the culture, and how can your client learn from them? How does your client need to adapt their style to the culture and values of the organization? What does your client already do naturally that will easily fit with the culture?

Align with the key players. Who are the formal and informal leaders in the organization? Who holds the most political power? Who is seen as up-and-coming talent? Who is on the most important projects? Who on the client's team is performing well and has the potential to keep growing? Who on the client's team appear to be in the wrong role or have a poor attitude? Who is on the way out? Work with your client to start thinking about their power base in the organization and how to build relationships with key people. For instance, one of my coaching clients took on a new role, leading a division where there was animosity with the parent company. One of his top priorities was to travel frequently to headquarters to build bridges with the people leading the parent company. As a result of this work, relationships between his business unit and the parent company improved significantly compared with those of his predecessor, and he was able to request more resources and support to help his organization be more successful. At the same time, he built a relationship with an executive at headquarters who happened to become CEO within the year; his strong relationship worked in his favor once this former peer moved up.

Discover and avoid political land mines. Managers and executives in new roles sometimes have to tread lightly, especially in highly political organizations. There are pet projects, sacred cows, special agendas, powerful people who might get offended, conflicts between managers that can force people to pick sides, and managers who have more power than their titles might suggest. It is hard to see these issues, which is why the metaphor of a buried land mine makes sense. However, you can coach your client to ask questions to learn more about the political landscape and not go in naively.

Take enough time to observe and discover. One mistake that some new managers and executives make is to rush in and change things too soon. Coach your client about how long they have to observe, learn, and make smart decisions. The window of opportunity to learn before acting varies with the situation. I worked with a reverend who specialized in turning around struggling churches; he would wait eighteen months to get to know his congregation before making any significant decisions. That's probably the far end of the acceptable window; most executives have a couple of months to observe, assess, and map out a plan. In some cases, the window is smaller, but you can coach your client to list some hypotheses about the main issues in their area of responsibility and then take the time to test those hypotheses before reaching conclusions.

Create a development plan to keep improving. Marshall Goldsmith's book *What Got You Here Won't Get You There* concisely explains why every manager and executive needs to keep developing. It is unlikely that a client taking on a new role will know everything there is to know about the industry, business, or leadership. At some point during their first ninety days, come up with a development plan for the client to succeed in the role and also set the stage for success into the future.

Packages for Different Stages of Career Exploration

Career coaching clients come with different goals. Some want to start from scratch and uncover completely new career possibilities. Others know what they want to do and want coaching to land the ideal job. Still others know what they want to do and how to get there and would like a coach to hold them accountable. Clients who have years of experience will have different expectations than twenty-somethings coming out of college. Executives will have different needs than frontline employees who want to secure their first management role. You might also land an engagement with a gatekeeper to clients, such as a recruiting or outplacement firm, and they might want a set package for a set number of sessions or hours of coaching.

For this reason, if career coaching will be a major part of your coaching practice, you should come up with some set packages and pricing for your clients. You can mix and match one-on-one coaching with some group coaching, offer webinars or teleclasses with instruction, and add in some live workshops too.

Give some thought to packages for the following situations:

- **Soup to nuts.** Develop a coaching program for your target market that takes them through the whole process of identifying who they are, what they want to do, navigating the transition, and getting the new role. Include success in the new role as an optional upgrade.

- **Nuts and bolts.** Offer a package to develop marketing messaging and collateral for your clients.

- **Nuts and bolts plus accountability.** After developing the messaging and collateral, help your clients to secure the position. Include success in the new role as an optional upgrade.

- **Accountability only.** Provide group and one-on-one coaching to keep clients who are actively seeking work to stay on task, get support, leverage their networks, and reduce the time it takes to land the right position.

- **Outplacement.** Come up with a package of ten to fifteen sessions to help outplaced workers make the transition and find a new situation.

- **Success in a new role.** Offer clients a 90-day coaching package to help them succeed in their new role.

Part Eight

BUSINESS COACHING

Overview

Business coaching helps business owners grow their companies, increase what their companies are worth, and have their businesses be less dependent on them. It adds a technical layer of coaching to the leadership coaching topics already discussed.

The topics in this section include:

- Assessing the business to know where the coaching should focus.

- Understanding the client's aspirations and goals for the business and what might be standing in the way.

- Helping clients clearly understand the business model, including how many units they have to sell to break even, what drives revenues, what drives profits, and what drives cash flow.

- Working with the client to test and roll out ideas to improve the key drivers in the business model.

- Developing a compelling strategy.

- Coaching clients to get leverage on their time and have the business be less dependent on them.

One model that I use in business coaching that covers the above areas and leadership coaching is the CASTLE Model for Business Growth and Success.

CASTLE is an acronym for:

- <u>C</u>ontrol
- <u>A</u>spirations
- <u>S</u>trategy
- <u>T</u>actics
- <u>L</u>everage
- <u>E</u>volution

Control refers to the business owner's mastery of the financial performance of the business, from knowing his or her breakeven volume to understanding and improving the key levers that have the most impact on revenues and profit. Most business owners do not pay enough attention to projecting and meeting key metrics. Your first role as a business coach is to help your clients get control of their business and grow it proactively, while focusing on the numbers that really matter.

Aspirations are the business owner's long-term goals for the business. Without high aspirations for the business, the business owner will not be motivated to make any changes or difficult decisions required for lasting success. You will help business owners get back in touch with their passion for starting the business, set their most ambitious goals, and—if they have lost their spark—help them be excited again about going to work in the morning.

Strategy is a plan for the business to compete and dominate its market. You can provide enormous value by helping your clients clarify their positioning in the market, target customers, products, services, and what they do best. For larger companies, you can work with the owner on an overall strategy, as this book described in an earlier chapter. For smaller companies, you might start with the marketing strategy, which helps the client determine the best message and positioning to succeed in the market.

Tactics are ways your clients will achieve their metrics to create a profitable enterprise and get visible in their marketplace.

Leverage refers to a variety of ways for business owners to build a business that runs without them. With proper leverage, business owners can focus on setting direction and standards, make more valuable use of their time, build an enterprise that has significant worth, and achieve their aspirations. Most business owners have jobs, not businesses. Perhaps your most important role as a business coach is to show the business owner how to shift from, as Michael Gerber describes in his *E-Myth* series of books, working in the business to working on it.

Evolution describes how the business owner will continue to learn and develop, including new skills, attitudes, beliefs, and knowledge.

In a business coaching engagement, the CASTLE Model normally begins with the A (Aspirations), the C (Control the numbers), and the T (Tactics to improve the business). Coaching clients on their aspirations creates a positive environment filled with potential and enthusiasm. Following up with Control and Tactics—if the client is not strong in these areas—gets the business in shape for ongoing growth. From there, coach and client can work on bigger-picture areas, such as strategy, leverage, and the evolution of the business owner as a leader.

Assessing the Client's Business

Before your first session with a client, assess their business and determine the progress they are making. It also identifies areas of potential need. Finally, the assessment helps you to build a relationship with the client by preparing in advance.

There are two parts to the assessment: a data request and a written questionnaire. In both parts, reassure the client that you only want information they already have. If the client can't answer a question or provide a piece of data, let them know that your coaching sessions will fill in any gaps.

Data Request:

- Three years of financial statements
    - Income statement
    - Balance sheet
    - Starting and ending bank balances for the year or cash flow statement if available
- Projections and goals, along with any goal-tracking tools already in place
- Business plan
- Marketing and advertising materials, including website address
- Product/Service list and pricing
- Organization chart

- Job descriptions
- Recruiting advertisements
- Manuals and operating procedures
- Performance review forms
- Training program manuals

Assessment Questionnaire

Shown below is a questionnaire that usually gets to the heart of the issues with the business from the owner's perspective. Feel free to add to it, simplify it, or change it to fit your needs and the needs of your target market.

- What would you like to get out of this coaching relationship so that it is one of the best experiences of your professional career?
- What are your one-, three-, and five-year goals for the business?
- What is your ultimate vision for your business?
- Why did you start, buy, or get into this business?
- What sets your products/services apart from the competition?
- What are your top talents that help make the business successful?
- What excites you the most about the business?
- What do you like doing most in your business?
- What do you like doing least in your business?
- What are the top strengths of your business?
- What are the top weaknesses of your business?
- What are the main external threats your business faces, for instance, from competitors or government regulations?
- What are the main opportunities your business has to grow and improve its position in the market?

- What are your top five frustrations with your business?

- What is the one thing that keeps you up at night about your business?

- How would you assess your team?

- How do you use technology in your business?

- What are the key numbers that drive revenues, costs, and cash flow in your business?

- What is your breakeven volume?

- What are the top five customer complaints you receive?

- What is your annual employee turnover?

- Estimate the top uses of your time right now in your business. How would you like to change how you use your time?

- How would you describe the culture of your company? How close is this description to the culture you want to have?

- What is one behavior you could start or stop doing that would help you have more impact with your employees and executive team?

Aspirations

Aspirations are client dreams and visions regarding where they want to take the business.

Aspirations determine passion and motivation. The amount of effort clients put into the business is directly related to how high their aspirations are for the business. High aspirations mean passion, and passion means motivation to do what needs to be done to get results.

Set aside a coaching session to discuss aspirations. Ask your client these questions:

- Why did you start the business?

- When you started the business, what was exciting to you in terms of what your business made possible?

- What makes you passionate about running this business? What gets you most excited?

- What difference do you want to make through your business? How do you want your customers to be better off from the products you offer? What is the overall purpose of the business (e.g., Disney wants to make people smile)?

- How big do you want your business to get?

- What do you want your business to be famous for? What do/ should you do best?

- How do you see your business developing over the next five and ten years? What is your overall vision for the business regarding the items shown below?

- Number of locations

- Number and types of products/services

- Reputation in the market

- Distribution channels

- Values of the organization

- Types of employees the business attracts

- Types of customers

- Media attention and overall visibility

- Revenue growth

- Profit

- Value of the business

- What is the endgame of the business? Do you want to sell it and, if so, to whom and for how much? Do you want to go public? Do you want to transfer ownership to your children?

- What else gets you excited about the business?

- What are your personal goals?

- How do you visualize your retirement? When do you want to retire? How much will you need?

- How much money do you need to save for your children's schooling?

- Take a moment to list the top 20 material goals you have in your life, for example, travel, recreation, your home, memberships, hobbies, and charitable giving. List the dates by when you want to have these and how much they will cost.

Challenge your clients to get beyond any limiting beliefs or perceptions and really dream about where they want to take their business and what they want to achieve!

Once your clients do this work, you can coach them on anything they already know that might be holding them back. Here are two good questions to ask:

- *What is currently standing in the way of your aspirations?*
- *What beliefs or perceptions do you already know you have that are holding you back from taking your business to where you want it to go?*

Note that if the client isn't aware of any limiting beliefs, they will come up as you work with the client to implement strategies and tactics. You will hear them in the excuses the client makes for why things aren't working or why they didn't take action as well as blanket assertions or judgments they make about people, success, money, customers, or time

At the same time, once you move into more technical aspects of business coaching, you and the client can refer back to their aspirations as a way to motivate them to overcome any setbacks and keep making progress. No problem seems too big if the aspirations are inspiring enough.

Define the Business Model and Key Drivers of Business Success

The meat of business coaching begins by getting control of the numbers that drive every business. This work is not necessarily glamorous, especially compared with landing new customers or developing an exciting new strategy to penetrate new markets. Before a business can grow, however, it has to be viable. To be viable, the business owner has to have a firm grasp of the numbers.

Getting control of the numbers is not merely an accounting exercise. Accounting focuses on the past. As a business coach, you start with history and then go much further. You help your client understand the financial levers that will make the business grow profitably. You also help the client look to the future by setting goals for key metrics, comparing results to those goals, and making adjustments when goals are not met (or when goals are not ambitious enough).

It will be important for you to keep the above point in mind. Your clients will ask you how what you do differs from what their accountant does. The answer is that you go much further than accountants. Accountants look at the past, often for IRS purposes. In contrast, you use numbers to help businesses advance powerfully into the future and achieve their goals. Also, you are in a coaching role, which means you are not there to create more reports or analyses. You are there to help the client grab hold of the most important numbers in the business and use them to grow revenues, profits, and the value of the enterprise.

A large percentage of the time you spend coaching clients will focus on how they are doing compared to their financial goals. If your clients aren't tracking their numbers and measuring progress based on them, they won't be able to take control of their destiny and ongoing success. They won't know how they are doing, where they are going, or the best way to get there.

You must emphasize to your clients that you expect and need them to track the metrics that they will need to get results from their work with you.

Note that you do not have to be an accountant to help businesses track and improve these metrics, but it can help to have a background in accounting so that you can do some additional number crunching, especially by calculating a variety of financial ratios. It is actually more powerful, though, to help business owners focus on the few financial metrics that make the most difference to their success. Some business owners get so lost in their financial statements that they fail to focus on the most important numbers.

In fact, you should emphasize to your clients that your role is to help make things simpler and more practical for them!

Here are the key parts of a business model that every business must define and improve:

- Breakeven Volume
- Revenue Model
- Profit Model
- Cash Flow Model

Breakeven

The first place you start with any client is the Breakeven Volume, which tells you and the client how many units they have to sell to cover all their costs. You should work with the client to calculate Breakeven Volume on an annual, monthly, weekly, and daily basis.

Many clients think they understand the concept of breakeven, but they do not. For instance, some clients don't see any difference between fixed and variable costs and just want the bottom line on their income statements to be greater than zero. Others assume that as long as their bank account doesn't go down every month, they assume they are breaking even. Still others don't know how to use the tool strategically to think about such issues as seasonality, how to change their operating model to lower fixed costs, or how to increase revenues to cover costs more easily.

To calculate Breakeven Volume, you need to know three numbers:

- Unit sale price
- Unit cost
- Total fixed costs

Unit sale price is the average sale price for the business. Take total revenues for the year and divide by total units sold. If a company sells many different products, you still arrive at a single unit sale price with this method; you can look at individual products after doing the analysis at a general or macro level. If a company sells services (such as a law firm), divide revenues by the total number of engagements or the total number of hours billed.

Unit cost is the direct, or variable cost, of each unit sold. To calculate unit cost, take the total Cost of Goods Sold and any other direct costs (e.g., shipping cost to customers, direct commissions) and divide by the number of units sold. For professional service firms, variable cost can be almost negligible because the main costs are fixed (e.g., salaries and rent). If the firm pays commissions or is in the temporary staffing business, however, include the cost of the commission or the temporary staffing wages that the client pays in this calculation.

Fixed costs are all the recurring costs of the business: salaries, rent, utilities, advertising and marketing, insurance, and interest. It is imperative that your client include their own salary in fixed costs.

Breakeven begins by calculating unit sale price less unit cost. This is called unit contribution and is the amount of money that the business takes in as a direct result of selling a product. You could also divide the company's gross profit by units sold to arrive at this number.

Next, divide unit contribution into fixed costs, which gives your client their historical Breakeven Volume. You can divide by 12 to get the monthly Breakeven, by 52 to get the weekly, and by 365 (or total days the business is open) to get the daily Breakeven.

For example, assume a client calculates the following numbers:

Revenue/Unit	$5.00
Cost/Unit	$2.00
Unit Contribution	$3.00
Fixed Costs	$100,000
Breakeven/Yr	$33,333
Breakeven/Month	$2,778
Breakeven/Week	$641

Unit contribution is $5 per unit minus $2 direct or variable cost per unit, or $3 per unit. Annual Breakeven Volume on $100,000 of fixed costs is 33,333 units ($100,000 in fixed costs divided by unit contribution of $3). Weekly Breakeven Volume is 641. If the business is open five days per week, it needs to sell just over 128 units per day to break even.

Once you have the Breakeven Volume, you have some questions to ask your client:

- How does Breakeven Volume compare with current volume? Is the client breaking even, losing money, or exceeding breakeven?
- What is the distribution of volume over time? That is, it would be interesting to graph volume on a daily, weekly, and monthly basis.

This will show how much unit sales tend to change by day of the week, week of the month, and month of the year. If you have this information, you can work with the client to increase units sold during down times.

- When are times that the client does not break even, and why?

- What are some creative ways the client could run the business to have a dramatic improvement in breakeven? For instance, a restaurant owner might ditch the expensive infrastructure required to run a retail location and switch to a food truck. A publisher might switch from selling $10 books to packaging information products at $200 per unit.

- How would Breakeven Volume change if the client:

  - Raised prices by 5%, 10%, and 15% across the board?

  - Changed product mix to focus on high-revenue and high-margin items?

  - Increased number of transactions by 5%, 10%, and 15%?

  - Decreased direct costs that go into making the product—but without hurting quality?

  - Reduced fixed costs by 5%, 10%, and 15%?

- How does Breakeven Volume change if you add to fixed costs all of the personal bills you need to pay along with money you need to save for retirement, college savings for children, and any other long-term goals?

The overall purpose of looking at breakeven is not to have an academic discussion. It is to get the client to think about ways to reduce the number of units needed to break even or to have an easier time covering variable and fixed costs.

Revenue Model

After exploring breakeven, you and the client can delve into the client's business model, starting with revenues.

Your role as a coach is to help the client break down revenues into a formula, or a revenue model. There are many ways to do this. One of the simplest is to combine the sales funnel with the value of a customer.

The sales funnel tells your client what it takes to get a new customer. Imagine a funnel that is large at the top and narrow at the bottom. Next, imagine your client's entire target market hovering like a cloud above the sales funnel. If your client does the right things, some portion of the market will become aware and interested in the client's business. They will enter the top of the funnel as suspects. Next, a smaller portion of these people will turn into qualified leads. They have the money, decision-making authority, and serious desire to buy. From there, some percentage will make a purchase and fall through the narrow bottom of the funnel, having converted to customers.

From there, if your client knows how much each customer is worth to them, they can calculate a formula that predicts revenues. The numbers that make up this formula include how many units a customer buys during each transaction, how much they pay per unit, and how often they come back to purchase in a set period of time.

By multiplying all these things out, your clients have a very basic revenue model:

Number of suspects x Conversion rate to qualified leads
= Number of suspects who become qualified leads
x Conversion rate to customers
= Number of leads who become customers

Number of customers x Number of Units Purchased Per Transaction
x Average Unit Price x Transactions Per Customer Per Year
= Gross Revenues

From gross revenues, we can subtract returns and bad debt—if applicable to your client—to get a net revenue number.

Gross Revenues - % Returns - % Bad Debt = Net Revenues

This generic approach is one of many that works for many businesses. We will soon explore ways to enrich it or try other models.

This approach to looking at the revenues of a business is valuable because unlike accounting statements it doesn't start with revenues. It gets down to the numbers that drive revenues. For a business to increase revenues, it has a number of options:

- Increase the number of people who are aware and interested
- Increase the number of people who are qualified leads
- Increase the conversion rate (the percentage of qualified leads that become customers)
- Increase the number of units a customer purchases each time they make a transaction
- Increase price per unit or have customers buy more expensive units
- Increase the number of transactions a customer makes each year (e.g., increase loyalty)
- Decrease returns and bad debt

As a business coach, you will work closely with your clients to brainstorm ways for them to work on each of these six options to bring in more revenues. This is the tactical part of business coaching and will be discussed soon.

Before getting into how to do that, it is important that you set up a system for your clients to track these numbers. This can take work and some creativity, but you have to remind your clients that they can only improve what they measure. In some cases, they may have to do periodic surveys to get at some numbers. For instance, consider a retail store owner trying to calculate their conversion rate. If they don't have an automated system to count how many people come into the store, they may have to manually count how many people come into the store (leads) and how many people actually buy (customers) to discover the actual conversion rate.

Also, many clients will over- or underestimate the numbers if they guess. For instance, many salespeople are overly optimistic about their conversion rate and disappointed or even skeptical when actual data is used. You can't let them guess.

The above approach is only a start—an example to get you comfortable with the approach. Before you impose a formula on your client, introduce the concept by giving the example above. Then ask the client what drives their revenues.

For instance, if the client runs a chain of hamburger restaurants that sell only one product—hamburgers—then the drivers of revenues are:

- Number of stores
- Number of people who come into each store to buy a hamburger
- How many hamburgers each person buys
- The price of the hamburger

The client can increase revenues by opening more stores, increasing foot traffic to each store, getting people to buy more hamburgers, or finding ways to offer more expensive hamburgers.

If the client runs a home healthcare business, drivers include:

- Number of referral sources to the business (e.g., physicians, hospitals, nursing homes, estate planners)
- How many patients each referral source brings

- The type of insurance the patient has
- How much the insurance pays for a visit
- How many visits the patient receives
- How many added services the patient receives per visit

This type of client can increase revenues by increasing the number of referral sources, getting more referrals from each source, getting more patients with insurance companies that pay the best, increasing the number of visits the patient receives, and increasing the number of services provided during a visit (e.g., adding a tech with a nurse).

For an online media company, drivers of revenues might include:

- Number of visitors to the site
- Advertising rates per thousand visitors
- Number of advertising opportunities
- Leads to prospective advertisers
- Conversion from leads to actual advertisers
- How many advertisements each client purchases
- How much they pay per advertising spot
- How many spots they buy
- How long they remain an advertiser

These models can get complex. If in doubt, go back to the generic example at the start of this section that combined the sales funnel with the value of a customer. From there, interview your client about what they think are the key drivers of revenue and construct a model with them.

Another way to approach this work is by asking the client how to make structural improvements to the revenue model. A good revenue model has the following characteristics:

- Recurring revenue, for instance, as with insurance and cable companies that get ongoing payments

- A dominant strategic position, for instance, with proprietary products or a strong brand that makes it easier to attract customers and raise prices over time

- Raving, loyal customers who keep coming back and keep referring others to the business

- High switching costs, for instance, the way that cell phone companies lock customers into a long-term contract

- A wide distribution network that makes the company visible to as much of the market as possible

Once you and the client get into tactics and strategy, you can work on improving the revenue model even more. Everything fits together with business coaching once the foundations are in place.

The Profit Model

As a business coach, you will spend most of your time with clients on increasing revenues. This makes good sense because if revenues grow profitably, then everything else tends to take care of itself. However, revenues are not sufficient for the viable, let alone successful business.

The primary objective of any business is to generate profit, without running out of cash. One dollar of increased revenue does not lead to one dollar in increased profits because of the costs that cut into revenues. However, one dollar of increased productivity goes directly to the bottom line. Therefore, your clients need to be constantly aware of their profitability and especially the costs that eat into profits.

On the next page are the numbers you should ask your clients to track:

- **Gross profit margin.** The percentage of sales left to the business after direct costs.

- **Gross profit.** The dollar amount left to the business after direct costs. For instance, if a business sells $10,000 worth of cupcakes and ingredients to make the cupcakes cost $4,000, the gross profit is $6,000, and the gross profit margin is 60%.

- **Fixed costs.** All other recurring costs to the business: e.g., salaries, rent, utilities, advertising and marketing, interest expense, depreciation, dues and subscriptions, licensing, professional fees, contractors.

- **Pretax Profits.** What the business takes in after all costs except taxes

- **Pretax Profit Margin.** Pretax profits divided into net revenues.

Clients should set targets for gross profit margin and fixed costs. Gross profit margin can be improved through a number of tactics, including raising prices, negotiating better supply costs, and cutting waste. Fixed costs tend to stay the same until a certain level of sales is reached, but fixed costs can be decreased with such tactics as better negotiation, smarter use of space, and automation.

You can also use this work to plan capacity. Ask the client to think about how fixed costs will change as different revenue figures are hit. At what unit and sales volume will the client need more space? What kind of staff will be required at different sales volume levels (e.g., a new salesperson, more manufacturing personnel, additional financial support)? What else will change as volume increases?

Finally, taxes can take a huge bite out of your client's net income and are not the domain of most business coaches. Make sure that your clients have an excellent accountant and assign them homework of meeting with their accountant to reduce their tax burden and increase deductions.

Cash Flow

In business, cash is its lifeblood. If a business runs out of cash, it has a heart attack. Your job as a coach is to make sure that the business has plenty of blood running through it and isn't at risk of a heart attack.

Your clients need to know two rules about cash:

- Profitability and cash flow are not the same thing.
- Most businesses fail because they run out of cash before they become viable.

Let's start with the first rule. A business can make an excellent profit and still have negative cash flow. That's because a business can drain cash through investments that don't show up on the income statement and flow through to profits. Investments in equipment, office fixtures, and inventory all take cash, and all show up as assets before they show up on the income statement.

This fact of life directly relates to the second rule. A business with a sound revenue and profit model may still run out of cash. The owners may invest too quickly in growing the business through large equipment and space purchases, rapid hiring, or spending lots of money on untested advertising.

Your role as a coach is to help your clients understand their cash flow, avoid running out of cash, and improve it. Key metrics to track at all times, especially at the beginning and the end of each month, include:

- **Cash on hand.** How much cash does the business have in the bank?
- **Cash going out.** How much cash will the business need to cover operating costs, buy inventory, and make any planned investments? This should be projected on a weekly, monthly, and quarterly basis.
- **Cash coming in.** How much cash is expected to come in through accounts receivables, new sales, and financing sources. This should also be projected on a weekly, monthly, and quarterly basis.

- **Ending cash.** How much cash will be left at the end of the week, month, and quarter after cash going out and cash coming in?

In the cash flow model below, note that the business used in this example has a problem.

CASH FLOW MODEL	PERIOD: PROJECT
Starting Cash on Hand	**$1,000**
Cash Going Out:	
Salaries	$15,000
Fixed Costs	$5,000
Accounts Payable	$2,000
Inventory Purchases	$2,500
Investments	$500
Repayment of Debt Principle	$ -
Taxes	$ -
Other	$ -
Total Cash Going Out	**$25,000**
Cash Coming In:	
Net Cash Sales	$15,000
Accounts Receivable Paid	$5,000
Investor Capital	$ -
Debt Capital	$ -
Total Cash Coming In	**$20,000**
Ending Cash on Hand	**$(4,000)**

In the period being projected, this business is going to have a cash deficit of $4,000. If they don't do a better job planning for cash, and if nothing changes, they are going to have a heart attack.

What are the options? They include:

- Delay payments to suppliers (stretch out accounts payable).

- Order less inventory (and use existing inventory more efficiently

- Defer investments.

- Increase the amount of sales paid in cash.

- Collect accounts receivable more quickly.

- Get an investment or a loan.

If the situation gets really bad, more drastic measures are needed (e.g., layoffs).

Coach your client every month to make sure that a heart attack due to a lack of cash is not imminent. Even better, coach them to create a business that is strong, has increasing cash flow, and no signs of heart disease at all.

If you want to go deeper with your client, the following three ratios will help you and your clients make decisions about improving cash flow:

- **Days' receivables.** The number of days it takes to collect sales. Take sales for the year and divide by accounts receivables at the end of the year, which will give you receivables turns. Divide this number into 365 to get days' receivables. For instance, if a company has $100,000 in sales during the year and $10,000 in accounts receivables, it turns over its receivables 10 times in a year; 365 days divided by 10 turns = 36.5 days' receivables. As an alternative, you might calculate this ratio using only credit sales (as opposed to total sales) to see how long it takes to collect credit sales specifically.

- **Days' payables.** The number of days it takes your client to pay suppliers. It is calculated similarly as days' receivables except that you divide purchases made on credit by the average accounts payable balance.

- **Inventory turns.** How quickly your client turns over inventory. The best way to calculate this ratio is by dividing rolling 12-month cost of sales by current inventory. So, if a company's cost of sales over the past 12 months is $50,000 and current inventory is $2,000, the company turns its inventory 25 times a year. You can divide this number into 365 to see how many days it takes to turn inventory.

By knowing these numbers, you can brainstorm with your clients about ways to collect cash from customers more quickly, stretch out payables to suppliers (without alienating the supplier), and increase inventory turns (e.g., by ordering more efficiently, simplifying the product line, focusing on high turnover items, and cutting down on waste).

When you meet with clients, get them into the habit of projecting and planning cash flow on a weekly and monthly basis. Make sure they are in control of every nickel that goes out the door and don't spend anything that isn't in the plan.

The Dashboard

Now you and your client have in place a dashboard to track and improve results. They include:

- Revenue Projections
- Profit Projections
- Cash Flow Projections

At least once a month, you and your client should review these numbers. Then compare actual results with their goals, set new goals for the coming month, and develop tactics to improve.

Also, don't forget about breakeven volume. Frequently check with clients to see how far above or below breakeven is their unit volume.

Reminder to get behind the numbers

As a coach, part of your ongoing development will be to help your clients understand how numbers drive their unique businesses.

Sometimes you will need to adjust the generic business model to fit a specific type of company. For instance, with a law firm, you might treat each partner as a separate business entity. Assuming you can get each partner to have X leads, convert Y% of these leads to clients, and generate $Z per client per year, you can multiple the number of partners by the average revenue per partner to come up with a number of total firm revenues. Then you can work with each partner to help them meet their targets. You can apply this same model to almost any professional services firms (e.g., real estate, accounting, consulting, and engineering). It also applies to any multiunit business; create a business model for each unit to uncover variability in performance, and then get each unit performing at a consistent level of excellence.

Similarly, different businesses within an industry compete differently, and the numbers reflect their choices. For instance, the traditional jewelry store turns its inventory only once or twice each year and makes up for its slow turnover with very high margins. In the past few years, however, a number of large wholesale diamond and jewelry stores have emerged. Their model is to reduce margins and make up for lower margins with higher inventory turnover. These higher turns allow these businesses to negotiate lower prices from suppliers and choose to either lower prices further or increase margins.

You will see the trade-off between margins and inventory turnover in a number of industries: all purpose stores (where Wal-Mart is a master of low margins and high turnover); hardware stores (Home Depot invented the model of lowering prices and increasing inventory turns); and supermarkets (where margins are as low as 1% and inventory turns drive profitability).

If you order annual reports for publicly traded companies in industries that interest you, you will be able to benchmark a variety of different ratios to get a sense for how the "big boys" do things. In your target market, you can offer to benchmark companies in your industry for free to establish your name or for a fee, providing anonymous benchmarking for your clients about where they stand in terms of revenue growth, revenue per employee, profit margins, debt, inventory turns, costs per employee, and much more.

The bottom line is that you want to work with your clients to discover the metrics that matter most to their businesses and that give them the best results with the least amount of effort. Be sure to ask your clients which metrics they track to measure success. For instance, in hospitals—one of the most complicated businesses in the world—key metrics include cost per patient day, average patient length of stay, and daily census; and these metrics are further broken down by specific categories of disease and insurance carriers.

Again, most small-business clients will be delighted with the formulas presented so far. As you progress in your practice, refine these models for your specific clients and their needs.

Test and Roll Out Ideas to Improve the Numbers

At this point, your client should be tracking and measuring the key numbers for success. Now you can work with them to introduce the ideas that will help them achieve their financial goals.

These ideas should tie back directly to the main metrics that your clients need to control. For instance, if you and the client are using a generic business model, these ideas should tie back to:

- Increase Revenues:
    - Increase the number of people interested and aware.
    - Increase the number of qualified leads.
    - Increase conversion from leads to customers.
    - Increase price per unit.
    - Increase units per transaction.
    - Increase transactions per customer (customer loyalty).
    - Reduce returns and bad debt.
- Increase Profit Margins:
    - Increase the gross profit margin.
    - Decrease fixed costs.
    - Increase the pretax margin.

- Increase cash flow:
  - Decrease cash going out.
  - Increase cash coming in.

If you are going to get into business coaching, you should keep and build a file of ideas proven to improve results in your target market. If the client fails to come up with their own ideas, you are ready to add value. Don't push your ideas onto the client. Use active inquiry to challenge the client to come up with their own ideas, or look around and see what competitors and successful businesses in other industries are doing.

The idea of this part of business coaching is that your client treats the business like a science experiment. They should set up a laboratory to constantly test new ideas at low risk and low cost, and then learn as much as possible from the results of the test. There are three possibilities after each test:

- Discard the idea because it is not something viable for this business.

- Tweak the idea and retest because it was close and there might be a way to improve the approach.

- Roll out the idea as part of the company's ongoing operations because the idea was a success.

The coaching process follows this flow:

- Choose which metric or metrics the client will improve during the coming month. Do this during the monthly review of the numbers.

- Work with the client to come up with ideas to improve those numbers. Again, you can assist the client with your own ideas, especially if you have expert knowledge, but the best approach is for the client to come up with their own ideas. Otherwise, there is a risk that they will implement the ideas halfheartedly and blame you when they don't work.

- Develop an action and accountability plan to turn the idea into a test.

- Define the results that will indicate that the test is a success.

- If the client resists new ideas, work to understand why. One of the biggest sources of resistance will be time. Many clients are so focused on the minutiae of running the business that they don't have time to implement anything new. If this is the case, you will need to work with them on building leverage and using their time better. You can also challenge them to delegate the work to others in the company.

- During coaching sessions, before discussing other topics, help the client stay accountable for testing ideas. Coach them on overcoming challenges to implementation.

- Each month review the results of the completed tests and challenge the client to keep testing. Remind the client to think about this process as having a laboratory and working to turn the business into a science. Some clients will be able to test no more than one idea per month to improve the business, while others have the energy and time to test five or more. Meet your clients where they are, and if they are only testing one idea at a time, gradually challenge them to test more ideas.

One hint: Many clients naturally want more leads. Challenge them to resist this temptation. What good is a lead that doesn't buy? What good is a lead that buys but doesn't come back because the company's product or service was poor? The best approach to growing a business is to create a solid operating model that delivers great service at maximum profit and keeps customers coming back. After that, it makes sense to focus on converting qualified leads to customers. Once these elements are in place, then the business owner and company will make optimal use of any leads that it generates.

Strategy

Strategy defines which customers a company serves, the products it offers these customers, how it will compete in its marketplace, the values it will follow in everything it does, and top priorities to make progress. A previous section in this book discusses strategy for larger organizations. Here, despite some overlap, we discuss how to coach smaller business clients about strategy.

Three areas need to be covered:

- How the company competes
- Strategic planning
- Marketing foundation and strategy

How the company competes

One of the first matters to discuss with your clients is how they compete and what they do best. There are really only two ways to compete in any market:

Strategy #1: Dominate by going head to head. In this strategy, you need to have a 3 to 1 advantage over your competitors in some attribute that matters to your customers. For instance, FedEx has established a 3 to 1 perceived (and real) advantage over others in terms of reliability or getting packages there overnight. Meanwhile, the U.S. Post Office has a 3 to 1 advantage in terms of cost when a package doesn't have to be there overnight.

You can dominate on all sorts of dimensions: personalization, the shopping experience, operational efficiency (e.g., Wal-Mart and Southwest Air), product leadership (e.g., Nike and Intel), source of supplies (e.g., many cement companies), depth and breadth of experience (e.g., McKinsey Consulting), and customer intimacy (e.g., IBM).

One way for smaller companies to dominate is by finding a niche. With a niche, your client chooses a focused target market and dominates it. For most business coaching clients, the niche strategy is the most viable.

For instance, focus on a specific industry with a deep solution for that industry. You can reach your target market easily, speak their language, provide top-notch solutions to their specific problems, and beat generalists.

Examples include a software company that focuses exclusively on products for restaurants, a sales training firm that serves only law practices, and a book publisher focused only on nonprofit executives.

The niche strategy also works well locally. For instance, your client could be the realtor who focuses on a particular subdivision and knows it better than anyone else.

Another approach to the niche strategy is to focus on a particular demographic or psychographic group, such as gender, ethnicity, religion, hobbies (e.g., golf, motorcycle riders), and political affiliation.

If your client lacks a 3:1 advantage over their competitors, they need to try the next strategy. Unless they want to compete based on "hustle and heart," most business owners can't sustain a business with a 1:1 advantage or worse. They end up as a commodity, a me-too product, and have problems, such as price wars (like some airlines).

Strategy #2: Change the game. If your client can't dominate, for instance with a niche, they have to change the game. This means either changing the rules of the game completely or bundling products to provide superior value in new ways.

For instance, Microsoft changed the game with its Office product line. Before Office, many costly, separately run office applications were available (such as Lotus 123 and Word Perfect). Microsoft essentially put them out of business with an affordable suite of products available in a single convenient package.

Similarly, TIVO changed the game with its DVR technology. Netflix is changing the video rental game with a unique new service. The Internet has also changed the game in a number of industries, from mortgages to insurance, book sales, dating, and media.

Strategic planning

After you introduce the above concepts to your clients, you can ask a series of questions to help them clarify their strategy. Note that you can overwhelm your client with hundreds of strategic questions. It is much more powerful to boil down strategy to a few key questions focused on the customer, solutions for the customer, the company's unique edge, and the type of company the owners want to create (e.g., values).

- **Describe your vision for the company one more time (from your work on aspirations).**
- **To make your vision a reality, who will be your customers?**
    - Do you define your target market by industry, title, geography, demographics (e.g., age, ethnicity, gender), or psychographics (e.g., a mind-set or belief system, such as liberal, conservative, green, motorcycle rider, golfer)?
    - What is the ideal customer for your company?
    - What are emerging customer groups?
    - What problem does your customer have that you solve? What does this problem feel like for them?

- Which segments of your target market are easiest to reach and through what means?

- How does the customer learn about you and try your product?

- What makes your customer loyal for life?

- Why don't these customers buy from you? What makes them skeptical?

- What options besides you does your customer have to solve their problem?

- What is your profile of the ideal customer?

- Who are NOT your customers? Which customer segments should you de-emphasize (because they are not profitable, too risky, or in a declining marketplace)?

- **What are your products and/or services?**
  - What results do these products achieve for your customers?
  - What logical benefits do your products provide?
  - What emotional benefits do they provide? How do they make your customer feel?
  - Which products best address the needs of your most profitable customers?
  - Which products should you de-emphasize?

- **What does your company do best for your customers?** Examples include proprietary product, proprietary or exclusive source, location, convenience, consistent service, price, speed, unique or exclusive distribution channel, research and development/new products, licensing intellectual property, customization, homemade/made from scratch product, depth or breadth of expertise, proven results, size or scale, knowing the needs of a particular customer segment better than anyone else, and personalization. Be careful of vague answers from your clients. Ask for specific examples. "Good service" and "fair prices" are not acceptable answers.

- **Given the above, is the company going to compete based on dominance in a particular attribute or by creating a game-changing strategy?**

- **What is the primary benefit you offer customers that is unique and better than what anyone else offers and that is compelling to the customer?** A benefit is something the customer gains from the features of your products or services that includes an emotional component: look better, feel better, enjoy peace of mind, be more secure, enjoy more time, save money (greed), feel younger and more alive, savor the tastes of Old Italy. . . . This edge should be significant to customers (not just to the business owner), measurable, and meaningful.

- **What proof can you offer customers to back up your claims of being the best (e.g., a guarantee, testimonials, articles about you, case studies, and quantifiable results)?**

- **What are the values of your company?** What attributes will define how you behave, treat others, and do business (e.g., competitive, friendly, accountable, fun, fanatics about service, creative, and/or risk takers)?

- **Given your answers to the above, what priorities does your company need to set to:**

    - Emphasize a more focused and profitable customer base?

    - De-emphasize unprofitable customers?

    - Emphasize the most profitable products and services?

    - De-emphasize less profitable products and services (unless they lead to larger purchases down the road)?

    - Be the best in a certain key attribute and deliver the desired primary benefit to the customer consistently?

    - Shore up any internal weaknesses that prevent satisfying customers?

- Get proof of being the best and delivering the promised benefits?

- Bake the values you want for your company into the fabric of everything you do?

- **Who will be accountable for making these priorities happen and by when?** Note that your clients may feel "stuck" about doing more right now until you focus on developing leverage. That's okay. For now, just make sure they know what they have to do to create the company they want to have.

The above questions are crucial for grounding your clients in what their business is about and what it needs to do to excel.

As a coach, part of your ongoing development should include doing research in your community or area of expertise about how different companies compete, especially the companies in your target market. For instance, in my community, real estate companies compete in a number of different ways:

- The leader in the market focuses on upscale and waterfront properties. They are a local firm that has been in the market for three decades. Their realtors are all highly professional, well-educated, seasoned individuals. The company has invested heavily in technology. It has also formed an alliance with Sotheby's Auction House. This firm dominates the upscale niche in our local market and has forged lasting relationships with local developers of upscale properties.

- The second-largest firm is a national real estate brokerage firm and competes based on its national scale and local service. They have a national reputation and advertise heavily on television. Newcomers to our area know this firm by name and trust its reputation.

- The next largest firm competes based on the experience of its realtors, who on average have a decade more experience than the typical realtor and the track record to prove it. This firm competes based on its advantage in experience and seasoning.

- A successful niche firm specializes in attracting buyers from the UK and Germany, where real estate is very expensive, and the dollar trades favorably.

- A game-changing firm represents only buyers in the market. They focus on the large influx of retirees and act as a buyer's representative.

- Similarly, another firm competes on price, offering just a 3% commission and no-frills service.

- Finally, another firm specializes in serving investors, with a focus on short sales, foreclosures, and properties that can be flipped.

You should research a variety of top industries in your marketplace to be able to speak intelligently about how different types of companies compete. An even better idea is to do some research on a volunteer basis for a local industry association. You can interview business owners about how they compete and present the findings as a speech to members. You establish yourself as an instant expert and can use the above strategic framework (along with other frameworks in this book) to solidify your credibility.

In *Good to Great*, author Jim Collins notes that the best companies have three things in place: passion for the business, something they do better than anybody else, and a viable business model. We have now covered these three aspects of a business. Your clients got in touch with their passion when you discussed aspirations with them. During your strategic conversations, they determine what they do best, and in your coaching about controlling the numbers, they determine a viable business model based on the key levers, or metrics, for profitability and cash flow.

Marketing foundation and strategy

The final strategic piece with business coaching clients is to help them hone their marketing message and strategy. Your work with tactics to improve the business model will cover some of this ground, but it helps to have your client develop a solid foundation for marketing.

Shown below are areas to cover to help your clients develop a strong marketing foundation and strategy:

Target markets. What are the target markets? What problems do they have that the company addresses? What is the cost of these problems to the organization and the business owner? How much pain is there?

Solution and primary benefits. What is the company's solution to these problems? What are the primary logical, personal, and emotional benefits that customers experience as a result of these solutions?

Competitive advantage. How does the company's product and services stand out? What is the best positioning based on criteria that matter most to people in the target market?

Proof. What proof can the company offer to back up the above claims?

Core marketing message. How can the company put together the above elements, especially the problem, solution, benefits, advantage, and proof, to compel people to learn more. What is the call to action? What is the headline?

Guarantee or pledge. What kind of guarantee or pledge can the company offer to give comfort and reduce the perceptions of risk that potential buyers might experience?

Story. What is the history of the company? How can the company's unique story be used as a marketing tool?

Elevator pitch. What is a 30-second statement that tells people what the company does and its benefits?

Tagline. What's a concise tagline that captures the company's primary benefits or edge?

Logo. What would be the best logo to capture the essence of the company?

Help the Business Owner Build Leverage

At this point, your clients are making excellent progress in controlling their key business metrics and making improvements, while also keeping their strategy and aspirations in focus.

Now they are ready to build a business that runs without them. The three main benefits of doing this are as follows:

- The client will have more time.

- The business will be set to grow and make more money for your client.

- The business will be worth more money when the client is ready to sell it.

To build leverage, most business owners need to do what Michael Gerber advises in his *E-Myth* series of books: Stop working in the business, and start working on it. In other words, most business owners are technicians, not CEOs. Your clients have to start thinking more like CEOs and less like technicians.

To be successful, they need to work on the following leverage points:

- Generate the attitude of an effective CEO.

- Use time more effectively.

- Develop an organizational structure of roles who work "in the business."

- Recruit talent who are accountable for meeting objectives in their role.

- Develop routine processes with standards.

- Develop repeatable systems to get consistent results.

- Use technology wherever possible to automate routine functions.

- Build a team that is aligned, involved, and motivated.

- Continue to evolve the owner's role to a leader who sets overall direction, motivates, attracts and retains talent, continuously raises the bar, and builds the business the way a CEO would.

Let's look at each.

Leverage Point #1: Generate the attitude of an effective CEO

To effectively grow a business that runs without them, your clients will need six attitudes. Take time to explain these attitudes, and ask these questions:

- Which attitudes do you need to change?

- How does this attitude express itself in your work and with others?

- What are the costs of this attitude? What will the business look like if you don't change it?

- Are you willing to change it (many business owners are not, and this precludes serious business growth)?

- What is possible if you change the attitude?

- What behaviors will change if you have this attitude?

- What support do you need to change this attitude?

- Would you rather have results or [insert the attitude and its payoffs here]?

The attitudes are:

- **Commitment to taking massive action.** "Massive action" is a term borrowed from Tony Robbins. It means that the business owner takes action way beyond ordinary to achieve a result. This kind of action requires a serious commitment to achieving one's aspirations and goals. It means that when the competitor is home watching television, your client is focused on growing the business. When the last employee has gone home, your client is working on developing systems and processes to make the business run on its own. Massive action is required because your clients will hit a point of having one foot in the door as a "technician" working in the business and one foot in the door while transitioning to work on the business. Until the client makes the transition, there will be more work.

- **Control over the ego and desire for status.** Many business owners don't want to turn over the business to others. They want to be the hero coming in every day and fighting fires. Until the business owner realizes that results are more important than being the key man or woman, the business will not reach the next level.

- **Trust.** "No one can do it as well as me," is what many business owners think. They may be right, but that is no excuse. The business owner needs to recruit talent who can do the job and then support that talent with key performance indicators/standards, processes, training, and coaching until they get the job right. If brain surgery is a trainable skill, so is almost any other business role.

- **Ability to take risks and deal with imperfect information.** Some business owners fear anything other than the status quo. Things are good now, so why fix it if it isn't broken? Similarly, many business owners want 100% complete and perfect information before making a decision, which leads to analysis paralysis. Unfortunately, if a business isn't growing or improving, it is dying (or the competitors are circling to kill it). Business owners need to get outside their comfort zone and take risks to grow the business and create leverage. They are either serious about making change or they are serious about stagnating.

- **Willingness to be unpopular and face conflict.** Building leverage means working with people to get things done. This means confronting people with your expectations, how they do and don't meet those expectations, and what performance you expect in the future. Business owners need to be comfortable with conflict to have these conversations. In building leverage, they will need respect but not popularity.

- **The right balance of monitoring vs. need to control**. If business owners don't step in from time to time to monitor results and insist on higher standards or changes, they are really just abdicating authority. Abdication is not acceptable, but neither is micromanagement and too much control, which will prevent employees from developing or feeling empowered to think on their own. The business owner needs to find the right balance between micromanagement and abdication, which begins with an attitude that might be called "controlled surrender" or "interested detachment."

As a coach, you will constantly bring your clients back to these attitudes. Almost any hurdle they face in developing leverage will start with having an attitude that gets in the way and keeps others from doing their job effectively.

Leverage Point #2: Time

To convince business owners that they are working in the business and to help them determine if they are spending their time optimally, it is very helpful to assign a time study to your clients.

There are two types of time studies you can do, and the second one is more accurate.

First, they can estimate the top activities they do each day and each week as a percentage of time.

Second—and this is preferred—they should record how they spend their time every day for a week, at 15-minute intervals. A simple journal might look like this:

Time	Activity

Once you have this data, compile it to understand exactly how your clients spend their time. How much time is spent "in" the business as more of an employee instead of "on" it as a true CEO? (Note: Michael Gerber of the *E-Myth* book series is the one who came up with this distinction of in vs. on.) Categorize each task based on the following questions:

- "In": Someone else (or a computer) could be trained to do this, and the activity is not building on leverage (e.g., answering customer phone calls, taking orders, making the product, shipping the product, tactical marketing, selling, working with suppliers, bookkeeping).

- "On": This is a leadership/CEO task that only I should do (e.g., setting standards, setting directions, reviewing ideas from employees, developing or reviewing projections, recruiting and retaining top talent).

At the same time, ask the client these questions for each task:

- Did this task have to be done at all?

- Could this task be delegated?

- Did it have to be done right then, or could it have been deferred?

- Did it have to be done as perfectly as it was done, or was there a way to do it in less time that was "good enough"?

- Would a routine process help to make sure this task is done efficiently and consistently every time according to set standards?

Next, take a look at how many hours each day and week the client is putting into the business. Ask clients how many hours they want to put into the business and how they would spend extra time.

Finally, ask clients to develop an allocation of their time to build the business rather than continue to work in it.

For instance, let's say a computer programmer wants to expand the business. His current allocation of time might look like this:

Activity	Percentage of Time
Coding	60%
Client proposals	10%
Client billing	5%
Answering client phone calls	10%
Business development	15%
Total Time Per Day:	12 Hours

Working with him, you might discover that his vision is to grow his firm to be a leader in programming in his region. To do that, he realizes that he needs to spend his time in new ways and reduce his daily "grind" from 12 hours to 10 hours per day:

Activity	Percentage of Time
Recruiting and training programmers	30%
Recruiting and leading a sales force	30%
Recruiting and leading a marketing and administrative team	20%
Nurturing top client relationships	10%
Getting visible in the community	10%
Total Time Per Day:	10 Hours

Now he has a vision of where he wants to take his firm and how he will spend his time in the future.

Of course, he now faces a tricky situation. He has to simultaneously handle current clients while evolving to the new model. Perhaps step one is that he hires one salesperson and one new programmer (who can take over his current clients) while he continues to handle client billing. From there, he can continue to grow the business by developing programming methodologies and systems, creating a marketing process and system, and recruiting additional talent.

Remind your clients that priorities show up in action. Someone who says he wants to lose weight and spends time sitting and watching television instead of working out and also spends time at fast-food restaurants instead of preparing salads has not made losing weight a serious priority. Similarly, if the client is not spending time on ways to build leverage in his business, then leverage is not (yet) a priority for him

Finally, reassure your clients that understanding how they use their time is only one step in the process. The other points of leverage show how to actually shift one's time to more valuable business-building activities!

Leverage Point #3: Organizational Structure

To begin developing organizational capacity and leverage, your clients need to have a solid understanding of how they will structure their company.

A typical organizational chart lays out various positions or functions, including CEO, Finance and Accounting, Marketing, Operations/ Production, Human Resources, Selling, Procurement, and Technology.

In most small organizations, a few, and sometimes only one, owner(s) wear all of these hats. They often find themselves burning out while trying to do several different jobs. For the owners to create leverage, they need to assign other people to key functions in the organization, whether by hiring employees or engaging contractors/part-time help.

During one of your coaching sessions, challenge your client to draw the ideal organizational chart for the business. Tell that person not to worry about who is in the business but instead to focus on the functions that need to get done.

Next, work with the client to develop a capacity plan. At what revenue milestone will the client be ready and willing to hire people to fill the chart? In what sequence? Generally, it makes sense to start with commission-only (or low base pay) salespeople. As the sales force grows revenue, more people can be added, but sometimes there is a catch-22, and the owner needs to invest in hiring key people before cash flow from sales justifies it. You need to let your clients make up their own mind about when to fill the slots on their chart. The cost of not hiring capacity is that the owner will continue to spend time working "in" the business, which will lead to eventual burnout with a business that is not worth as much as it could otherwise be worth.

At the same time, most clients will have worries and fears about hiring people. The most common fear is that they can't find good help they can trust. Let the owner know that this may be true, and that it is common to have to invest in people who sometimes leave or don't work out, but in an upcoming section, you will learn how to help your clients get the right people on board.

A second problem with midsize firms is that they have convoluted organization structures. For instance, a restaurant chain might hold restaurant managers responsible for traffic and yet might not give them the authority to manage their own marketing budget (e.g., a centralized corporate marketing function does the marketing). Likewise, some family businesses create positions for family members who do not really pull their own weight. Similarly, in some organizations, some employees report to so many managers that they feel pulled in different directions. Your role in such situations is to help simplify the organization chart. Focus on the "what," i.e., the roles that need to be in place for success. Then work on the "who" later.

Leverage Point #4: Talent

Once business owners know who needs to be on board, they can begin to recruit, train, and develop talent. Jack Welch of General Electric used to say that his number one job was finding and motivating top talent. Jim Collins' books *Built to Last* and *Good to Great* talk about the need to get the right employee on the right seat on the bus.

Every business owner must do certain things well to recruit, train, and develop talent, and your coaching can cover these areas.

- **Get the right people on board in the right place.** Placing standard classified ads is not enough to find good people. To get top people, your clients need to do the following:

    - Find top people through referrals, by defining the type of talent and passion they need, and telling their network about it. Have your best employees and trusted colleagues source candidates from their network.

    - Place ads that focus on passion, excellence, or other values that the company has. Don't just list a basic job description. Have a headline that tells people you want passion for your industry or their function.

    - Make candidates work to get an interview. It is too easy today to send resumes to hundreds of potential employers. Your clients don't have the time or need to sift through junk applications. You want to let unqualified people weed themselves out, while the truly enthusiastic applicants get through. Therefore, coach clients to do the following:

        - Get a recorded phone line that asks candidates to leave a message talking about their background, why they want the job, at least one thing that sets them apart, and their contact information.

- Ask the best ones to submit a resume and references. Check the references.

- Have a quick screening interview by telephone with successful candidates

- Invite the remaining candidates in to a "Super Tuesday" (or whatever day of the week) recruiting day. Your client can set aside a single day to hold interviews. Candidates can rotate to meet each manager, complete an observed team assignment or case study, and even make presentations in front of the business owner and other candidates about why they are the best choice for the job.

- During interviews, ask candidates to tell stories that demonstrate their talent, passion, and times when they have made a difference with their talents and skills. Look for specific results, not just tasks.

- The above process is standard practice in top-tier consulting firms and is proven to find the "best of the best."

- Make offers on the spot so that candidates don't have to wait

- Follow up with unsuccessful applicants to thank them for their time.

- Become known as one of the top employers in your area so that you are a "magnet" for top talent.

- **Provide appropriate training.** Even if the business owner has a small business, they can and should still provide outstanding training. The owners can even start a corporate university, just as large corporations do. Training should include detailed instructions about expectations, processes, standards, and best practices. The business owner or top employees should train staff to emphasize the importance of training, which should include time for employees to add their own suggestions; for instance, one company requires new hires to submit one idea for improving something in the company within a week of their start date.

- **Make sure everyone know what is expected of them and has the authority to succeed.** Every employee should have a contract that details the following:

  - Responsibilities.

  - The metrics that will determine their success. Every employee should be focused on at least one and up to five performance metrics. Ideally, these metrics tie to revenue and profit growth and can also include quality, customer satisfaction, and response time, among others. Include details about how often the employee will be measured against these metrics.

  - The authority the employee has and does not have. Authority must match responsibilities and metrics. Nothing is worse than having responsibility without authority!

  - A clear line of accountability that specifies who will oversee the employee.

  - Bonuses that the employee receives for achieving metrics and goals.

- **Provide ongoing development.** Develop a curriculum for ongoing professional development for every employee. In addition, make sure that managers sit down with employees at least every six months to create a development plan for the employee. The development plan should specify.

  - Key competencies required in the job.

  - Development needs of the employee.

  - Tactics to address the need (e.g., training, new assignment, volunteer work, mentorship).

  - Date to reassess.

- **Provide constant feedback.** Employees want to know if they are meeting expectations. Too many managers defer feedback until the annual performance review, which leads to surprises and frustration. It is much better to focus on "teachable moments" when you can acknowledge the employee for a great job or use a specific situation to correct behaviors and get back on track.

- **Create a sense of team and lead!** Employees look to the business owner to provide leadership. The next section, along with your Center for Executive Coaching program, provides details about how to coach business owners to build teams and lead effectively.

An exercise you can do with your clients is to have them list every employee and then assess that person based on the following questions:

- On a scale of 1 to 10, how well is this person performing in his or her current position?

- On a scale of 1 to 10, how much leadership potential does this person have? Could he or she take over a piece of the company at some point? The whole company?

- Is the employee in the top 25%, top 50%, bottom 50%, or bottom 25% in terms of performance?
    - If the employee is in the top 75%, what is the plan to challenge, develop, reward, and retain that employee? Which employees that the company values might be "flight risks"? What is the plan to keep them on board?
    - If the employee is in the bottom 50%, what is the plan to get that employee to perform better, move him or her to a more suitable position, or transition him or her out of the company?

Illustrative Assessment of Employees

Name	Performance (1 to 10)	Leadership (1 to 10)	Percentile	Plan

Leverage Point #5: Processes

To genuinely build leverage, every business needs to standardize the most common processes. While every process will have exceptions, business owners should still do their best to make routine 80% of the tasks that go into a specific process. An old classic to read to get more information about process design is *Reengineering the Corporation*. Another excellent book about process redesign in a manufacturing setting is *The Goal*.

Here is how to help your clients document their processes:

- Have your clients identify their most important processes. These have a set start and end and result in an end product. Examples include handling a customer call, manufacturing a process, taking an order, shipping an order, starting a new project, bidding on a project, setting a restaurant table, prepping food, opening the store, closing the store, making a sales call, hiring staff, on boarding staff, and more.

- Choose one process.

- Map out the way the process should happen from start to finish. Specify what gets done. Don't worry so much about how the process is done now. Focus on the right way to do things.

  - Wherever possible, minimize handoffs to new people and locations. The fewer people touching a process, the fewer errors

  - Balance the process so that the slowest steps take place first. The process has fewer bottlenecks (large bottlenecks mean more room for errors).

  - Add resources to steps in the process that have bottlenecks to balance the process.

  - Use automation wherever possible to routinize tasks.

- Consider ways that new technology can simplify the process.

- Specify where each step in the process should happen and who is accountable.

- Set specific, measurable standards for each step in the process and the end result based on what the customer of the process (even internal customers) expect, including:

  - Time for completion (from the end user's point of view)

  - Time to hand things off (AGAIN: handoffs should be minimized, as they are one of the largest sources of errors

  - Error rates

  - Allowable waste

  - Quality indicators

  - Cost

- Develop instructions to ensure that things get done right the first time. In relative terms, it costs $.01 to fix something before a process starts, $.10 to fix something in the middle of the process, and $1.00 to fix something at the end of a process.

- Assign someone to own the process.

- Measure and improve the process. Track complaints related to the process over time, and systematically improve the process until things are done right 100% of the time.

- Raise standards over time.

- Repeat with the next process.

Until your clients have documented their most important processes, they will not be able to train staff, make consistent improvements, or have a firm with intellectual property and systems that makes it valuable. Keep pushing your clients to map out at least one new process each week.

Many clients will suggest that they have consistent processes in place. A little research can quickly find out if they are telling the truth. For instance, I visited a client restaurant that thought they provided great service. When I sat down for a meal, this was my experience: it took ten minutes to get water and a menu, it took twenty minutes to get bread, I got a different dish than I ordered, I was "handled" by three different wait staff, and my food was overcooked and dry.

If you can't mystery shop the business yourself, insist that you interview some customers about service and quality. You will find out how the business is perceived in the market and how well it delivers what it promises.

WARNING #1: In an ideal world, processes should be set up to make the business owner redundant. Unfortunately, this almost never happens. Business owners must not abdicate responsibility for monitoring the business once processes are in place. They must still roll up their sleeves and make sure that employees are meeting standards.

WARNING #2: Don't let your client go overboard with "manual mania"! Too many procedures per employee will lead to confusion. For instance, we recently saw a television show about a beauty salon with a 200-page manual that every stylist had to master to know what to say to a client and when. The consultant hired to turn this salon around immediately ripped up these manuals. They were simply too confusing for the stylists, who couldn't keep track of everything in them, weren't interested in memorizing scripts (they wanted to style hair!), and were savvy enough to know that a manual couldn't cover every interaction with a sophisticated client. When left to improvise with clients, the stylists were excellent at putting clients at ease and being professional. A lead stylist was able to monitor consultations and the general work in the salon and make sure that conversations were productive. Use common sense! Sometimes procedures get in the way, and sometimes they are crucial.

Leverage Point #6: Systems

A business needs repeatable systems or ways of doing things on an ongoing basis to generate results for the business. Examples of systems include:

- A marketing system that has the business repeat set marketing tactics on a regular schedule.

- A selling system that follows a set process to close new business.

- A procurement system that gets the right amount of inventory of supplies when the business needs it and at the best price and quality.

- A billing system that collects receivables on time.

- A system to maintain equipment and technology on a regular basis.

- A hiring system to find top talent.

- A training system to develop that talent.

- A reward and recognition system to acknowledge and thank top talent, while removing people who are not achieving their performance goals.

- A system to get financial data on time.

- A management system to give feedback to talent.

The more systems your client has in place, the less time they have to spend reinventing the wheel. There is obvious overlap between systems and processes, but don't worry so much about this overlap. Just make sure that your client is thinking about ways to systematize everything possible in the business so that it is repeatable, has set activities happening at set times, and is as routine and "idiot proof" as possible.

Leverage Point #7: Technology

Technology is available to assist for almost every business task. Take time during a coaching session to develop an action plan to identify, research, and implement time and money-saving technology.

Each industry has its own technology, and you can rely on your clients to be up-to-date on technology that can help their business. At the same time, use this list to jog their mind:

- Technology to make ordering easier.

- Technology to make billing easier.

- Customer Relationship Management systems to keep track of customers.

- Contact management technology.

- Point of sale technology for retail stores and restaurants.

- Computer-based machines for manufacturing.

- Shipping automation (e.g., postal meters, in-house FedEx software and processing).

- Shipment processing software to batch and process shipments.

- Electronic medical records (for medical practices).

- Accounting software (such as QuickBooks).

- Online banking, bill processing, and downloads to accounting software (e.g., Bank of America).

- Online payroll processing.

- Bar code scanning for inventory control and supply chain management.

- Tax software.

- Online meetings.

- Online payment processing.

- Automated check depositing.

- Online ordering from vendors.

- Automatic ordering.

- Human resource management systems to track applications, track performance reviews, and track employee information.

- Auto-responders to automatically stay in touch with customers and prospects.

- Contact databases and email systems, such as Constant Contact, to create graphically pleasing email newsletters and broadcasts

- Online calendars and scheduling.

Sometimes technology makes sense as an investment, and sometimes it doesn't. As the coach, you can be a sounding board to help the client make smart choices.

Leverage Point #8: Team

Ultimately, success in business comes down to every employee being aligned and working as a team. As a coach, you can survey employees to assess how well they understand the business direction, feel involved, and feel that they are part of a high-performance team. At the same time, the *Wisdom of Teams* by Katzenbach is a great book to read to get up to speed on the best thinking about teams.

Assess your client to make sure they are doing the following things to promote teamwork:

- Clearly stating the direction the client taking the company.

- Setting clear outcomes and objectives for the company and every employee.

- Communicating frequently with every employee about results, changes, new ideas, and new directions.

- Integrating new employees onto the team. Don't just give new hires a handbook and a desk with a phone. Create some fanfare when a new employee joins. Make sure they leave the first week knowing everybody they need to know to succeed, that they are energized, that they know the company's values, and that they feel part of a special business.

- Involving employees in generating new ideas, giving input about company direction, and suggesting improvements.

- Clearly letting employees know how they are doing and what they can do better, not just during annual reviews but at least weekly and during "teachable moments."

- Cross-training employees so that teammates can cover for each other.

- Giving employees the authority to handle exceptions and do what they need to do to meet their metrics.

- Encouraging risks and failure. For any company to grow, it has to take risks, which means that employees need to take risks too. Ideally, the client has created an environment that allows employees to take risks and make mistakes (so long as an employee doesn't repeat the same mistake over and over again).

- Providing time for employees to meet, get to know each other, and bond.

If your clients have the right structure, right people, right processes, right systems, right technology, and right team in place, they can focus on leading the business in the right direction. They can stop working in the business and start building the value of the enterprise.

Leverage Point #9: Leadership

Once your client has made progress with the other eight points of leverage, the coaching can focus on leadership. In fact, it will be hard to avoid the subject of leadership throughout this coaching process.

Leadership means:

- Setting and communicating strategic direction and goals so that everyone in the company understands and is on board. Ideally, clients involve their teams in providing input and dialog about direction and what the company should do best.

- Continuing to recruit, train, and retain top talent, and developing them to be able to take over the company or a piece of the company

- Reviewing the numbers to make sure the business is achieving its goals and involving the team to make midcourse directions

- Trusting others to get the job done, based on processes with standards and job descriptions with specific performance metrics

- Providing coaching and mentoring to top talent, directing people who need new skills (or having someone else direct them), and removing people who are not performing or are not a good fit with the culture.

- Creating the culture by modeling the company's values and expectations for professionalism and excellence.

- Raising standards.

- Finding someone who can take over as CEO. This is the hardest part of leadership, but every business owner should be working to groom and develop internal candidates for the CEO role. The best scenario is one in which two or three people compete for the role and have specific goals to meet to be chosen.

Ask your clients to describe their job description as a leader. Then go back to how they have historically spent their time and how they will need to spend their time in the future. Are they doing what they need to do to fulfill their job description?

The Evolution of the Business Owner

Most of the coaching up to this point is designed to make sure the business evolves. The final step now turns to ensuring that the business owner keeps evolving too.

For businesses, evolution relates to constantly improving strategy, operations, financials, and the value of the business.

For business owners, evolution means continuous learning and development, especially in areas related to being a better business manager and leader.

There are many ways to help the business owner evolve as a leader. First, all of the coaching you do with the leader to improve the business will come back to how well your client leads. As things come up, you have the opportunity to explore what holds your clients back and strengths they can build upon to be better.

Second, at a certain point in the coaching, you might implement a behavior and/or perceptual coaching process as described previously in this book.

Finally, every three to six months or so, you can sit down with your clients and have them complete their personalized professional development plan, which can be set up in many different ways. You can start with a 360-degree feedback process, assessment, and Leader's Dashboard, as described in other parts of this book. You can also create a custom plan. For instance, one approach is to work with your clients to define how they will improve in the following areas:

- A better attitude or attitudes
- New skills to be a better manager and leader

- Greater knowledge about business, a specific industry, and key technical or functional aspects of the business

- Increasing their network, business relationships, and overall sphere of influence.

Examples:

Attitudes	Skills	Knowledge	Network
professionalism positivity resilience creativity innovation relationship building competitiveness comfort with conflict responsibility accountability focus	influence selling generating leads networking business writing proposal writing managing time communication computer software motivating others holding people accountable coaching mentoring business decision-making running meetings recruiting top talent	industry analysis competitive analysis trends in technology marketing finance legal issues human resources process redesign business analytic tools accounting strategic thinking	join business and industry associations get on a nonprofit board get on a committee at an association join social and community service clubs reach out to school alumni volunteer on a government advisory committee

Have your client fill in the following form to develop a plan:

Area to Improve	Specific Improvement	Expected Benefit / Result	By When	How to Improve
Attitudes				
Skills				
Knowledge				
Network				
Other				

Special Cases in Business Coaching

As a business coach, you will come across a number of special cases that you need to handle. The most common include:

- Conflicts between two partners
- Conflicts that come up in family businesses (which make up a significant percentage of our economy)
- Whether or not to bring in an investor/equity partner
- How to handle slow economic times
- Investment decisions
- Opportunities to acquire another company
- Exiting the business

Here are some pointers on effective ways to deal with each situation.

Conflicts between two partners. Two or more partners often have conflicts at some point in any business. For instance, one partner may be a visionary, while another might be focused more on details. The two might develop resentments because the visionary is thinking long term, while the other gets stuck fighting fires. Similarly, one partner might lose interest in the business and want to move on. Third, it is common for one partner to have more ambitious goals for growth than the other partner, and this can lead to conflict. You can provide valuable mediation to these partners.

The key for any partnership is that both partners contribute equally to the business and especially to the equity value of the business. If one partner is not pulling their weight, it might be time to leave the business. Similarly, if partners have different visions for the business, it might be time for a split.

Ideally, you can help partners see each other's point of view and mediate a solution to keep the business progressing. In many respects, you are like a marriage counselor in this situation. As in a marriage, it is costly, complicated, confusing, and disruptive to everyone involved when the relationship ends in a divorce. Sometimes "divorce" in business is the best solution, but often you can help the partners redefine their relationship and continue to work together to improve the business.

Key questions to ask include:

- Where does each partner want to take the business? Are their visions compatible? If not, is one partner willing to accept and build upon the other's vision?

- Does each partner think the other is pulling his or her own weight? If not, why not, and what can be done to meet expectations?

- What are the talents of each partner? What are ideal roles for each partner? What talents and roles does the business need, and is there a match between the talents and the desired roles of each partner? (If not, maybe a buyout is in order, or maybe the partners need to agree upon new roles and goals for each other.)

- How can both partners better understand each other's communication style and accept it?

- What requests does each partner have for the other?

Interview each partner separately, and then bring them together for discussion. Your role is to make sure each partner listens to the other, understands the other partner's position, and tries to come up with constructive alternatives to make progress.

If partners decide to split, your role is to ask key questions to make the split amicable before attorneys get involved. Questions include:

- What do the original operating agreement and articles of incorporation say about a split?

- How will the business be appraised to arrive at a fair price?

- What are the payment terms to buy out the partner (e.g., time period, interest rate, payment, earnout based on key numbers being reached)?

- How long will the exiting partner remain at the business before leaving to ensure a smooth transition?

- Will the exiting partner retain any equity in the business or sell their entire interest?

- What collateral will the exiting partner have if the remaining partner(s) don't pay?

- Can the exiting partner start or join a competitive venture? For how long? In what market?

- Can the exiting partner use or own any intellectual property or other assets of the business? In what ways?

- Can the exiting partner take clients or recruit employees?

- Can the exiting partner work with vendors of the company?

Conflicts that come up in family businesses. The majority of businesses in the USA are family owned, but family businesses can be messy affairs. They come with lots of baggage, including jealousy, resentment, and entitlement among various members of the family. Issues include family members who don't carry their own weight, differences in risk tolerance, differences in ethics, differences in willingness to pay out cash vs. investing it back into the business, treating family and nonfamily fairly (or recruiting nonfamily members into key business roles), and determining who will succeed the founder or current business CEO.

You can provide extremely valuable advice by helping separate family issues from business issues. Questions to ask include:

- What is the outcome you want to achieve with this issue? Forgetting the people involved, what are the key action steps and roles needed to achieve this outcome? Who needs to be accountable, and for what metrics? Who is best suited to achieve these goals and be accountable?

- Do all family members have clear roles and accountable for clear metrics? If not, how can you create clear roles and accountability? What happens if a family member fails to perform and meet his or her goals or is not accountable? When is it okay to terminate a family member who isn't carrying his or her weight? Is this the same way a nonfamily member would be treated? If not, why not?

- Are all family members involved in the business now really needed? What is the ideal organizational structure for the business? What are the talents and ideal roles for participating family members? What are the gaps where outside professionals need to be recruited? Which family members really aren't contributing to the business or don't have a clearly defined role and should transition out?

- For conflicts: What does each party in the conflict think about the issue and how to resolve it? Is there a middle ground so that everyone wins?

- How will a new successor be chosen to take over the reins of the business from the current CEO?

Whether to bring in an investor/equity partner. Some business owners jump too quickly into a partnership or equity investment.

Equity is expensive to give away and should only be given in exchange for lasting contributions to the value of the company. When business owners trades cash for equity, they give up control, have to manage the new investor's expectations, have potential liabilities and lawsuit risk, and complicate their business.

Also, different investors bring different benefits to the party. A one-time investment from friends and family is not worth as much as an investment from a well-connected, seasoned business professional or strategic partner. Plus, investments from friends and family almost always come with strings, including a high risk of seriously damaging the relationship if the investment capital is not returned.

Your role is to ask your clients what they are giving up in exchange for investment and whether or not it is worth it today, in a year, in five years, and in a decade. Make sure they consider the downside risk of taking the investment and whether or not they can find alternative ways to raise capital (e.g., from key customers, debt capital, or by slowing growth).

Also, make sure your client is getting a good deal. What kind of return is the investor expecting? How does he or she value the company three and five years down the road? If an investor is willing to invest $100,000 in a company and expects a 25% return every year, that person will expect the investment to grow to $125,000 after one year, $156,250 after two years, and $305,176 after five years. If the investor believes that the company will be worth $1 million after five years, that person will expect to own 30.5% of the company in exchange for a $100,000 investment ($305,176/$1 million). However, if the business owner believes the company will be worth $2 million after five years, then that person will only be willing to give up 15% of the company in exchange for a $100,000 investment, assuming that a 25% return is considered reasonable.

How to handle slow economic times. The best way to handle slow economic times is by building up cash reserves and business credit during good times. Cash becomes a competitive advantage during slow times. Encourage your clients to live a conservative lifestyle and keep money in the business so that they are ready for the natural downturn in any economic cycle. This is especially true for highly cyclical businesses—construction and housing, luxury items (boats, SUVs, exotic travel), and consumer products and services.

At the same time, make sure your clients have processes in place to provide consistent service to clients. They can then rely on clients' loyalty for repeat business and referrals during down times.

Once slow times come, your clients need to be prepared to work harder than any competitor to win their share of a shrinking pie. If in good times they invested one unit of effort to get back one unit of results, now they need to be prepared to invest five to ten units of effort to get back one unit of results. This is especially true for marketing initiatives.

Tips include:

- Make sure everybody in the organization is prepared to work extra hard to generate business.

- Focus on existing customers. Delight them and work to increase revenues from your current customer base.

- Ask current customers for referrals.

- Put your marketing efforts on "manual" instead of automatic. Visit customers and nurture the relationship. Let people know how much you appreciate their business.

- Do not cut marketing costs. Companies that advertise during down times build perception as strong players in the market, but you should continue to test and refine your marketing programs to improve your cost per order.

- Use down times as an opportunity to be contrarian. Buy out competitors. Build capacity (e.g., Intel is famous for building chip capacity during slow times to emerge ready to handle demand during good times). Just be sure to preserve cash.

- Get rid of all nonperforming employees.

- Use the downturn as an opportunity to identify high-potential employees. Reward them for their contributions when good times return.

- Streamline processes and focus on delighting customers with consistent service and results.

- Help struggling customers improve their business.

- Approach vendors for improved terms.

Investment decisions. Suppose your client asks you if they should invest $100,000 in a new piece of equipment. How would you help them answer the question? You need to consider many separate issues:

First, what is the hard dollar return of the new piece of equipment? How long will it take for the company to pay back its investment? What percentage return does that represent? (Similarly, if instead of equipment the owner is considering hiring a new salesperson, the same questions still apply. How long will it take for the salesperson to earn back their salary? How much will the salesperson have to sell every year, month, and week?).

Second, what are the soft returns of the new piece of equipment? How much time is saved? How will customers benefit?

Third, are there ways to spend the $100,000 that can generate better returns?

Fourth, has the client considered all costs required to make the investment? For instance, some capital equipment requires extensive remodeling of a plant (e.g., increasing the load capacity of the floor). Others come with expensive annual fees and high preventive and replacement maintenance costs. What about energy costs, environmental risks, government requirements like licensing or permits for new construction, and the need for training?

Fifth, what is the downside? Too many business owners fail to consider the downside risk of an investment. What can go wrong? What if it takes twice as long to generate returns, and those returns are half as much as expected? What if the equipment costs twice as much as anticipated? What if production is delayed or stopped during installation or additional investments are required to make the new equipment compatible with the rest of the company's equipment or technology?

Help your client anticipate all risks, and develop a conservative, medium, and ambitious scenario for any major investment. Also help them prioritize which investments are most critical for helping the company compete and win in the market.

Opportunities to acquire another company. Most acquisitions fail to achieve results. The reason for failure has nothing to do with financial analysis. Rather, mergers typically fail because two very different cultures with very different values and operating procedures usually mix like oil and water.

As a business coach, you provide invaluable service in assessing the cultures involved in a merger by asking these questions.

- Would you define each entity as entrepreneurial, collaborative, bureaucratic, or dog eat dog? How different are the cultures?

- How does each entity reward success?\

- How does each entity compete? Are the operating models too different to make for a sound merger?

- How does each entity define excellent performance?

- How different are the clients/customers and decision makers who buy from each entity?

- Will the executive teams of each entity be willing and able to collaborate? What about the two CEOs? Who is the "dominant" CEO in the merger?

- Does each entity have significant strengths that will benefit the other?

- What might cause conflicts among the employees of each entity? How can these be addressed?

- Who are the flight risks if a merger happens? Which key people will probably leave because their roles are redundant or they can "cash out"?

- What is the transition plan to ensure a smooth merger? How long is the plan? What will be the communication plan?

- How will employees be trained on the capabilities of the other entity?

- What is the new organizational structure? Will each of the "boxes" and "silos" really communicate and work together? What can be done to make sure they do?

For more complex situations, a previous chapter in this book covers mergers in more depth.

Exiting the business. Finally, the dream of just about every business owner is to sell the company to a larger company for a huge price and then retire comfortably.

The work you do as a business coach will help your clients' companies put into place the structures they need to prepare for a sale.

If, however, your client wants to exit the business, you can help in other ways as well. For instance:

- Be sure the company has all of its processes and systems documented.

- Make sure all employees have employment agreements in place, including non-competes.

- Have clean financial records, including auditable expense receipts and payroll documents.

- Have all assets clearly documented.

- Have an employee policy manual that every employee has read and signed.

- Have detailed position and job descriptions.

- Document all performance reviews at least annually.

- Most importantly, make sure the owner is not needed to run the business. No one wants to buy a business that depends on the former owner.

- Help the owner be clear and realistic about the price he or she expects for the business. Too many owners use publicly traded NYSE comparables to value their company (e.g., 18 times earnings). Small and midsized private companies rarely sell for anything close to that multiple. Rather, typical valuations start at one to three times "owner's benefit" or the annual benefit (income, health benefits, travel and entertainment, car allotment, dues and memberships) that the owner receives from the business; the price often includes financing and an earnout or a payout if the new owner achieves certain milestones. You can also form an alliance with a business brokerage in your area so that you have resources for your client when it comes time to sell. The brokerage can give you some rules of thumb for valuing the business and help you assess how easy it will be to sell the business when the owner is ready.

During your coaching meetings with a client who wants to sell, set a timeline for selling and develop a detailed work plan with the client to get comfortable with a selling price and get the company "in shape" for sale. If you can, identify likely businesses or investment groups (e.g., private equity) that might like to purchase the company.

Finally, note that if owners have followed your coaching, they should have plenty of free time while other people run the business. They might enjoy taking in cash while spending time on other things. Alternatively, they could take out a large loan using cash flow from the business as collateral and enjoy the proceeds of the loan tax free while the company pays down the loan over time. Once the loan is paid off, they can repeat the process and enjoy another tax-free windfall. In other words, they may never have to sell the business. Once they have freed themselves from working in the business, they can continue to own it and enjoy the leverage—and cash flow—that they have created.

A Typical Business Coaching Agenda and Flow

Now that you understand what the coach covers with clients, here is an agenda for a typical 50-minute coaching session:

- Get an update about what is new in the business. New customers? New products? New insights? New marketing results? New hires? New issues?
- Once the client has a system in place to collect the key numbers, review them.
- Review any homework and discuss it.
- Choose one of two options:
    - If there is a pressing issue to discuss, handle that.
    - Introduce a new topic.
- Assign homework to help the client grasp the new topic, or set goals for the next session based on a current issue.
- Ask them what they got out of the session.
- In between the sessions, fax the client some reading materials for the next session, along with an inspirational quote or some encouraging words.

Note that your conversations will shift with the client over time. Initially, you will spend lots of time introducing new concepts and helping the client get in control of the numbers. Once you have gone through the entire CASTLE model with a client, you shift to working on building leverage while ensuring that the client maintains control of the key numbers (and they show improvement). You also spend more time on current issues.

A client should never leave you. Always find a new aspiration that the client has, and work on that with them. An evolving business is a strong business. When owners stop evolving or the business doesn't evolve, the business tends to stagnate, and competitors catch up. Keep challenging the client to improve.

At the same time, some clients may want to transition to a less intensive program after you help them make significant progress. After perhaps a year of coaching, you can decrease the frequency of meetings from weekly to biweekly and eventually monthly. After a year or two, transition clients to a Leadership Circle or to group coaching.

FINAL NOTE: GET YOUR CLIENT TO AGREE TO NEVER MAKE A MAJOR BUSINESS DECISION WITHOUT YOUR INPUT. YOU NEED TO ESTABLISH YOURSELF AS A KEY PERSON ON THEIR TEAM, LIKE THEIR BANKER OR EVEN SHADOW CEO. THEY ARE TO CONTACT YOU REGARDING ANY MARKETING CAMPAIGN, NEW HIRE, STRATEGIC CHANGE, PURCHASE OVER $1,000, NEW TECHNOLOGY, SPECIAL CONCESSION TO A CLIENT, ETC., ETC. YOU ABSOLUTELY NEED TO BE A KEY PERSON ON THE CLIENT'S TEAM, INVOLVED AS A SOUNDING BOARD FOR EVERY DECISION THE CLIENT MAKES!

Conclusion:

The Crucial, Deceptively Simple Leadership Skill
For Breakaway Performance

The purpose of this book was to demonstrate that coaching is a crucial, deceptively simple leadership skill for breakaway performance. I sincerely hope that you see the power of coaching.

It is crucial because it can help individuals, teams, and the entire organization shift to higher levels of performance. Coaching can turn a manager into a leader who develops leaders and sets up the organization for ongoing success.

It is deceptively simple because it takes practice to let your clients come to their own insights and take accountability for their development and performance. It is easy to slip into other roles that are not coaching and can get in the way of results. True coaching incorporates a bit of martial arts because the best coaches use the client's energy and ideas to help them be successful. They do less and get more.

Finally, coaching - done right - achieves breakaway performance. People in organizations, as well as solo professionals, achieve more when they have support, a sounding board, different perspectives, and the opportunity to think through issues. They also achieve more when they have an environment and process that lets them determine the best course of action for them to develop, achieve ambitious goals, and help the organization progress. Coaching creates that environment and provides that process.

You have now read numerous examples of ways that coaching can bring value. It helps individuals become more effective leaders through coaching on behaviors, perceptions, communication, focus, thinking, and time management. It helps leaders develop stronger relationships to make things happen with the help of others. It also can be a key component in accelerating organizational initiatives, from engaging employees to succession planning and leading change.

If you agree that coaching is powerful, your next step is to practice, practice, and practice some more. Get training to become a better coach. Find colleagues and practice coaching one another. Get a coaching mentor who will observe you in action or listen to recorded coaching conversations that you have. From there, keep encouraging other leaders and managers to master this skill.

It is worth the effort. One coach can help many people get better than they already are. Many coaches can transform an organization.

Addendum One

Seven Habits and a Five-Step Action Plan for a Culture of Success Through Coaching

Creating a culture of success through coaching is relatively simple in theory but hard to implement. This addendum defines what a culture of coaching means and then suggests the high-level action steps required. First, organizations with a culture of coaching have the following habits:

Employees at all levels are open to receiving feedback, input, and advice. In fact, they regularly request it from others. It is not easy to hear tough advice and feedback from others. Most leaders, managers, and employees don't do it well. While the guidelines for receiving feedback are straightforward and the type of skill that is taught in $99 hotel seminars (e.g., thank the other person, treat the advice as a gift, direct it in the way that is most valuable to you, and focus on the issue and not the personal), many people get defensive and are closed to receiving feedback professionally. A culture of coaching starts with employees at all levels being open to advice and feedback. In other words, they are coachable.

Actively strive to get better. Second, a culture of coaching is about mastery. Employees want to keep getting better. They keep raising the bar and demanding the best from themselves and each other. This trait requires an organization with attractive career paths and opportunities for growth and development.

Be willing to stop digging in your heels with stubborn and already known positions and instead conduct a deep, creative inquiry into root causes and innovative solutions. It is easy to have conversations about what's known. It is also easy to stubbornly stick to the same position about an issue so that the issue never gets resolved; for example, watch the political parties in the USA dig in their heels about crucial challenges for the country. In some organizations, employees roll their eyes before a colleague even speaks because they already know what he or she will say. Coaching is about having conversations about what's not known. It is about putting one's position aside and having a dialogue to go beyond rigid thinking and attitudes. Coaching challenges people to leave the past in the past; work together to create new ways of approaching problems; and balance relationships, results, and ego.

Use coaching along with other approaches to develop leaders to grow the organization. A culture of coaching is about developing new capacities in employees. New leaders keep emerging to grow the organization and also allow current leaders to continue to grow and develop in the most strategic ways possible. See the chapter about succession planning for an illustrative approach.

Get important conversations going. The book *Good to Great* by Jim Collins uses the metaphor of a flywheel to talk about one role of a leader. The leader's job is to ask crucial questions about what the organization does best, its values, and its purpose. As the conversations build, so does momentum, the way a flywheel takes a while to turn but eventually becomes a powerful force. A culture of coaching encourages employees to ask deep questions and work together to answer them while always leaving room for new insights and creative approaches.

Create the culture you want to have. A culture of success through coaching is only one aspect of an organization's culture, the same way that coaching is one skill that a manager should possess. Leadership still has to define the complete culture they want for the organization. A previous chapter discusses how to do this work.

Use coaching as a tool to help people get better and continuously improve the organization. Finally, in a culture of success through coaching, people coach each other to ongoing success. This can happen through formal coaching relationships with internal and external coaches, but most of the time it happens through ongoing dialogue with managers, colleagues, and employees. Everyone plays a coaching role.

Action steps to create this kind of culture include the following:

- Train senior leaders and managers to be effective coaches.

- Reward people for modeling coaching behaviors, especially when they solve key issues or develop top talent through coaching.

- Senior leaders need to model the coaching behavior they expect to see.

- Use coaching as a tool to create other aspects of the desired organizational culture.

- Use both internal and external coaches as one of many tools to help people develop.

As with any kind of culture change, the obvious but hard truth is that senior leadership needs to make coaching a priority and a focus. Otherwise, none of the above action steps matter.

Addendum Two

Eight Keys to Creating
a World-Class Internal Coaching Group

As coaching has become an accepted tool to develop talent, many organizations have created internal coaching groups. Internal coaches usually work with leaders just below the senior level, while senior leaders work with external coaches to ensure confidentiality about sensitive initiatives. In our experience at the Center for Executive Coaching, there are eight keys to success when creating an internal coaching group.

Make sure that senior leadership supports the internal coaching group. Senior leadership must view coaching as a crucial function in the organization. Ideally, every senior leader should have a coach to demonstrate how important it is to be coached. If senior leadership doesn't respect coaching or the internal group, neither will others in the organization.

Choose great people to be internal coaches. The U.S. Marine Corps chooses top marines to train new recruits. For a top-tier internal coaching group, insist on only the best people. Some organizations shift mediocre performers to the role of coach. As a result, they lack credibility, and employees don't want coaching from them. Whether you hire coaches from outside the organization or from within, make sure that they are highly respected.

Free up internal coaches to have the time to coach. Too often, internal coaches are given multiple responsibilities, from working on employee assistance to recruiting new candidates. Sometimes this is because it takes the coach time to transition to their new role from their previous job; unless employees make a clean break, they are often stuck straddling two different job descriptions. At other times, the organization doesn't give coaching enough respect and layers on multiple responsibilities. Regardless of the reason, these other obligations often crowd out the coach's ability to coach. If you are going to create an internal coaching group, free up internal coaches to coach full-time.

Don't include progressive discipline or employee assistance under the umbrella of coaching. Coaching is a privilege. It is an approach to make good people better. When organizations combine leadership development with such areas as progressive discipline or any other interventions for struggling employees, they do a disservice to the profession of coaching and what it can accomplish. Separate coaching from other activities. Coaching should focus on helping good people get even better.

Pick a few focused initiatives that are tied to the organization's strategic priorities. Don't set up your coaching group to be a call center to take a call and try to answer questions. Don't dabble in too many initiatives. Coaching should support major organizational initiatives in a focused way. Identify areas where the organization can make key improvements or accelerate progress, especially with strategic priorities. Perhaps certain employees need to develop new competencies to benefit the organization. Perhaps there is a key strategic initiative that has gotten stuck. Or, maybe specific types of people, such as high-potential managers, could make major improvements in their effectiveness that would drive stronger results and competitive positioning. Use coaching to advance these initiatives. That coaching is then tied directly to providing value as defined by the organization.

Use a consistent approach. Some internal coaching groups hire coaches who have been trained in many different ways, which leads to inconsistent results and impact. Choose a coaching methodology and approach, and insist that all coaches use it. At the same time, be flexible enough to test and incorporate new tools, assessments, and methodologies.

Tie coaching to other approaches for developing talent and strengthening the organization. Coaching, training, mentoring, and professional development should all fit together and work toward common goals. Sometimes coaching alone is the best approach. Coaching can often reinforce training programs or other organizational development initiatives. In some cases, a full-court press with multiple approaches is needed to get results.

Measure and track results, and hold the coaching group accountable for having impact in the organization. Coaching is always about getting results, the same as any other function in the organization. Each coaching relationship should start with a clear intent and outcome. From there, track results of every relationship. Tracking results means more than asking clients about whether or not they were happy with the coaching. Specific, measurable improvements should show up in the organization from each coaching engagement. Results can range from tangible financial improvements to how confident and competent the client feels about using a new skill. Regardless, coaching should be as accountable as any other function in an organization.

Addendum Three

Create Your Own Coaching Frameworks

You have seen a number of frameworks you can use to coach clients. Creating frameworks is an important skill for anyone who wants to become the go-to professional in the market and one that you should develop.

Once you have your own framework(s), you can enjoy some fantastic benefits:

- Become unique and stand above other coaches.

- Become an expert, not just a coach.

- Charge more.

- Own an asset that makes your firm valuable and creates the potential for a stream of revenue.

- Turn your framework into products, seminars, speaking engagements, group coaching, training, licensing arrangements, certifications, and on and on.

- Build leverage in your firm by hiring other coaches who will use your approach.

The graphic below shows you four famous frameworks: Lencioni's Dysfunctions of a Team, Covey's Seven Habits, the DuPont Return on Investment Model, and the Boston Consulting Group Cash Cow Framework. These are only a few examples of frameworks that have made lots of money for their creators.

Examples of Frameworks

The Role of the Leader

Inattention to Results — Focus on Collective Outcomes

Avoidance of Accountability — Confront Difficult Issues

Lack of Commitment — Force Clarity and Closure

Fear of Conflict — Mine for Conflict

Absence of Trust — Go First!

Lencioni: Five Dysfunctions of a Team

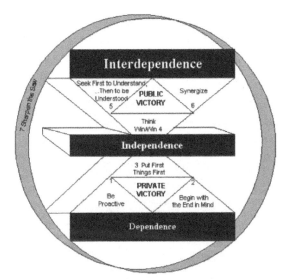

Covey: Seven Habits

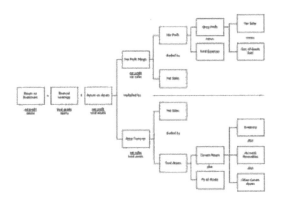

Dupont Return on Investment Model

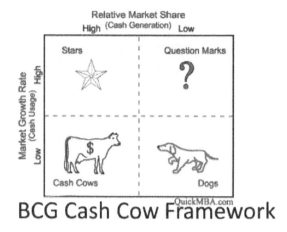

BCG Cash Cow Framework

Budget some time to create your own framework. Think about a problem that your target market faces, and develop an elegant framework. Start by describing the problem clearly. Then explain the root causes and how to solve them.

Give this framework a catchy name, create a graphic that makes it look professional, market it on your website and in other collateral, write articles about it, develop a coaching process to incorporate it into your work with clients, and keep moving ahead from there.

Here are some examples for you to practice:

- How the leader of a company can foster more and quicker innovation, for instance, by developing and/or launching more new products/services more quickly.

- How women (or insert any other demographic group here) can rise to the top, even as a minority in a specific industry or type of company.

- How a university administrator can create a more entrepreneurial culture in his department.

- How the leader of a highly competitive and individualistic culture can encourage more collaboration.

- How to resolve a conflict between two colleagues or business units.

- How to help a newly hired executive assimilate into a very different culture from his or her previous company. How a company can include social responsibility into everything it does (or you can substitute environmental sustainability for social responsibility).

Addendum Four

Coaching Case Studies

- How would you handle the following cases? Design a coaching plan for any of the following challenges that a client might share with you:

    - My team has conflicts.
    - My team is getting results.
    - My employees aren't doing what we need them to do.
    - I need to influence my colleagues to provide more support.
    - I have high employee turnover.
    - My manager and I are not getting along.
    - I have been getting feedback that some of my behaviors are hurting relationships.
    - My career is at a standstill.
    - I have a conflict with a colleague.
    - I feel that I can't trust my employees.
    - I need to change our culture.
    - Change isn't happening quickly enough.
    - I don't have a strong enough base of support among leadership.
    - Our board is not effective.

- We need a strategic plan.

- We are unable to execute.

- We are about to merge with another entity, and I am worried about what will happen.

- I am overwhelmed with too many priorities.

- I am not managing my time effectively.

- We need a succession plan.

- Your client is a strong one-on-one communicator and manager, but this person is presenting next month to a group of a hundred managers and is nervous. Your client's presentation style is highly analytical and dry. How can you help?

- Your client, a hospital administrator, works seventy hours per week and wants to work fifty. Your client's office is a complete mess, with stacks of paper and memos all around and a to-do list that is two pages long. How can you coach this person to be more effective?

- A 360-degree assessment shows that your client is great at using facts, logic, and reasons to persuade people to get things done. Your client uses this style in just about everything they do, from telling employees how they are doing and getting buy-in for big ideas to setting direction for their unit and coaching employees. What approach would you use to broaden your client's toolkit and make them more flexible?

- Your client fears that their organization is losing ground to the competition and is good but not outstanding in terms of price, quality, and productivity. How can you coach this person to help the company regain a strong market position?

- A superstar employee just lost another direct report due to his tendency to explode in anger and be dismissive and blaming when things go wrong. Your client, the CEO and manager of this person, is worried about the tone he sets, not to mention that two former employees have threatened lawsuits. One has also raised the issue of sexual harassment. Meanwhile, the superstar employee in question is very well connected politically in the organization, especially to some key board members, so the client needs to tread lightly. Also, his performance in terms of bottom line numbers is excellent. It doesn't help that your client tends to avoid conflict. What is your coaching strategy?

- The executive director of a major nonprofit is having trouble improving his relationship with the new chairman of the board. His style is process oriented, thoughtful, and consensus driven, while the new chair is bottom line oriented and quite abrupt. The chair wants much more involvement in the organization than the previous chair, and the executive director is concerned about the board getting too involved in daily operations. Both individuals are in agreement about the organization's mission and priorities. How can you help mediate this conflict?

- Your client has the following issues: His fortune of $4,000,000 has dropped to a negative net worth, while his company, once a rapidly growing software firm, has hit a wall due to the economy. He complains, "I can't get my people to do what I want them to do, especially in terms of growing sales. I don't know who is responsible for what, and I don't know how to get them to perform." His people respond that the client is a great technology guru but not good at conflict, stating expectations, or telling people what he wants them to do and where they are falling short. How do you help?

- You are coaching a high-potential junior partner at a consulting firm. She is brilliant and great at generating leads but has a major problem: When anyone debates with her, she becomes arrogant, angry, and dismissive. She does this with partners, lower associates, administrative assistants, and even clients. You have been called in to provide her with feedback and design a process to help her improve. What do you do?

- The owner of a $200 million distribution firm wants to develop a plan to hand the business over to his daughter. She has worked in the business for three years now, but she isn't very open to advice from the owner. He wants you to work with the two of them to determine how to groom her to take over. How would you proceed?

- The owner of a consulting firm wants your help in designing a sales process that turns every consultant in the firm into a business development expert as well as a consultant. This is a common model in the industry, but in this firm, most consultants are like deer in the headlights when it comes to anything related to sales. A few partners can sell, but they are too busy to mentor up-and-coming associates. What questions would you ask to assess what is in place and what isn't, and what kind of engagement would you propose?

- An investment banker calls you in to coach the CEO of a company with a proprietary technology to extract gold from mining sludge. The CEO is a former stock broker, who happened to meet a scientist with a license to the technology in question. He is a great promoter, but his weaknesses include an inability to write (dyslexia?), a lack of credentials or presence for Wall Street bankers, and a complete inability to construct a business plan and course of action. What is your strategy to help this person?

- The CEO of a hospital, your client for a couple of months, approaches you and says, "I think that one of our nursing units is overstaffed. Could you speak to our chief nursing officer and understand her staffing plan, how that compares with industry benchmarks, and ideas she might have to reduce staffing in this area?" How will you conduct this meeting with the CNO?

- Your client has just been promoted from a VP in corporate to the general manager of a major division, with profit and loss responsibilities. What questions will you ask to help him succeed?

- The CEO sends you in to coach one of his new direct reports, someone who has been called in to develop a new service line for a consulting firm. The service line is outside the CEO's expertise, and the relationship between the two is not strong. It turns out that the new employee was explicitly told he wouldn't have to sell, but now market conditions in the company require that everyone gets involved with business development. How do you coach this new report?

- The CEO of a bank, and a long-time client of yours, announces that he is having the worst week of his life. His bank is getting destroyed by the credit crunch, especially after going heavily into subprime mortgages. His wife is threatening to get a divorce. His oldest son is failing school and unlikely to make it to a four-year college without some remedial work. Layoffs at the bank are imminent. The CEO can't decide whether or not the bank will survive or if a merger is needed, and the FDIC is planning an inspection and audit of the bank within the month. The CEO is in a panic and doesn't know how to even focus. How do you help?

- You meet the CEO of the largest employer in your county. What questions can you ask immediately to establish credibility and show the CEO that you are a worthy relationship to have?

- Your client, a director of a large operational division, is feeling burnt out and disenchanted. She had been working on a reorganization that was meant to save the company a substantial amount of money as well as streamline operations. After eighteen months of conscientiously doing all that was required (consultations, communication, report writing, justifications, number crunching), she has been told that the reorganization cannot proceed because of various HR issues, mostly to do with staffing and pay grade issues. You have been coaching her on refocusing her energy on that which is under her control. She's on board with that, but you sense that she is emotionally withdrawing from the senior management team. For instance, there is a two-day retreat coming up, and she doesn't intend to go. She says, "What's the point? Nobody listens to me anyway." Your view: detachment is good, disengagement isn't. How do you coach her on this? Oh, and she has just three years until retirement.

- You have the opportunity to coach executives at a Fortune 500 company. They have sent you their list of "general competencies." You have coached your other clients on some of these but not all of them. Should you not take the job? How should you proceed? How do you set up a coaching engagement if the client has a list of existing competencies?

- You are an internal coach in a Fortune 500 company. You are frustrated because executives and managers don't seem to see you as a trusted advisor. It drives you crazy when they hire outside coaches and go around you because you know you are as competent as the external coaches they hire. How can you establish your credibility at this company?

- A branch manager of a major investment firm wants to advance his career to manage multiple branches. He wants to be what he calls a "leader of leaders." What would be your coaching plan for this client?

- Your client, the president of a company with $50 million in sales, reports to the CEO of a parent company with $500 million in sales. He oversees seven companies that were purchased to create an organization that can provide one-stop shopping to its clientele. He wants your help with the following: how to build stronger relationships with the parent company after his predecessor burned many bridges between the two organizations; how to appropriately assert to the parent company, whose executive team is close knit and has been pushing their own chosen managers into the subsidiary without the client's approval (and his CEO will be leaving soon and doesn't want to get involved in these conflicts); how to assess his own management team and determine who stays and who might not be a good fit; and how to present a coherent strategic vision to the parent company and board within a couple of months. How would you prioritize issues with this client and get traction on these issues?

- A client wants your help with a strategic plan. He has engaged you to interview key managers and then facilitate a retreat. You usually require at least two days, if not a series of three meetings, to complete strategic planning with a client. In this case, the client only wants to dedicate a half day to developing the plan. How do you proceed?

- You are coaching two partners in a business. One partner participates actively in the coaching and is positive about it. The other misses meetings, is negative during sessions, and doesn't seem particularly coachable about key issues. The first partner wants your advice about what to do to get the second partner more engaged in the coaching as well as in key issues that are hurting their relationship. What is your approach?

- A 360-degree verbal assessment of your client revealed a behavioral problem. When you present this issue to the client, he expresses surprise. He doesn't believe that he has this problem and gets defensive about it. Where do you go from here?

- You are coaching an HR director who has a very different style than the other seven members of the executive team. While the rest of the team tends to make fast decisions, speak with a bottom line style, juggle multiple priorities, and take risks, your client is the opposite. He takes a long time to make a decision. He is risk averse and tends to work methodically on one project before moving to the next. His communication style is process oriented, step-by-step. How do you coach this executive to adapt?

- You are coaching a CEO who has just received advice from his physician to slow down a bit. He gets about three hours of sleep a night and is constantly working. At home, he emails colleagues about work issues almost constantly. He seems to be doing the job of three executives, and it is taking a toll on his health. His rationale is that he was called in to turn around his organization, which has facilities in three states. This forces him to travel, while also wearing the hats of strategic thinker, operations leader, contract negotiator, political liaison, and visionary. How would you help the CEO to take his physician's advice and get more control over his time?

- A 24-year-old comes to you for career coaching, paid for by his parents. He has been flailing a bit in a string of different jobs since graduating from college. He has dozens of ideas about potential careers, including the Peace Corps, medical school, law school, technology start-ups, and one or two more. For each idea, he sees pros and cons and won't commit to any single idea. All he knows is that "I want to have a huge impact." How do you get him unstuck?

- How would you coach the owner of a business who wants to make major gains in sales and profits in the next few years?

About the Author

Andrew Neitlich is the founder and director of the Center for Executive Coaching (http://centerforexecutivecoaching.com), a leading coach training organization. The Center for Executive Coaching has been training coaches for a decade and is an Approved Coach Training Program (ACTP) with the International Coach Federation and also approved to provide training hours for the Board Certified Coach (BCC) certification. Members include professionals who have held leadership roles in many organizations, including FedEx, Aflac, Microsoft, Cisco Systems, Ascension Healthcare, Kaiser Permanente, the United States Air Force, Florida Institute of Technology, University of Minnesota, the United States Department of Defense, Macy's, the NBA, and Deloitte Consulting. Andrew also developed the Coach Master Toolkit, a library of practical, results-driven coaching methodologies. He has trained over 1,000 coaches around the world.

Andrew received his MBA from Harvard Business School in 1991. In addition to leading the Center for Executive Coaching and running a full leadership coaching practice, he is the author of the following books: Elegant Leadership: Simple Strategies, Remarkable Results; The Way to Coach Executives; Guerrilla Marketing for Coaches; and Guerrilla Marketing for a Bulletproof Career (both with Guerrilla Marketing founder Jay Conrad Levinson). He lives in Sarasota, Florida, with his family and plays lots of tennis.

For Additional Resources about Coaching, Coach Training, and Coaching for Your Current and Future Leaders.

The Center for Executive Coaching is available to train you and your team in the best practices of executive and leadership coaching. We have a number of solutions, from full training and certification to the use of our Coach Master Toolkit, along with online training programs for managers to learn coaching skills. We can also provide you with top-tier executives and leadership coaches to help your leaders and high-potential managers get even better.

For more information, visit us at http://centerforexecutivecoaching.com
or contact Andrew Neitlich directly
at andrewneitlich@centerforexecutivecoaching.com.

Made in United States
Orlando, FL
29 January 2025

57926898R00249